COSMOPOLITANISM IN PRACTICE

Global Connections

Series Editor: Robert Holton, Trinity College, Dublin

Global Connections builds on the multi-dimensional and continuously expanding interest in Globalization. The main objective of the series is to focus on 'connectedness' and provide readable case studies across a broad range of areas such as social and cultural life, economic, political and technological activities.

The series aims to move beyond abstract generalities and stereotypes: 'Global' is considered in the broadest sense of the word, embracing connections between different nations, regions and localities, including activities that are trans-national, and trans-local in scope; 'Connections' refers to movements of people, ideas, resources, and all forms of communication as well as the opportunities and constraints faced in making, engaging with, and sometimes resisting globalization.

The series is interdisciplinary in focus and publishes monographs and collections of essays by new and established scholars. It fills a niche in the market for books that make the study of globalization more concrete and accessible.

Also published in this series:

Violence and Gender in the Globalized World
The Intimate and the Extimate
Edited by
Sanja Bahun-Radunovic and V.G. Julie Rajan
ISBN 978-0-7546-7364-4

Cosmopolitanism in Practice

Edited by

MAGDALENA NOWICKA
Ludwig Maximilian University, Munich, Germany

MARIA ROVISCO
ISCTE – University of Lisbon, Portugal

ASHGATE

Published by
Ashgate Publishing Limited
Wey Court East
Union Road
Farnham
Surrey, GU9 7PT
England

Ashgate Publishing Company
Suite 420
101 Cherry Street
Burlington
VT 05401-4405
USA

www.ashgate.com

British Library Cataloguing in Publication Data
Cosmopolitanism in practice
  1. Cosmopolitanism 2. Acculturation 3. Globalization -
  Social aspects
  I. Nowicka, Magdalena II. Rovisco, Maria
  306

Library of Congress Cataloging-in-Publication Data
Cosmopolitanism in practice / [edited by] by Magdalena Nowicka and Maria Rovisco.
    p. cm.
  Includes bibliographical references and index.
  ISBN 978-0-7546-7049-0
  1. Cosmopolitanism. I. Nowicka, Magdalena. II. Rovisco, Maria.

  JZ1308.C68 2008
  306--dc22

                                                                    2008031183
ISBN 978-0-7546-7049-0

Mixed Sources
Product group from well-managed forests and other controlled sources
www.fsc.org Cert no. SA-COC-1565
© 1996 Forest Stewardship Council

Printed and bound in Great Britain by
MPG Books Ltd, Bodmin, Cornwall.

Contents

Notes on Contributors

Ulrich Beck is Professor of Sociology at the Ludwig Maximilian University in Munich and the British Journal of Sociology Visiting Centennial Professor at the London School of Economics and Sciences. From 1995–1998 he was Distinguished Research Professor at the University of Cardiff. In 1996 he got the honorary degree of social science from the University of Jyvskyl/Finland. Beck is chief-editor of *Soziale Welt*, editor of the Edition Second Modernity at Suhrkamp (Frankfurt a.M.); associate editor of the *Journal of Environmental Policy & Planning* and of *Socijana Ekologija* (Zagreb).

Mark-Anthony Falzon is a Senior Lecturer in Social Science at the University of Malta. He holds Masters and doctoral degrees in social anthropology from the University of Cambridge. During his time in Cambridge he was the holder of various awards, including an Overseas Studentship in Social Anthropology, a Wenner-Gren major award for fieldwork, and a Smuts Memorial Fund award. He is a Fellow of the Cambridge Commonwealth Society and a Life Member of Clare Hall. He has conducted anthropological fieldwork in Malta, London and Mumbai and is the author of a number of scholarly articles and book chapters on diaspora, cities, cosmopolitanism, and more recently hunting in the Mediterranean. His monograph, *Cosmopolitan Connections: The Sindhi Diaspora 1860-2000*, was published by Brill in 2004 and Oxford University Press in 2005. His edited volume, *Multi-sited Ethnography: Theory, Praxis and Locality in Contemporary Social Research*, will be published by Ashgate in 2009.

Dr Stef Jansen is Senior Lecturer of Social Anthropology at the University of Manchester (UK). On the basis of long-term ethnographic research in Bosnia-Herzegovina, Croatia and Serbia since 1996, his work aims to develop a critical anthropology of the transformations of home-making with regard to nation, place and the state, on the postsocialist intersections of hope and belonging. His publications include numerous journal articles and book chapters on these themes as well the co-edited volume *Struggles for Home: Violence, Hope and the Movement of People* (with Staffan Löfving, Oxford: Berghahn, 2008). In Serbian he has published the monograph *Antinacionalizam: etnografija otpora u Beogradu i Zagrebu* (Beograd: XX Vek, 2005) and a Croatian collection of his translated articles is forthcoming (Zagreb: Institut za Etnologiju i Folkloristiku, 2009).

Ramin Kaweh holds a Post-graduate degree from the University of Kent in Canterbury. Currently a Ph.D. student in the Department of International Relations at the London School of Economics and Political Sciences, he previously worked with the United Nations and the World Trade Organisation in Geneva, Switzerland, and also with UNESCO, as well as with the private sector, consulting international organizations and NGOs. He now works with Dynargie Switzerland, a branch of a global consulting and training company.

Paul Kennedy is reader in sociology and global studies at Manchester Metropolitan University. He is also the director of the Institute for Global Studies based in the sociology department at MMU and which has a number of highly research active staff working on various aspects of global studies. Until recently he was also the secretary of the Global Studies Association, which he also played a considerable role in founding in 2000. He has written and/or edited several books including the following: *African Capitalism: The Struggle for Ascendancy* (Cambridge University Press 1988), *Global Sociology*, with Robin Cohen (Macmillan 2000) and *Cross Border Communities*, co-edited with Victor Roudometof (Routledge 2002). He has also contributed chapters to a number of books and continues to publish in journals. His most recent research project has examined the transnational links, affiliations and identities of young Europeans with a background in higher education and who work in Manchester.

Kira Kosnick is Junior Professor at the Institute of Cultural Anthropology and European Ethnography, Frankfurt am Main. She was previously Lecturer in Cultural Analysis at the Nottingham Trent University. Her work focuses on minority media practices, Turkish migration to Europe and social formations in transnational contexts. Among her publications is the book *Migrant Media: Turkish Broadcasting and Multicultural Politics in Berlin* (2007).

Rob Kroes is Professor emeritus and former chair of the American Studies programme at the University of Amsterdam, until September 2006. He is a past President of the European Association for American Studies (EAAS, 1992–1996). He is the founding editor of two series published in Amsterdam: *Amsterdam Monographs in American Studies* and *European Contributions to American Studies*. He is the author, co-author or editor of 34 books. Among his recent publications are: *If You've Seen One, You've Seen The Mall: Europeans and American Mass Culture* (1996), *Predecessors: Intellectual Lineages in American Studies* (1998), *Them and Us: Questions of Citizenship in a Globalizing World* (2000), and *Straddling Borders: The American Resonance in Transnational Identities* (2004). With Robert W. Rydell he co-authored a book entitled *Buffalo Bill in Bologna: The Americanization of the World, 1869–1922* (2005) A forthcoming book is *Photographic Memories: Private Pictures, Public Images and American History* (2006).

Daniel Levy is Associate Professor of Sociology at the State University of New York at Stony Brook. He received his PhD from Columbia University (1999). As a political sociologist, he is interested in issues of globalization, collective memory studies and comparative-historical sociology. Among his recent publications are: "The Transformation of Sovereignty: Towards a Sociology of Human Rights" *British Journal of Sociology* 57 (4): 657-676 (2006) (with Natan Sznaider). *The Holocaust and Memory in the Global Age* (with Natan Sznaider, Temple University Press 2005). Together with Max Pensky and John Torpey he is co-editor of *Old Europe, New Europe, Core Europe: Transatlantic Relations after the Iraq War* (Verso, 2005). He co-edited (with Yfaat Weiss) *Challenging Ethnic Citizenship: German and Israeli Perspectives on Immigration* (Berghahn Books, 2002). Forthcoming is his *The Collective Memory Reader* (Oxford University Press – with Jeffrey Olick and Vered Vinitzky-Seroussi). His next book deals with the intersection of *Memory and Human Rights* (with Natan Sznaider).

Magdalena Nowicka holds a Ph.D. in sociology from the Ludwig Maximilian University, Munich. She is currently a Research Assistant at the Institute of Sociology, Ludwig Maximilian University, Munich. She has degrees in European culture studies and international relations from Warsaw and Krakow universities, and is author of a number of articles on European integration, collective identity, geographical mobility and transnational social formations. Her recent publications include *Transnational Professionals and Their Cosmopolitan Universes* (2006) and an edited volume *Von Polen nach Deutschland und Zurück. Die Arbeitsmigration und ihre Herausforderungen für Europa* (2007).

Maria Rovisco is a Research Fellow at the Department of Sociology, ISCTE – University of Lisbon. She gained her doctorate in Sociology from the University of York. In 2006 she was a Fulbright Visiting Fellow at the Center for Cultural Sociology at Yale University. She has published articles on the tradition of European films of voyage, cosmopolitanism and Europe, and questions of borders and identity formation. She is currently working on a project on the Arts and the Public Sphere. Her main research interests focus on cultural sociology, cosmopolitanism, the idea of Europe, and social theory.

Natan Sznaider is Professor of Sociology at the Academic College of Tel-Aviv – Yaffo. His recent publications include *The Compassionate Temperament: Care and Cruelty in Modern Society* (Rowman & Littlefield 2001). He co-edited *Global America: The Cultural Consequences of Globalization* (with Ulrich Beck and Rainer Winter) Liverpool University Press (2003). He is the author of *Memory in the Global Age: The Holocaust* Temple University Press (2005) (together with Daniel Levy).

Steven Vertovec is Director of Max Planck Institute for the Study of Religious and Ethnic Diversity, Germany. Former Professor of Transnational Anthropology at the University of Oxford and Director of the British Economic and Social Research Council's Centre on Migration, Policy and Society (COMPAS). He is Co-Editor of the journal *Global Networks* and Editor of the Routledge book series on Transnationalism and Editor or co-editor of sixteen volumes including *Conceiving Cosmopolitanism* (2003) and *Citizenship in European Cities* (2004). His most recent volume is *Transationalism* (2008).

Gillian Youngs is Senior Lecturer in the Department of Media and Communication at the University of Leicester, UK. Her main research areas are Feminist International Relations, Globalization and Inequality, Global Political Economy, Information Society, and Women and Feminist Theory and Information and Communication Technologies. She is currently leading an ESRC seminar series entitled 'Ethics and the War on Terror: Politics, Multiculturalism and Media' (2006–2008) in collaboration with Simon Caney (University of Oxford) and Heather Widdows (University of Birmingham). A founding co-editor of *International Feminist Journal of Politics* in 1999, she was lead co-editor 2003–2005. She continues to serve on the board of the journal as well as on the editorial boards of *Political Geography*, *Journal of Global Ethics*, *Development*, and *Communication, Culture and Critique*. Her policy-related, consultancy and project work has involved her with the cultural, communications and education sectors of UNESCO and UK and international NGOs. Her major publications include *International Relations in a Global Age: A Conceptual Challenge* (Polity, 1999), the edited volume *Political Economy, Power and the Body: Global Perspectives* (Macmillan, 2000), *Global Political Economy in the Information Age: Power and Inequality* (Routledge, 2007), the co-edited volume *Globalization: Theory and Practice* 3rd ed. (Continuum, 2008).

Foreword

How can we understand the difference between the discourse of 'globalization' and the new code word 'cosmopolitanization' or 'cosmopolitanism'? Are the latter just another example of the 'newspeak' (Orwell) in the social sciences? Not at all: the more we reflect on what 'globalization' means for the social sciences, the more the new cosmopolitanism wins its distinct meaning and importance.

We can distinguish four phases in how the word 'globalization' has been used in the social sciences: first, denial, second, conceptual refinement and empirical research, third, 'cosmopolitanization' and fourth, epistemological shift. The first reaction of the mainstream was to deny the reality, or relevance, of (economic) globalization, and to declare that nothing that fell under the heading 'globalization' on the social scientific agenda was historically new.

This explanation began to lose credibility in the second phase, when social scientists, in the most diverse disciplines, began to subject phenomena of globalization to conceptual analysis and to situate them in the theoretical and empirical semantics of the social sciences (for example, Held et al. Global Transformation, 1999). Through this sophistication, it comes to mind that a new landscape of societies is in the making. Its dominant features include interrelatedness and interdependence of people across the globe; growing inequalities in a global dimension; emergence of new supra-national organizations in the area of economy (multi-national co-operations), politics (non-state actors such as International Monetary Fund, World Bank, the World Trade Organization, the International Court of Justice), and civil society (advocacy social movements of global scope, such as Amnesty International, Greenpeace, feminist organizations and Attac); new normative precepts like human rights, new types and profiles of global risks (climate change, financial turbulences), new forms of warfare, global organized crime and terrorism.

In the third phase, there emerge important social scientific consequences in which the common denominator is 'cosmopolitanization'. How can this key concept be defined? 'Cosmopolitanization' means (a) the erosion of clear borders separating markets, states, civilizations, cultures, and the life-worlds of common people, which (b) implies the involuntary confrontation with the alien other all over the globe. The world has certainly not become borderless, but the boundaries are becoming blurred and indistinct, and more permeable to flows of information, capital and risk. Certainly, this does not mean that everybody is becoming a 'cosmopolit'. Often the opposite seems to be the case: a wave of re-nationalization and re-ethnification in many parts of the world. But at the same time it does mean that there is a new need for a hermeneutics of the alien other in order to live and work in a world in which violent division and unprecedented intermingling coexists, and danger and opportunity vie. This may influence human identity construction, which needs no longer to be shaped in opposition to others, as in the negative, confrontational dichotomy of 'we' and 'them'.

In my books (for example *Power in the Global Age*, 2005; *The Cosmopolitan Vision*, 2006 and *A God of One's Own*, forthcoming) I emphasize that cosmopolitanization does not operate somewhere in the abstract, in the external macro-sphere, somewhere above human heads, but is internal to everyday life of people ('mundane cosmopolitanism'). This mundane cosmopolitanism is not only to be found in people's heads (even though this is not a bad place to be), but can be found, foremost, in people's hearts. This means that cosmopolitanism is as much a reasonable option as it is a sentiment. The same is true for the internal operation of politics, which at all levels, even the domestic level, has to become global, taking into account the global scale of dependencies, flows, links, threats, etc. ('global domestic politics').

The awareness of these changes lags behind objective reality, because people are still thinking in terms of the 'national outlook' which suggests that nation-states are universal and the most important 'containers' within which human life is spent. Similarly, most of sociological research is still applying the rules of 'methodological nationalism', treating societies, confined to the borders of nation-states, as natural units of data collections and analyses. But this is a blind avenue: just as nation-based economics has come to a dead end, so too has nation-state sociology.

To the extent that this has been reflected, the fourth phase witnessed an epistemological shift. This insight gained momentum as the unit of research of different social scientific disciplines become arbitrary, when the distinction between internal and external, national and international, local and global, lose their sharp contours. The question for globalization research following this epistemological turn is: what happens when the premises and boundaries that define these units disintegrate? My answer is that the whole conceptual world of the 'national outlook' becomes disenchanted; that is, de-ontologized, historicized and stripped of its inner-necessity. However, it is possible only to justify this, and think through its consequences, within the framework of an interpretative alternative which replaces ontology with methodology, that is, the currently prevailing ontology and imaginary of the nation-state with what I propose to call 'methodological cosmopolitanism'.

This book, which has been edited and introduced by Magdalena Nowicka and Maria Rovisco, introduces a new fifth phase, namely the question of what does cosmopolitanism in practice mean. The contributions to this volume do not simply describe and analyse 'mundane cosmopolitanism' in a series of empirical cases, but acknowledge that in the process of cosmopolitanization – the erosion of borders and involuntary confrontation with others – people become more and more aware of an alternative cosmopolitan imaginary pointing towards the inadequacy of the national framework. Thus cosmopolitanism is not merely latent and unintentional in the context of a globalized world, but also a viable option for the reflexive handling of encounters with others in unknown situations in everyday life.

I highly recommend this book not only to those, who are interested in the discourses of globalization and cosmopolitanism, but also to those, who try to understand the fundamental changes of the world we live in.

Ulrich Beck

Acknowledgements

We are particularly grateful to Ulrich Beck, Frédéric Vandenberghe, Joost Van Loon and Mark-Anthony Falzon for reading and commenting on previous drafts of the Introduction. We are also thankful to Neil Jordan, our editor at Ashgate Publishing, for his support with the project.

Introduction
Making Sense of Cosmopolitanism

Magdalena Nowicka and Maria Rovisco

Investigations of actually-existing cosmopolitanisms (Robbins 1998) and of cosmopolitanism as a research method to study the social beyond the national are now at the heart of the research agenda of the social sciences. This renewed scholarly interest on the notion of cosmopolitanism draws attention to changes in the social world, from the expansion of global markets, transnational networks, and new patterns of collective attachment, to the expansion of new forms of global governance. A great deal of research has identified and described migrants and members of transnational communities as 'cosmopolitans'. However, it is often unclear how this condition involves a genuinely felt moral commitment to the world. Other research has focused on cosmopolitanism as an ethico-political project that underpins new institutional and political arrangements at a worldwide scale. These are visible, for example, in the way human rights conventions turn into international laws, and in the implementation of international criminal tribunals to stop humanitarian crises and wars against humanity. Yet, in this research agenda, individuals are often deemed only significant as abstract subjects of an emerging cosmopolitan world order and there is little sense of the role that ordinary individuals and social groups play in the making of this new cosmopolitan order (see Nash 2006).

Overall, and despite a considerable body of research that has already emerged from within a variety of disciplines, cosmopolitanism remains largely a prescriptive concept concerning the development of a new world order or a descriptive concept that enables one to label and distinguish between cosmopolitans and non-cosmopolitans (Hannerz 1992; Roudometof 2005, 116). The problem of treating cosmopolitanism purely as a social category to describe and analyse particular types of groups is that the term is routinely used to refer to some kind of identity that singles out 'cosmopolitans' in opposition to 'locals' or 'nationals' (see Jones 2007, 74–75). But how are cosmopolitan ideas, narratives and values, which are institutionally-embedded, shaping everyday life experiences and practices? How are ordinary individuals and groups making sense of their identities and social encounters in ways that can be said 'cosmopolitan'?

The aim of this book is to illustrate some of the ways in which cosmopolitanism can be used as an analytical tool to explain certain identity outlooks and ethico-political practices that are discernible in a variety of social and institutional settings. This collection of chapters focuses on empirically grounded research and engages current debates and new research findings on a variety of cosmopolitan practices, meanings, ideas and narratives. In terms of structure, the chapters have been grouped into three parts – Mobilites, Memories and Tensions – each part reflecting a major concentration of study on cosmopolitanism from a variety of theoretical and methodological approaches.

The purpose of this Introduction is to introduce the reader to the themes of this collection of chapters, especially in light of the major trends and issues of concern to scholars researching the topic of cosmopolitanism. While the first part sheds light on the analytical framework and theoretical interventions that underpin this volume, the second part sets out the organizing themes of the book and illustrates some new directions in the research agenda.

Cosmopolitanism as Practice and Moral Ideal

Cosmopolitanism in Practice is concerned with cosmopolitanism at two analytical levels: (1) cosmopolitanism as a practice which is apparent in things that people do and say to positively engage with 'the otherness of the other' and the oneness of the world; (2) cosmopolitanism as a moral ideal that emphasizes both tolerance towards difference and the possibility of a more just world order.

As a moral ideal, cosmopolitanism can be traced back to the thinking of the ancient Cynics and the Stoics, re-appearing, more forcefully, in various forms, within Enlightenment universalism (cf. Stade 2008; see also Fine and Boone 2007). In Enlightenment thinking, the notion refers to a normative ideal which purports that every singular human being is worthy of equal moral concern and ought to have an allegiance to the community of humankind. Kant (1991), for instance, defends that all human beings are equipped with the ability to discern what is morally demanded from them and envisions a loose confederation of nations obedient to cosmopolitan law. In the current research agenda, the idea of cosmopolitanism is more commonly tied to claims concerning the recognition of difference or the rise of new supranational arrangements and social movements founded on the human rights regime.

It is important to stress that cosmopolitanism – understood as a moral ideal – and cosmopolitanism – as enacted in the outlooks and practices of ordinary individuals and groups – are dimensions of cosmopolitanism which, although analytically distinct, are intrinsically related at the level of empirical reality. In this sense, and in some particular contexts more than others, concrete individuals embrace and mobilize – with different degrees of reflexivity – certain cosmopolitan values and ideas which allow them to develop a cosmopolitan imagination and a moral standpoint. Where in some social settings cosmopolitan sensibilities remain latent, in other contexts, they are more actively and consciously displayed by people. These are visible in the ways people manage their sense of living in 'one world' and with 'others', while being also articulated in the collective actions and 'reflexive capabilities' (Klöger 2005) of the members of those transnational networks of social movements who struggle against global injustices through various forms of ethico-political practice (Vandenberghe 2006; Kurasawa 2007).

All in all, cosmopolitan sensibilities, orientations and ethico-political outlooks presuppose an ontological dimension (Rapport and Stade 2007) and can be readily captured in personal narratives. It is against this background that this book seeks to address some of the links between cosmopolitanism as moral ideal, institutionalized forms of cosmopolitanism, and cosmopolitan identity outlooks, which remain largely unelaborated in the literature (cf. Cheah 2006, 492). Theoretically, the contributions to this volume are particularly concerned (although not exclusively) with cosmopolitanism as grounded category (Škrbiš et al. 2004) – as something that people do and is 'in the making' – rather than an abstract idea (cf. Pollock 2000, 593). Hence, cosmopolitanism can be used as an analytical tool to explain a particular mode of self-transformation that has been observable in everyday social and political life for a long time (cf. Rumford 2005, 4).

Cosmopolitan Perspectives

It is useful to briefly sketch the main intellectual traditions of thinking and theorizing cosmopolitanism for the purpose of giving the reader a better sense of how this collection of chapters suggests ways of widening the discussion. It is under the umbrella of three perspectives – moral cosmopolitanism, political cosmopolitanism and cultural cosmopolitanism (see also Kleingeld 1999; Delanty 2006) – that distinct theoretical orientations and empirical analyses have developed in disciplines as diverse as international relations, sociology, anthropology, political science and cultural studies.

Moral cosmopolitanism is the philosophical perspective that posits that all human beings ought to be morally committed to an essential humanity above and beyond the reality of one's particularistic attachments (such as nationality, kinship, religion) (see Nussbaum 1996; Turner 2002). As a moral standpoint, cosmopolitanism does not necessarily entail a duty to reshape the international political world order. Yet it does involve political duties, insofar as morality provides guidelines for one's actions in one's capacity as a citizen. This cosmopolitan ethic does not prescribe a set of readily applicable principles but it requires everyone to judge each situation in context and to act reflexively (Kleingeld 1999, 516). Moral cosmopolitanism has shaped and informed cultural and political cosmopolitanism approaches. In positing the moral equality of all human beings and all cultures, it sets the ground for the view of cosmopolitanism as a competence based on tolerance and openness towards 'other' cultures and value-systems, a perspective that is commonly found among the advocates of cultural cosmopolitanism. In a different vein, moral cosmopolitanism also involves a strong notion of universal morality that is implicated in calls for a cosmopolitan world order.

While rejecting both cultural relativism and ethnocentrism, cultural cosmopolitanism approaches are concerned with the problem of the recognition of difference and the respect for the variety of cultures (Kleingeld 1999, 517). A great deal of theorizing – informed by notions such as 'vernacular cosmopolitanism' (Bhabha 1996; Nava, 2007), 'rooted cosmopolitanism' (Appiah 1998, 2006; Beck 2003), and 'actually-existing cosmopolitanism as a reality of multiple attachments' (Robbins 1998) – attempts to transcend the tension between universalism and particularism. The underlying question here is, as Werbner (2006, 496) puts it, 'whether there can be an enlightened normative cosmopolitanism which is not rooted [...] in patriotic and culturally committed loyalties and understandings'. Some authors have shown how past and present cosmopolitanisms shape distinct worldviews and identities in a variety of times and places (Mignolo 2000; Pollock 2000). Falzon (Chapter 2, this volume), for example, suggests, in a case study of the Sindhi diaspora, that spatial unboundedness *per se* does not make the cosmopolitan grade and that actually-existing cosmopolitanisms are always located within some historical and geographical framework.

Other scholarship stresses the need to overcome the gendered, class and ethnocentric biases that blight the literature. For example, the figure of the cosmopolitan as a typically privileged, male and upper class citizen (Kanter 1995; Calhoun 2002; Hannerz 2004; Sklair 2000) has been challenged by research that points towards the existence of cosmopolitan attitudes among ordinary and working-class groups (Werbner 1999; Lamont and Aksartova 2002; Sassen 2006) and focuses on the vernacular, emotional, and everyday expressions of cosmopolitanism (Nava 2002, 2007).

Other authors (Pollock et al. 2000) offer a critical reading of triumphalist and neoliberal notions of cosmopolitical coexistence. It is in this vein that Cheah (2006) criticizes Habermas's (2001) vision of a cosmopolitan global public sphere which remains oblivious of the neoliberal logic of global capitalism, especially with regards to the imbalance in power relations created by an allegedly cosmopolitan North that is sustained by global exploitation of a postcolonial South in structural conditions of deep inequality. There is here a call for 'cosmopolitanism from below' which is not utopian, elitist or Western-centred and that has political implications of its own (Werbner 1999; Bhabha 1996; Nava 2007).

Overall, anthropologists and sociologists have been primarily concerned with the less reflexive aspects of cosmopolitanism which are apparent in mundane practices and lifestyle options on the micro-scale of daily interactions. In contrast, other authors, particularly political scientists and IR scholars writing within the tradition of political cosmopolitanism, understand cosmopolitanism as an ethicopolitical ideal that seeks to respond to the limitations of the nation-state unit in addressing global challenges and problems. In this context, cosmopolitanism emerges as a political project that fosters new forms of supranational and transnational governance (e.g. NGOs, the human rights regime) as well as the emergence of a robust global civil society (see e.g. Held 1995, 1999; Archibugi et al. 1998; Kaldor 2002; Rumford 2007).

Some advocates of political cosmopolitanism posit the development of a global legal order which can be seen as the institutional embodiment of cosmopolitan values of equality, solidarity and human rights, as well as the expression of a universal political consensus (Habermas 2001). This perspective is inspired by the cosmopolitan vision of Kant, which can be found in his writings on perpetual peace, and remains an authoritative approach within political cosmopolitanism. In Kant's view, cosmopolitan law regulates not only the relation between states, but also the interaction between state and individuals. The latter have the right to attempt to establish relations with other states and their citizens, but not the right to enter or settle in a foreign territory (cf. Kleingeld 1999, 513). Kant conceives the global federation of republic states as a form of political organization based on cosmopolitan right (*ius cosmopoliticum*), which is negatively defined as the right of 'hospitality', i.e., the right of a stranger not to be treated with hostility (Kant 1991). This cosmopolitan vision still holds sway in contemporary arguments suggesting that individuals and states ought to be morally and legally bound to international law agreements (Beck 2002). Finally, other authors point towards the development of a cosmopolitan citizenship that ought to be accompanied by an ethical change underpinning ways in which concrete citizens of different national states live and act towards 'others' regardless of national boundaries and in transnational contexts (Benhabib 2002, 183). Nash (2006), for example, suggests that the international human rights system can only set the ground for the development of a more cosmopolitan world order if ordinary people are able to identify themselves with the values that constitute this system.

It is important to note that the chapters included in this volume are not representative of traditional 'schools of thought' (namely, the 'moral', the 'cultural' and the 'political'). While many contributors deal with themes and issues that are typically developed and encountered in cultural cosmopolitanism approaches, in practice, we find that some contributions deal with issues of concern to more than one of the perspectives above outlined.

Overcoming disciplinary divisions, recent approaches to cosmopolitanism underpin, in a more forceful fashion, the claim that the social sciences need to break with the research lens that takes the national frame (collectives and systems of classification) as the given unity of analysis (Martins 1974; Chernilo 2006; Beck 2002, 2004; Beck and Sznaider 2006). The advocates of the so-called 'cosmopolitan turn' emphasize the limitations of the national *imaginaire* (Robins 2006, 19) and reject the assumption that human groups live in closed and self-contained spaces, and that cultures 'are clearly delineated as identifiable entities that coexist, while maintaining firm boundaries' (Benhabib 2002, 8). More importantly, there is here a call for an epistemological turn that occurs 'within an interpretative framework in which [...] "methodological cosmopolitanism" replaces the nationally centred ontology and imagination dominating thought and action' (Beck 2004, 132). This is predicated on a new 'grammar' that is enacted in actual challenges to boundaries – between internal and external, local and global, us and them – which become more complex, pluralized and ambivalent as we enter the twentieth-first century. This new 'grammar' equips the social sciences with the capability to grasp the 'real-world of cosmopolitanisation' (Beck 2004,

133). This new research lens is also concerned with aspects of a cosmopolitan imagination that is articulated in cultural models of world openness that enable novel understandings and explanations of the local/global nexus (Delanty 2006).

In its scope and aims, the present volume is indebted to this emerging cosmopolitan research agenda and its methodological presuppositions, which lay the ground for understanding cosmopolitanism as an analytical tool to study a particular mode of self-transformation.

Cosmopolitanism as a Mode of Self-Transformation

This volume involves, above all, an attempt to move beyond the tendency to purely identify and describe a social category of cosmopolitans. The contributions to this volume illustrate how cosmopolitanism can be seen as a *mode of self-transformation*, which occurs when individuals and groups engage in concrete struggles to protect a common humanity and become more reflexive about their experiences of otherness. This capability enables people to reflexively rework the boundaries between self and other, us and them (cf. Lamont and Aksartova 2002), and, thus, come closer to the reality of others and the world taken as a whole in fields often loaded with tensions and emotions. Self-transformation implies a sense of continuous self-scrutiny both with regards to the ways one positively engages the otherness of other cultures and people, and to the ways one is committed to the building of a more just world in conditions of uneven globalization. A key assumption here is that people can *actually* become more cosmopolitan in ways that are both reflexive and emotional.

Furthermore, the fact that individuals may at times seemingly act in a non-cosmopolitan fashion or display non-cosmopolitan feelings does not necessarily mean that people are then becoming less cosmopolitan. There is evidence in the contributions to this volume that cosmopolitanism as a set of practices and identity outlooks is not to be seen as predicated on the transcendence of the particularistic and parochial ties, which are often associated to non-cosmopolitan feelings and dispositions. While this stance may render irrelevant the antinomies between universalism and particularism, cosmopolitanism and nationalism, one should not lose sight of the limits of the cosmopolitan imagination, a consideration that is sometimes overlooked in the literature. Jansen (Chapter 4, this volume), for example, shows that the grammar of difference in post-Yugoslav antinationalism, which is carried on by a group of self-professed urbanites, attempts to resist nationalist closure by deploying cosmopolitan openness in a way that implies closure to some types of difference. Cosmopolitanism – as expression of both an attachment to 'the World' and a characteristic of the civilized urban self – works here as a rhetorical resource in these struggles to value certain forms of belonging over others.

Cosmopolitan identity outlooks and practices that are observable in real life situations have to be seen in connection with the way cosmopolitan norms and values become increasingly institutionalized in the contemporary world. Formal organizations, such as the United Nations, have included cosmopolitan values in their mission, whereas transnational non-governmental organizations, grassroots social movements and informal networks of NGOs are also appropriating cosmopolitan values and ideas for accomplishing their causes and agendas. These are all forms of an institutional cosmopolitanism that is embedded in various formal rules, laws and organizational structures.

It is against this backdrop that *Cosmopolitanism in Practice* seeks to explore the connection, rather than the tension, between institutional cosmopolitanism and forms of 'actually-existing' cosmopolitanism. It does so by acknowledging that, on the one hand, there are cosmopolitan ideas already ingrained in formal structures, imaginaries and ethico-political projects and, on the other, that individuals deploy – with different degrees of consciousness and in a variety of contexts – a set of cosmopolitan practices and orientations. The contributors to this volume take up cosmopolitan self-transformations in terms of people's 'real life' struggles to bridge boundaries between self and other or to profess an allegiance to humankind, and do so with different analytical and empirical focuses. While some contributors highlight individual interpretation to explore cosmopolitanism as a mode of self-transformation (Chapters 1 and 2), other authors pay special attention to the cosmopolitan imaginaries that shape and inform cosmopolitan identity outlooks (Chapters 4, 5, 6 and 8) or the situational contexts and social structures that both enable and constrain cosmopolitan self-transformations (Chapters 3, 7, 9 and 10).

Mobilities

In this part, the contributors consider how patterns of mobility and interconnectivity shape the cosmopolitan identities of particular groups. Some authors have focused on networks, patterns of consumption, and complex flows and mobilities of people, capital, technologies and cultural forms to explain and theorize cosmopolitanism (Urry 2002, 2003; Szerszynski and Urry 2002; Thompson and Tambyah 1999; Molz 2006). Inspired by globalization theory (see especially Robertson 1995; Appadurai 1996; Hannerz 1996), other scholarship ties cosmopolitanism to processes of transnational contact by looking at migrants, exiles and refugees. Examining issues of class location, ethnicity and subjectivity, this research has theorized the cosmopolitanism of working class labour migrants (Werbner 1999; Kofman 2005) and the emergence of a cosmopolitan citizenship in transnational contexts (Ong 1998). This is a major area of interest which has generated a good deal of scholarship in sociology and anthropology. The essays presented in this part take up this agenda to show how active geographical mobility might enable as well as constrain the experience of cultural engagement with 'others' and 'the world'. Cosmopolitanism is often seen as a characteristic of the global elites insofar as it is them who enjoy less financial barriers to frequent travel (see e.g. Calhoun 2002).

Yet, as the contributions to this part suggest, the unobstructed movement of people across national borders is not *per se* always consequential in terms of fostering cosmopolitan self-transformations. The fact that some mobile people are being more exposed and aware of 'other' cultures and value-systems does not necessarily mean that the conditions for positive interaction and engagement with others are created *a priori*. We might also be aware of the existence of 'others' and yet find ourselves in a situation when we are unwilling to interact with 'them'. The research agenda is thus challenged by the need to understand to which extent wide exposure to the 'Other' *always* encourages more cosmopolitan openness and dialogue with other cultures and realities.

Magdalena Nowicka and Ramin Kaweh address this question by focusing on cosmopolitanism as a mode of personal interaction with culturally different 'others' in alien local contexts. By focusing on an instance of cosmopolitanism among highly mobile professionals of an international organization (the United Nations), they go on to show that cosmopolitanism requires a constant effort to overcome one's emotional distance towards 'others' despite the reality of their bodily co-presence. Arguing that the institutional context of the UN enhances the cosmopolitan self-identification of individuals who describe themselves as citizens of the world, the chapter contrasts narratives of world-openness with the reality of everyday practices of UN professionals in unfamiliar sites, and demonstrates how moments and expressions of openness alternate with experiences of closure towards 'others'.

In a similar vein, Paul Kennedy examines the different personal quests that propelled a group of around sixty continental Europeans from fourteen countries to ultimately settle in Manchester, and traces their 'cosmopolitan careers' by exploring the complex relationships and personal networks they develop with other non-British nationals and with the 'locals'. He goes on to show that, despite the rich cultural resources that skilled middle-class migrants bring with them, they also experience several difficulties in gaining entry to local social networks and that many gravitate towards other foreigners. He argues that it is through the incidence of encounters with both foreigners and locals that these continental Europeans forge their paths into local society and, ultimately, become more cosmopolitan as they attain greater levels of self-understanding, personal autonomy, and openness to aspects of the wider world.

Whereas Nowicka and Kaweh's and Kennedy's contributions stress the personal networks and life trajectories of a particular category of highly mobile people to probe their cosmopolitan identity, Mark-Anthony Falzon explores, through an ethnographic lens, the dynamics of the social processes that make the cosmopolitan grade and argues that there is no necessary contradiction between ethnicity and one's commitment to 'world society'. Looking at the case of Sindhis, he shows that belonging to this diasporic Indian group constitutes a powerful and well-trodden path into the cosmopolitan way of engaging with the world – even if mitigated by factors such as caste, resources, location, occupation and level of education. He probes the essentially paradoxical set-up in which a particular group that is known by its mobility and defines itself on the basis of kinship and locality produces a particular type of cosmopolitanism with far-reaching economic and social consequences.

Overall, the three chapters included in this part suggest that cosmopolitanism is better seen as a form of imagination – that one can exert and develop in certain transnational contexts – rather than an essential quality of mobile people.

Memories

The contributions to this part focus on the changing meanings of cosmopolitanism, especially with regards to the consideration that cosmopolitan self-transformations are tied to historically-specific cosmopolitan imaginaries and frames of memory. Cosmopolitan approaches often link the condition of globalization to postnational phenomena and the reality of an emerging cosmopolitan age. This is consistent with the fact that there has been in the literature a great deal of emphasis on cosmopolitanism as a condition of the 'present' that assigns meanings to a 'past' (understood as less cosmopolitan) and to a 'future' (expected to be even more cosmopolitan) (see Fine 2003; see also Jansen, Chapter 4, this volume). With the speed-up of new patterns of travel, tourism and communication via the electronic media, there have been important changes in the ways in which more and more people are able to come close to the reality of other cultures in a variety of world sites. But while there is ground to argue that the current stage of globalization – in its economic, cultural and technological dimensions – facilitates, in an unprecedented fashion, the rise of a banal and latent cosmopolitanism (Beck 2004, 134), a sense of the historical grounding of present and past cosmopolitanisms is often sidelined in the literature. As Pollock et al. (2000, 584) insightfully noted 'cosmopolitanism must give way to the plurality of modes and histories – not necessarily shared in degree or in concept regionally, nationally, or internationally – that comprise cosmopolitan practice and history'. In fact, while individuals can become more cosmopolitan in distinct world sites in rather banal ways (synchronic time), cosmopolitan identities, practices and ethico-political outlooks of various kinds are also tied to historically-rooted memories and imaginaries (diachronic time).

The chapters presented in this section are primarily concerned with ways in which the cosmopolitan imagination functions as a cultural resource that allows one to trace shifts in the meanings of cosmopolitanism with regards to historically specific socio-cultural contexts. Issues related to how concrete individuals and groups experience cosmopolitan self-transformations that are observable in concrete practices and outlooks, and issues related to the links between cosmopolitanism and spatial unboundedness, which were all at the heart of the previous Part I, are given somewhat less attention in this part. The focus is here placed on the temporal dimension and the discursive frames of actual cosmopolitan memories.

Stef Jansen's chapter draws on long-term ethnographic fieldwork in the post-war period in Bosnia-Herzegovina, Croatia and Serbia to look at non-dominant memories of home amongst a specific group of urbanite activists and other post-Yugoslav refugees. He argues that these are people who recall they had lived, until very recently, lives that they may now sometimes describe as 'cosmopolitan', but they feel they have been robbed of them in the context of the post-Yugoslav conflicts of the 1990s. He shows that the ethico-political practices and identities of these activists rely heavily on strategies of continuity with a remembered 'normal' cosmopolitan past, and that the grammar of difference of post-Yugoslav antinationalism attempted to resist nationalist closure by insisting on the previously open nature of national boundaries in a messy everyday life context, where national loyalties coexisted along urban-centred collective self-understandings.

Rob Kroes' contribution on cosmopolitan engagements of Europe through the lens of American mass culture shares some of the concerns of Jansen's paper, arguing that certain discursive frames and forms of representation are tied to historically-specific cosmopolitan imaginaries. Yet, while Jansen uses an ethnographic approach to suggest that the grammar of antinationalism underpins the imagination of a cosmopolitan past among post-Yugoslav refugees, Kroes underlines, through a historical and semiotic reading, how both a European tradition of high-minded cosmopolitanism and the vernacular memory of cosmopolitan 'Europes' have cut across lasting ethnic and national divides, but are yet unable to provide an overarching imagery of Europe that is potentially meaningful for all in the context of a wider EU. Looking at American iconography in public space, Kroes shows, more specifically, how American mass culture allows cultural exchanges and conversations across older dividing lines in Europe, while being also used as a subtext in forms of European resistance against global cultural icons. Ultimately, he argues that such cosmopolitan cultural exchanges are visible in a self-conscious and ironic appropriation of American mass culture in popular culture.

The chapter by Ulrich Beck, Daniel Levy and Natan Sznaider makes a rather more radical case for a cosmopolitan memory that is combined with memories manifested in many different places. They argue that the shared memories of the Holocaust provide the foundation for a cosmopolitan memory that is of universal applicability and involves an orientation towards a shared cosmopolitan future. Arguing that this new cosmopolitan memory lends political and moral authority to the human rights regime, the chapter analyses the historical roots of the transition from national to cosmopolitan memory by looking at instances of forgiving and restitution in the context of concrete legal practices. Specifically, the authors develop their argument by presenting two case studies – the Polish struggle for a cosmopolitan memory in the discourse on *Jedwabne* and the German reparation of the 1950s – in which they show how the discourses of guilt and forgiveness are indicative of a new historical awareness detaching itself from the boundaries of the nation-state.

Notably, the contributions to this part illuminate how cosmopolitanism has been, alongside nationalism, a powerful form of collective imagination in the western world.

Tensions

The chapters presented in this part discuss if and how cosmopolitan ideas and discourses actually foster cosmopolitan outlooks in settings blighted by ethnic, religious or gender tensions. The contributions contained on the previous parts of this collection were more specifically concerned with the role that dimensions of time and space consciousness play in the makeup of cosmopolitan identities or imaginaries. Whilst these remain issues of concern for the contributors to this part, the chapters here presented turn to a more close consideration of how, in the contemporary world, certain cosmopolitan discourses and ideas – which are increasingly articulated in institutional settings – enable specific individuals and groups to bridge differences with 'others' (cf. Lamont and Aksartova 2002, 1). They are indicative of a move in the research agenda that shows that cosmopolitan ideas and values are tied to particular worldviews, and investigates whether such ideas and values can actually foster cosmopolitan practices and identities (see Vertovec, Chapter 7, this volume).Cosmopolitanism is here understood in terms of new strategies and ways of coping with problems and challenges concerning the problem of the recognition of difference. In this context, cosmopolitanism proves useful as an analytical tool to deal with the question of tension and conflict in the social and political world, an aspect which is often neglected in the literature (cf. Delanty 2006, 33). If we accept that conflict and strain are intrinsic features of social life (Douglas 1966; Alexander 1992, 302) and not a condition, or a social malaise, that an emerging cosmopolitan world order would completely eradicate, we can see how cosmopolitanism is instantiated in some of the ways individuals and groups overcome social tensions between self and other, us and them.

This section begins with an essay by Steven Vertovec which makes a case for both display and fostering cosmopolitanism in Berlin via a case study of the public station SFB4 Radio Multikulti. With its ethnically diverse personnel and distinctive programming, broadcasted daily in several languages, Radio Multikulti handles a diversity of news topics, debates and world music which appeal to diverse local audiences. Drawing on Nussbaum's proposal for cosmopolitan education, Vertovec argues that this media experiment actually fosters cosmopolitanism in communicating cosmopolitanism – as a socio-cultural condition – that is reflected in representations of Berlin as a site of multiple cultural entanglements and vibrant ethnic and cultural diversity – and also – as an ideology – that is conveyed by Radio Multikulti's programming strategies. This programming agenda not only facilitates cosmopolitan orientations and affiliations but also the respect for human rights and anti-racism.

While Vertovec shows how a particular media environment fosters cosmopolitan imagination in the way Radio Multikulti helps its diverse local audiences to bridge racial and ethnic differences, Gillian Youngs's contribution, by contrast, places the limits of the cosmopolitan imagination at the centre of her argument. Departing from a critical reading of Virginia Woolf's *Three Guineas*, she shows, for instance, how masculine cosmopolitan imaginaries entail an abstract notion of the cosmopolitan individual that has prevented women's voices from participating more fully in the cosmopolitan debate. Youngs argues that at the heart of Woolf's arguments is a concern about the exclusions and limitations resulting from national masculine traditions of higher education – in particular, the fact that cultural and economic resources have been explicitly diverted away from women to men – and that these exclusions are consequential in terms of investigating the limits and possibilities of a cosmopolitan orientation on education in the so-called Age of the 'War on Terror'. She draws attention for the critical question, raised in *Three Guineas*, of how and why women's influence on bringing about a more peaceful world across local and national divides has been historically restricted, and demonstrates that Woolf's critical thinking on education, as a means by which cosmopolitan worldviews that are not shaped by masculine characteristics can bring about social change and self-transformation, is still relevant nowadays.

Like Youngs, Kira Kosnick's contribution is concerned with a particular expression of the limits of the cosmopolitan imagination. In her ethnographic study of migrant artists with a Turkish background who are residents of the city of Berlin she suggests that while young postmigrant artists of second and third generation display cosmopolitan affiliations and sensibilities in their life trajectories, cosmopolitanism is appropriated in the rhetoric of urban cultural policy as an ideology that actually prevents and conflicts with the accomplishment of such *actually-existing* cosmopolitan affiliations. Kosnick examines the tension between an urban cosmopolitan discourse that seeks to market Berlin as a world-open capital and an urban integrationist discourse aiming at discouraging transnational and diasporic identifications of migrants. She suggests, ultimately, that the localizing drive of these urban policy measures and discourses is subverted by the activities and orientations of artists and people with Turkish background who work in the cultural industries.

Whereas the contributions of Youngs and Kosnick engage the limits of the cosmopolitan imagination by focusing on particular ideological frames, Maria Rovisco's chapter highlights ways in which the situational context can actually constrain the cosmopolitan imagination of concrete people. By contrasting the accounts of youths who volunteer within the religious networks of the Catholic Church with the accounts of youths who volunteer within a nonreligious organization, she shows that young Portuguese volunteers, who participate in programmes of cooperation and development in Africa, adopt a cosmopolitan ethico-political outlook by drawing on cosmopolitan narratives, worldviews and ideas that are channelled and enforced in the institutional structures of the organizations where they volunteer. She goes on to make a case for a Christian cosmopolitanism that does not necessarily entail parochialism or religious intolerance. Whereas this type of cosmopolitanism is contrasted with the cosmopolitan outlook of nonreligious young volunteers, she also shows that the image of the cosmopolitan as someone that travels smoothly between cultures and value-systems, and as a consumer of global tastes, does not hold sway in view of the various challenges, uncertainties and tensions the volunteers face in the local sites where they care for others.

The chapters contained in this last part are representative of an emerging line of research that places the management of differences and tensions of various kinds (e.g., religious, ethnic and sexual) at the heart of the research agenda. Taking all chapters together, we hope to have shown that cosmopolitanism can be used as an analytical tool to study 'real life' self-transformations and that this has implications for future research on the topic. We also hope that the empirical evidence the contributors offer will generate fruitful discussions among scholars across the social sciences and beyond traditional disciplinary divisions.

References

Alexander, J. (1992), 'Citizen and Enemy as Symbolic Classification: On the Polarizing Discourse of Civil Society', in Lamont and Fournier (eds).

Appadurai, A. (1996), *Modernity at Large: Cultural Dimensions of Globalization* (Minneapolis: University of Minnesota Press).

Appiah, K.A. (1998), 'Cosmopolitan Patriots', in Cheah and Robbins (eds).

— (2006), *Cosmopolitanism: Ethics in a World of Strangers* (London: Allen Lane).

Archibugi, D., Held, D. and Kohler, M. (eds) (1998), *Re-Imagining Political Community – Studies in Cosmopolitan Democracy* (Cambridge: Polity Press).

Beck, U. (2002), 'The Cosmopolitan Perspective: Sociology in the Second Age of Modernity', in Vertovec and Cohen (eds).

— (2003), 'Rooted Cosmopolitanism: Emerging from a Rivalry of Distinctions', in Beck, Sznaider and Winter (eds).

— (2004), 'Cosmopolitan Realism: On the Distinction Between Cosmopolitanism in Philosophy and the Social Sciences', *Global Networks* 4:2, 131–56.

Beck, U. and Sznaider, N. (2006), 'Unpacking Cosmopolitanism for the Social Sciences: a Research Agenda', *British Journal of Sociology* 57:1, 1–23.

Beck, U. and Winter, R. (eds) (2003), *Global America? The Cultural Consequences of Globalization* (Liverpool: Liverpool University Press).

Benhabib, S. (2002), *The Claims of Culture: Equality and Diversity in the Global Era* (Princeton: Princeton University Press).

Bhabha, H. (1996), 'Unsatisfied: Notes on Vernacular Cosmopolitanism', in Garcia-Moreno and Pfeiffer (eds).

14   *Cosmopolitanism in Practice*

Calhoun, C. (2002), 'The Class Consciousness of Frequent Travelers: Towards a Critique of Actually Existing Cosmopolitanism', *The South Atlantic Quarterly* 101:4, 869–97.

Cheah, P. (2006), 'Cosmopolitanism', *Theory, Culture & Society* 23: 2–3, 486–96.

Cheah and Robbins, B. (eds) (1998), *Cosmopolitics. Thinking and Feeling Beyond the Nation* (Minneapolis: University of Minnesota Press).

Chernilo, D. (2006), 'Social Theory's Methodological Nationalism. Myth and Reality', *European Journal of Social Theory* 9:1, 5–22.

Delanty, G. (2006), 'The Cosmopolitan Imagination: Critical Cosmopolitanism and Social Theory', *British Journal of Sociology* 57:1, 25–47.

Douglas, M. (1966), *Purity and Danger: an Analysis of Concepts of Pollution and Taboo* (London: Routledge & Kegan Paul).

Featherstone, M., Lash, S. and Robertson, R. (eds) (1995), *Global Modernities* (London: Sage).

Fine, R. (2003), 'Taking the "Ism" out of Cosmopolitanism: an Essay on Reconstruction', *European Journal of Social Theory* 6:4, 451–70.

Fine, R. and Boon, V. (2007), 'Introduction: Cosmopolitanism: Between Past and Future', *European Journal of Social Theory* 10:1, 5–16.

Garcia-Moreno, L. and Pfeiffer, P. (eds) (1996), *Text and Nation* (Columbia, SC: Camden House).

Habermas, J. (2001), *The Postnational Constellation – Political Essays* (Cambridge: Polity Press).

Hacker-Cordon C. (ed.) (1999), *Democracy's Edges* (Cambridge: Cambridge University Press).

Hannerz, U. (1992), *Cultural Complexity. Studies in the Social Organization of Meaning* (New York: Columbia University Press).

— (1996), *Transnational Connections: Culture, People, Places* (London: Routledge).

— (2004), *Foreign News. Exploring the World of Foreign Correspondents* (Chicago: The University of Chicago Press).

Jones, P. (2007), 'Cosmopolitanism and Europe: Describing Elites or Challenging Inequalities?', in Rumford (ed.).

Held, D. (1995), *Democracy and the Global Order: From the Modern State to Cosmopolitan Governance* (Cambridge: Polity Press).

— (1999), 'The Transformation of Political Community: Rethinking Cosmopolitanism in the Context of Globalization', in: Hacker-Cordon (ed.).

Kaldor, M. (2002), 'Cosmopolitanism and Organized Violence', in Vertovec and Cohen (eds).

Kant, I. (1991), *Political Writings* (Cambridge: Cambridge University Press).

Kanter, R.M. (1995), *World Class: Thriving Locally in the Global Economy* (New York: Simon & Schuster).

Kleingeld, P. (1999), 'Six Varieties of Cosmopolitanism in Late Eighteenth-Century Germany', *Journal of European Ideas* 60:3, 505–24.

Klöger, H. (2005), 'Constructing a Cosmopolitan Public Sphere – Hermeneutic Capabilities and Universal Values', *European Journal of Social Theory* 8:3, 297–320.

Kofman, E. (2005), 'Figures of the Cosmopolitan: Privileged Nationals and National Outsiders', *Innovation* 18:1, 83–97.

Kurasawa, F. (2007), *The Work of Global Justice. Human Rights as Practices* (Cambridge: Cambridge University Press).

Lamont, M. and Aksartova, S. (2002), 'Ordinary Cosmopolitanisms: Strategies for Bridging Racial Boundaries among Working-Class Men', *Theory, Culture & Society* 19:4, 1–25.

Lamont, M. and Fournier, M. (eds) (1992), *Cultivating Differences – Symbolic Boundaries and the Making of Inequality* (Chicago and London: The University of Chicago Press).

Martins, H. (1974), 'Time and Theory in Sociology', in Rex (ed.).

Mignolo, W. (2000), 'The Many Faces of Cosmo-polis: Border Thinking and Critical Cosmopolitanism', *Public Culture* 12:3, 721–48.

Molz, J. (2006), 'Cosmopolitan Bodies: Fit to Travel and Travelling to Fit', *Body & Society* 12:1, 1–21.

Nash, K. (2006), 'Political Culture, Ethical Cosmopolitanism and Cosmopolitan Democracy', *Cultural Politics* 2:2, 193–212.

Nava, M. (2002), 'Cosmopolitan Modernity: Everyday Imaginaries and the Register of Difference', *Theory, Culture & Society* 19:1–2, 81–99.

— (2007), *Visceral Cosmopolitanism. Gender, Culture and the Normalisation of Difference* (Oxford/New York: Berg).

Nussbaum, M. (1996), 'Patriotism and Cosmopolitanism', in Nussbaum and Cohen (eds).

Nussbaum, M. and Cohen, J. (eds) (1996), *For Love of Country: Debating the Limits of Patriotism* (Cambridge: Beacon Press).

Ong, A. (1998), 'Flexible Citizenship among Chinese Cosmopolitans', in Cheah and Robins (eds).

Pollock, S. (2000), 'Cosmopolitan and Vernacular in History', *Public Culture* 12:3, 591–625.

Pollock et al. (2000), 'Cosmopolitanisms', *Public Culture* 12:3, 577–89.

Rapport, N. and Stade, R. (2007), 'A Cosmopolitan Turn – Or Return?', *Social Anthropology* 15:2, 223–35.

Rex, J. (ed.) (1974), *Approaches to Sociology: An Introduction to Major Trends in British Sociology* (London/Boston: Routledge and Kegan Paul).

Robbins, B. (1998), 'Actually Existing Cosmopolitanism. Cosmopolitics – Thinking and Feeling Beyond the Nation', in Cheah and Robbins (eds).

Robertson, R. (1995), 'Glocalization: Time-Space, Homogeneity-Heterogeneity' in Featherstone, Lash and Roberston (eds).

Robins, K. (2006), *The Challenge of Transcultural Diversities. Transversal Study on the Theme of Cultural Policy and Cultural Diversity* (Strasbourg: Council of Europe Publishing).

Roudometof, V. (2005), 'Transnationalism, Cosmopolitanism and Glocalisation', *Current Sociology* 53:1, 113–35.

Rumford, C. (2005), 'Cosmopolitanism and Europe: Towards a New EU Studies Agenda?' *Innovation* 18:1, 1–9.

— (ed.) (2007), *Cosmopolitanism and Europe* (Liverpool: Liverpool University Press).

Sassen, S. (2006), *Non-Cosmopolitan Globalities*, paper presented to the Conference Assuming Cosmopolitanism: Critical Encounters between Cosmopolitanism and Development, 23–24 November 2006, University of Manchester, Manchester, UK.

Sklair, L. (2000), *The Transnational Capitalist Class* (London: Routledge).

Škrbiš, Z. et al. (2004), 'Locating Cosmopolitanism: Between Humanist Ideal and Grounded Social Category', *Theory, Culture & Society* 21:6, 115–36.

Stade, R. (2008), 'Cosmos and Polis, Past and Present', *Theory, Culture & Society* 24:3–4, 283–5.

Szerszynski, B. and J. Urry (2006), 'Visuality, Mobility and the Cosmpolitan: Inhabiting the World from Afar', *British Journal of Sociology* 57:1, 113–31.

Thompson, C. and Tambyah, S. (1999), 'Trying to Be Cosmopolitan', *Journal of Consumer Research* 26, 214–39.

Turner, B.S. (2002), 'Cosmopolitan Virtue, Globalization and Patriotism', *Theory, Culture & Society* 19:1–2, 45–63.

Urry, J. (2002), 'Mobility and Proximity', *Sociology* 36, 255–74.

— (2003), *Global Complexity* (Cambridge: Polity Press).

Vandenberghe, F. (2006), *The State of Cosmopolitanism*, Paper presented at the XVIth. World Congress of Sociology, Durban, South Africa, July 2006.

Vertovec, S. and Cohen. R. (eds) (2002), *Conceiving Cosmopolitanism – Theory, Context, and Practice* (Oxford and New York: Oxford University Press).

Werbner, P. (1999) 'Global Pathways: Working Class Cosmopolitans and the Creation of Transnational Ethnic Worlds', *Social Anthropology* 7:1, 17–35.

— (2006), 'Vernacular Cosmopolitanism', *Theory, Culture & Society* 23:2–3, 496–8.

PART I
Mobilities

Chapter 1

The Middle Class Cosmopolitan Journey: The Life Trajectories and Transnational Affiliations of Skilled EU Migrants in Manchester

Paul Kennedy

Increasing migration flows, ever more multicultural cities and the forces of globalization combine to intensify human interconnectivities. Consequently we have never before experienced so many opportunities nor such a need to pursue mutual understanding across ethnic, national and other primordial boundaries. It is hardly surprising, therefore, that recent years have seen a surge of interest in cosmopolitanism. Central to this has been a noticeable tendency for scholars (for example, Cheah and Robbins 1998) to focus on what Hollinger (2002) calls the 'new cosmopolitanism'. Here, the preservation of cultural diversity and the universalist desire to find common ground uniting all humans are seen as equally valuable goals. There is also an acceptance that most people find it easier to bestow loyalty on their own ethnic or national group but this need not preclude the existence of certain cosmopolitanism possibilities. This broader perspective also focuses our attention on the possibility of 'multiple kinds of cosmopolitanism' (Delanty 2006, 27) – the many ways the local and the global can be combined. This chapter focuses on one particular and likely source of such influences, namely, the impact of migration and given that around 95 per cent remain at home. However, migrants' experiences also differ markedly and this is likely to affect their capacity to demonstrate various cosmopolitan orientations. Here, briefly, are two different cases which illustrate this point.

Economic migrants from poor countries tend to bring skills and cultural resources that do not always find a ready market and they may face racism and discrimination. Consequently they tend to forge 'highly particularistic attachments' (Waldinger and Fitzgerald 2004, 1178) which replicate the primordial affiliations they knew at home while building multi-faceted transnational links across territorial borders. Thus, we find multicultural societies which stitch the North and South together but in ways that produce mostly separate social enclaves.

In contrast, skilled migrants, especially those who migrate alone and who are not part of a company or other pre-existing organizational team, are in a very different situation. They possess high educational credentials, which can probably be exchanged for the economic capital and social linkages they may initially lack. Their training may equip them to be members of professional occupational cultures which are readily transportable across borders and permit collaboration irrespective of nationality (Hannerz 1990). Moreover, skilled migrants are unlikely to be influenced or assisted by their family or other home ties. Even if they possess a few friends and contacts overseas this does not resemble the multiplex bonds that often encapsulate the economic migrant nor can such expatriate contacts provide the kinds of automatic entry – through family, kin or ethnic-community-based business – into the jobs that skilled migrants may prefer and which they are qualified to seek. Skilled migrants are also increasingly required to valorize the more advanced sectors of the globalized knowledge economy. Yet most are not rootless members of transnational capitalist elites (Sassen 2000 and Sklair 2001). Finally, skilled migrants who are EU citizens enjoy free mobility and equal eligibility to the same employment and some welfare rights as nationals when living in a member country.

This chapter is based on the findings from a qualitative study of 61 skilled migrants from 13 EU member, or associated member, countries. In depth, semi-structured interviews were conducted in 2005. An overall framework of questions was used but they were designed so as to permit multiple responses and to allow the respondents freedom to develop some themes more than others where appropriate. Reliable data bases indicating nationality, gender, age and occupation were not available. EU nationals are not required to register with their consulates. Employers, too, do not compile lists including such information and the UK Data Protection Act prevents them from giving out contact details. The respondents were obtained by sending out emails to organizations, by approaching groups and associations which might offer useful leads and by visiting likely venues frequented by foreigners. Initial contacts were then followed up through a snowball technique. The study is therefore an exploratory one which makes no claims for wider validity though there is no reason to suppose that the respondents were markedly different from other skilled, young EU migrants elsewhere in Britain. Thirty-four women and 27 men were interviewed. The average length of stay was six years but with considerable variation around this mean. Fifty-four per cent were aged between 27 and 34 years, 23 per cent were between 22 and 26 years old and a similar percentage were 35 years or older. All but two were postgraduates and all were in work, mostly full-time. They were employed in a range of local economic sectors as professionals in private businesses, universities, medicine, nursing, dentistry and veterinary services, third sector enterprises and the creative industries and a few were employed in restaurants and shops.

The argument follows a grounded or inductive approach which draws on theoretical insights trawled from recent literature. The discussion begins by outlining a research framework for understanding middle class cosmopolitanism. It then draws extensively on the personal experiences and narratives of the respondents in order to explore these ideas.

Understanding Cosmopolitanism among Skilled Migrants

The Initial Reasons for Migration

It is useful to distinguish the initial reasons skilled migrants may have for moving abroad from those that shape their motives for remaining overseas later. Thus, their cosmopolitanism may be influenced far more by their overseas experiences than whatever orientations they possessed prior to migrating. To different degrees there are perhaps three key factors which may be crucial in prompting these initial moves. One involves access to an appropriate stock of cosmopolitan capital which might predispose some individuals to move overseas and equips them to deal with the difficulties involved. Then there are instrumental needs relating to job and career prospects, pushed partly by a dearth of such opportunities at home. Skilled migrants may face less pressing economic constraints than poor Southern migrants, but to the former these are nevertheless serious and real. Third, many individuals may be affected by a desire to find adventure and cultural diversity through travel. I elaborate on these motives later.

The Career of the Middle-Class Cosmopolitan

Whatever cosmopolitanism may be, it is important not to regard it as a quality that is fixed but as an evolving one. Rather, cosmopolitanism can perhaps be conceived as following a trajectory. In the case of migrants, for example, we can suppose that once overseas they move into a social field fraught with risks and unfamiliar situations and this may propel them in unanticipated directions. Accordingly, we can speak of the potential journey of the cosmopolitan so that over time many people first become one, and then, what began as a one dimensional orientation, might develop a momentum and become a more prominent and multi-faceted aspect of their subjectivity.

Cosmopolitanism as Self-Transformation

It can be inferred from this that cosmopolitanism involves self-transformation whereby individuals interrogate their identity, affiliations, subjectivity and life space (Delanty 2006). Of course, a heightened self-reflexivity and the need to construct one's own persona and life course (Giddens 1991 and Beck and Beck-Gernsheim 2002) are said to be ubiquitous processes in late modern societies and not just for those who migrate. However, for skilled migrants, constructing a do-it-yourself biography is likely to involve a far greater exposure to the 'other' or 'others' than is the case for those who remain at home. This, in turn, seems likely to influence the ways they then pursue their individual projects of self-realization.

Varieties of Middle-Class Cosmopolitanism Abroad

Some individuals may already possess certain cosmopolitan orientations prior to migration and these are discussed below. However, we can identify several qualitatively different kinds which may be either ignited or deepened by living overseas. First, cosmopolitanism may arise or become intensified where individuals establish social relationships with members of ethnic or national groups different from their own and are no longer content to merely gaze with aesthetic curiosity from the outside (see also, Kennedy 2005). The findings from the Manchester research suggest that the experience of building enduring transnational relationships gradually awoke in most a greater awareness and knowledge of other cultures, countries and indeed sometimes of the world or aspects of it. Accordingly, this shift towards world openness constitutes a second orientation but overlapped with, and was largely generated by, engagement in multiple social relations involving border crossings.

There is perhaps a third kind of cosmopolitanism where, fuelled by the interpersonal relationships forged with people from different cultures, individuals might begin to assume a degree of moral responsibility towards distant, unknown others in far away societies. Of course, close social interaction between individuals requires 'a field of moral forces' (Turner 2006, 139) to underpin recognition, trust, respect and reciprocity. This is a normal part of friendship. However, expressing a generalized ethical responsibility – or the preparedness not just to think and feel but also to act outside one's own society and towards unknown others – is perhaps much more difficult than engaging in interculturality and evincing a general openness to the world. Thus, it requires an especially high capacity for empathy that may be related to personality but may also be set in motion or deepened by a unique syndrome of life experiences.

Motives for Migration and the Role of Cosmopolitan Capital

Earlier I suggested three reasons why skilled migrants may see moving overseas as possible and desirable. In this section we explore these in respect to the Manchester respondents. A central theme concerns how far their propensity to migrate was partly or wholly fed by the possession of cosmopolitan capital accruing through earlier experiences.

Some migrants may have greater stocks of cultural and other resources which predispose them to cope with migration. Here, social class is likely to be important especially where individuals come from a middle-class background. This may endow them not just with educational credentials but also social confidence and an individual rather than a collective frame of reference. They bring a free-wheeling and culturally experimental approach to their lives. Certainly, more than half of the Manchester respondents had parents either or both of whom were professionals, company directors or people in high administrative positions. The parents of another quarter were lower civil servants, religious ministers, therapists, middle ranking police or army officers, small entrepreneurs and so on. A capacity to cope competently with one or more foreign languages would also seem to provide cosmopolitan capital and is likely to be associated with social class and educational attainment. Interestingly, in the case of the Manchester respondents, around one third claimed that their desire to learn or improve English – mainly people from the Southern European countries – was one of their main reasons for moving to the UK. A stay in Britain offered them a route to enhancing future career opportunities whether in the UK, back home or elsewhere.

Both these resources, a middle class background and English language proficiency, probably made it easier to engage in migration strategies. However, in neither respect were the respondents markedly different from the rest of their university-educated age cohorts across the EU and in the case of English language we have seen that many initially lacked a proficiency yet they still migrated. A third source of cosmopolitan capital, therefore, which may have been more unique to this particular group – though it is impossible to be certain – was perhaps their previous experience prior to reaching early adulthood, for example, studying abroad or childhood exposure to other cultures. Here, one third of the respondents had spent a period of around six months studying in another country on some kind of degree exchange programme. Britain was the recipient country in roughly half of these instances. Although mostly the respondents regarded these as brief interludes in their undergraduate training rather than as migration experiences, they had encouraged some to move overseas for work and/or postgraduate training later. In the case of childhood experiences 16 respondents reported one or more of the following: having bi-national parents (six cases), living abroad with their parents during childhood (seven cases), spending time at an international school with pupils of many nationalities (two cases) or coming from families with a history of migration across national boundaries associated with geo-political upheavals (two cases). Just under half of the sample fell into either or both of these two categories – short-term overseas degree study and/or childhood exposure to an overseas life.

While it is likely that these respondents were better endowed with cosmopolitan capital as a consequence of such experiences, care is needed in placing too much emphasis on this supposed uniqueness. First, student exchange schemes have been strongly encouraged by the EU for many years and large numbers have enjoyed this experience. Between 1987 and 2003 one million EU students engaged in an overseas exchange experience (Recchi 2006, 71). Second, the remaining respondents who had not enjoyed either or both of these experiences had nevertheless also become migrants. Third, a close examination of the explanations given by the respondents for migrating reveals that hardly anyone provided a single reason. Instead, most claimed a mixture of motives and this is clearly evident from the multiple responses recorded in Table 1.1.

Fourth, short or long term instrumental motives were the most frequently cited reasons for migration and these often overlapped. Adding work, educational and language factors together 87 per cent of the sample migrated for one, and often more, of these motives. This is in line with Beck's (2004, 134) discussion of 'forced cosmopolitanism' where migration is often driven more by economic necessity or 'real-world cosmopolitanism' (Beck 2004, 133) than the pursuit of 'harmony across national and cultural frontiers' (Beck 2004, 132). Breaking down this instrumental factor into its components, over half (51 per cent) claimed that employment or career advancement had been powerful motives. A further 41 per cent moved to the UK partly or entirely in pursuit of educational qualifications. Sometimes this was because they had obtained a university scholarship but more often it was linked to their dearth of appropriate qualifications required for gaining a university place at home or because they believed that a UK university offered the specific course and/or learning culture which were unavailable in their own country. Finally, in most cases the respondents who were endowed with cosmopolitan capital related to earlier educational or family experiences overseas were just as likely to point to instrumental factors when discussing their initial reasons for migrating as those who lacked such assets.

In addition to the possession of reserves of cosmopolitan capital and/or pressing instrumental needs, skilled migrants may also be influenced by the desire for overseas adventure including encounters with cultural 'others'. Indeed, it can be seen from Table 1.1 that this was the most frequently cited non-utilitarian motive for migration, often closely allied to a wish to escape the limitations of local or family life. Altogether 67 per cent talked in these terms. The strength of such desires, among migrants but also the general population, is perhaps largely explicable in the following terms. Contemporary citizens are constantly exposed to images of alternative life ways through the mass media, tourism, migration flows, consumerist images of the exotic spread worldwide by 'branded products and advertising' – which enable people to think of 'themselves as global' (Urry 2000, 185) – or because the visuality of the global made possible by physical-bodily, media and virtual forms of travel (Szerszynski and Urry 2006, 127) contain a potential for spreading cosmopolitan 'ways of thinking and perceiving'. Together these generate a 'banal' cosmopolitanism (Szerszynski and Urry 2002) – an everyday and taken-for-granted set of stimuli on which individuals rarely reflect very deeply. The respondents in the Manchester study seem just as likely to have been exposed to such influences as everyone else. Here, Recchi (2006, 76), among others, has pointed to the tendency for the current generation of middle-class young Europeans to regard moving overseas as a 'shortcut to capital accumulation', both economic and cultural, but also the chance to live an adventurous 'nomadic and globalizing lifestyle'.

Table 1.1 Factors affecting migration to Manchester or the UK

Motives/actors involved	Number	Sample percentage
Employment or career enhancement (Job situation difficult at home, better pay in the UK, more flexible system, job offer here)	31	51
Study related (Ph.D facilities good here, got scholarship, like the degree courses, etc.)	25	41
Language related (Already spoke English or wanted to improve English)	19	31
Some personal connections here (Already had friend/relative here, personal recommendation by someone met at home)	18	30
Romantic links – partner already based here	6	10
Desire to travel overseas, experience other cultures and lifestyles	28	46
Need to escape from home town, country	8	13
Desire to escape family pressures	5	8
Attracted by knowledge of British culture and history	5	8
Attracted by Manchester 'scene' (Music, football)	6	10
Total	**153**	+

Percentages don't add up to 100 per cent because of multiple responses.

Lived Experiences Overseas and Crossing Cultural Borders

The lived experiences of skilled migrants develop their own momentum and may propel individuals along a trajectory of personal and social change which either awakens cosmopolitan orientations or intensifies those they already possess. In this section we explore the interpersonal relationships formed by the Manchester respondents and the pathways they often followed in building a transnational social milieu.

Despite the cultural resources that skilled migrants bring with them, moving overseas – especially for the first time – is fraught with difficulties. This is especially so if they arrive alone and where any prior social contacts are few and mostly thinly dispersed. Only six respondents came to Britain already involved romantically with a British partner who could ease their absorption into local society and in every case they met this person outside the UK. Among the mountains that need to be climbed are the following: coping with the everyday mechanics of life in a strange country, where everything from bus timetables to gaining medical attention seems incomprehensible and especially where language facility is poor; having to become independent from parental support very quickly, especially if away from home for the first time; dealing with emotional emptiness after leaving behind friends, family and familiar places; and the need to build new social networks. Of course there are also advantages and we return to this theme later.

The Difficulties of Gaining Entry to Local Social Networks

One constraint on building a new social life was the difficulties encountered in forming social relationships with locals. This was often related, partly, to their limited language skills during the early period of stay. Language not only carries a people's shared meanings it also contains private codes, secondary meanings, localized colloquialisms and common sense understandings (Schutz 1964, 95).

A lack of fluency is likely to act as a constraint on everyday sociality as Pieter's account illustrates. He was a French-speaking Swiss who had lived in Manchester since 2001. Both through his business and football he had eventually formed a rich social network of local ties across the social class spectrum which was highly exceptional. Nevertheless, on his early stay he said:

> to be honest with you, if you want to…hold a conversation at a normal pace like English people…I think it takes time…it's not easy at all, and I think it is a lot of time thinking 'oh my God what the fuck are they on about'. And they just talk…so fast and is such a slangish way as well that it was just impossible for me after one year of English background to sort of be able to play an active role in a conversation like that.

A number of respondents also pointed to the difficulty of getting to know British people unless you had acquired and internalized the nuanced references to British culture. These included the following: humour and joke-telling skills, a detailed knowledge of sport teams, popular bands, musical trends and media celebrities and above all the situations and themes in UK television soaps and other popular programmes. The consumer and designer lifestyles made possible by a thriving credit card culture were also highly significant in British life. Either much of this was very difficult to understand and perform convincingly, and required a long period of learning, or aspects of it were unacceptable to the respondents thereby limiting their social acceptance. Manuel's comments later illustrate this argument.

However, language facility and cultural knowledge were not the only factors inhibiting entry to local networks. Thus, where migrants only remain for a short period – as with Erasmus students – the investment costs for both parties may seem high compared to the benefits of relationships. Second, locals are usually already encapsulated within a variety of flourishing networks built around family, friendship, school, neighbourhood, college, church and probably work as well. This tendency towards social closure is likely to be even stronger with respect to the local 'native' population who may have lived in the area most of their lives. Indeed, nationals from London or Scotland, for example, might face similar difficulties and this often made them more available as friends especially if they were co-participants in work or study venues. These and other issues are clearly demonstrated by the following accounts.

Vivienne was a German university language teacher aged 29. She had been in Manchester for barely a year. She commented:

> I know a lot of people especially through my church and flat mates some of whom also attend the church…but I've not been here long enough to make real friends. I think there's a Manchester problem. I don't really know English people. First, I'm in the language department – so no one here is English. And in this particular church it's the same problem, the same thing. I have a Danish friend, a Mexican friend or whatever but really to know English people it seems impossible in Manchester. Those who attend the church are quite young and mostly students…you have a lot of exchange students or doctoral students and lots of people staying here, coming over and staying here… It's so much easier to get involved with the non-English because they are coming here and they are open and looking for somebody – and the English they have their own groups.

Elvira had been in Manchester since 2002 and worked part time for a clinic offering physiotherapy. On her contacts with locals she said:

> in my first year I lived in halls and so I have a few British friends from there who are still close friends but they are all Londoners. I hardly know a single Mancunian…The only time I really interact with Mancunians is when I go to work for the physiotherapist job…I feel I belong to a set of international people. I've lived in many places, I have friends from all over the world. So whenever I encounter Mancunians they've lived here all their lives. Those that go to university here they'll stay here. Hence I don't have much in common with them…to make friends with them is a lot harder.

Gravitating Towards Other Foreigners

Partly because of their difficulties in penetrating local networks but also because of other shared problems during their early period of stay, many respondents formed relationships with other foreigners. Like them, they were away from home and were social outsiders. This tendency to gravitate towards other foreigners rather than – or in addition to – expatriates is probably more likely in the case of older migrants, among those who intend to stay for some time and/or those who have secured stable jobs. In addition, some organizations and firms assemble mixed nationalities for long term projects. This may be because the work involved requires a portfolio of language skills in order to deal with overseas clients or simply in order to find versatile, skilled employees. Examples of such organizations include: university research and postgraduate centres, third sector organizations, the national health service, multinational companies which specialize in servicing the needs of overseas affiliates and creative arts organizations. Certain kinds of leisure activities and locations may also attract foreigners and several such places were mentioned – the art-house cinema, certain restaurants, bars and coffee houses, the tango club in the city centre and various night clubs. The following accounts illustrate the dynamics involved in these processes and are fairly typical.

Antonio was in his late twenties and from Turin. He worked as a university research assistant. Talking about his friendships formed through the university he commented:

> The university is very mixed as you know, although I befriend more easily with people who are not English…perhaps, I think, we (the non-British) have less connections other than work with the British.

He went on to describe the networking processes which underpinned both expatriate relationships and those between foreigners.

> It just so happens because of the places where people meet and really the conditions and the opportunities they have. And there is also a word of mouth phenomenon, you can read emails or you can be asked when somebody comes to Manchester for the first time, where they could stay, and so there are chains and networks.

Wolfgang was German with a French partner and taught at a university. Asked about his social life in Manchester he replied:

> For a long time I met a lot of other Europeans, like Paulos, who's a Finnish musician, and I think it took me longer to become friends with people from England, or even with Mancunians, but I had the same experience in Stockholm and Helsinki, that first this international community creates a lot of meetings and parties…so you meet a lot of foreigners…and it takes time to really come close to the inhabitants.

These findings call into question Hannerz's (1990) influential argument that cosmopolitanism involves deliberately seeking encounters with the local cultural 'other' because it seems this can often be very difficult. How can migrants respond in the face of this local indifference? In the case of many respondents one solution was to distinguish between parochial people who, irrespective of their social class, had never left the region or city and British nationals who shared the identity of being 'strangers' from elsewhere and especially if these were educated and/ or people sharing the same work or professional experience. There was some indication from the study that there is also a third kind of 'local'. This is the person who has also lived overseas at some previous time and who is therefore more responsive and socially confident towards the foreigners they later meet at 'home' as well as better equipped to engage in intercultural exchanges. As we have seen, six respondents had met their British partner outside the UK and in four cases this occurred where both were in a third country. In addition, several other respondents who had long-term British partners reported that the latter had studied or travelled abroad before they both met.[1] The general significance of living abroad as a transformatory experience – especially for some certain kinds of skilled migrants – is discussed more fully later.

Another issue raised by these findings concerns why the experience of forging social affiliations with other foreigners helped to propel them in a cosmopolitan direction. Here, what is crucial is the fact that these very trans- and post-national relationships exposed them to cultural 'others' far more than if they had remained at home. Moreover, this happened at a time of strong emotional need. They had to navigate their way across these primordial boundaries and forge intercultural exchanges. But added to this there was the reality, noted by a number or respondents, that locations in Britain, and especially cities such as Manchester, contained a much greater national-cultural mix of people from across the world than they had encountered at home, thereby adding to their mélange of intercultural encounters.

Paths into Local Society

Despite the obstacles, most respondents eventually formed relationships with some British people. Several pathways led in this direction. One involved access to certain venues and situations which are especially conducive to meeting and befriending locals. We have seen that university postgraduate or research centres provide one such example but others include orchestras and bands, hospitals, IT companies, NGOs or cultural centres where foreign nationals offer language courses to interested locals (there are three in Manchester). Another route arose where the respondents formed romantic relationships with British partners – some of whom may have also lived overseas previously. Third, with the sheer passing of time and the accumulation of cultural knowledge, language skills and social contacts, through such things as buying a property, becoming involved with neighbours or forming work friendships, many respondents gradually became partly absorbed into British society. Each of the next two case studies illustrates one of these scenarios and they stand in for others.

---

1 Unfortunately the possible significance of this connection only became apparent some time after completing the interviews so a clearer picture is not possible without further research.

Marianne was a French teacher in her early thirties. Both in her first teaching post in Plymouth, after graduating in France, and some years later in London she found it hard to break into local networks. Describing her London experience she said:

> I met people at work but...people were living in different parts of London and going back home every night. They had their own circle of friends and so never went out to do things, or only once or twice a year...So I'd just go home and you were alone...I knew some French people on the same course...and I hung out with them. But it wasn't really a choice, it was the situation.

However, she is now married to a British partner she met in Budapest. They have a child and so she now shares school interests with other parents but is also involved with neighbours and local friends and relatives through her marriage. As she observed:

> I think when you are in a romantic relationship with someone then this person can introduce you to his or her own friends. But that's the only way through I know [into local social life].

Manuel was Spanish and worked in a cultural centre. He was unmarried and had worked and partly lived in the Manchester area for some years. His comments on how over time he had become partly embedded in the host society through friendships rather than romantic relationships, echo those of other respondents.

> I suppose I feel part of this country now, I feel integrated...whereas people I've met...they still feel foreign...I've got quite a strong accent and people assume I'm foreign but I don't feel that foreign...I suppose I know music, I know telly programmes, I know actors, there are so many things that have become part of my culture...it's kind of a hard job to get used to the weather, food, culture, the way of living. But I feel happy here now...I mean for example if my boss said you've got to go New York...I will do it...but then I will be paying all the visits to England because I've got my friends here.

Some indication of the extent to which the respondents had formed transnational relationships, including crossing the barriers into British society, is revealed by the following. Thus, when asked about their three or four closest friends in Manchester and/or the UK nearly one third did not include any fellow-nationals at all among this group – although these were often present in their wider networks. On the other hand, the closest friends named by over half were individuals who were partly, and sometime mainly, members of other foreign nations. Similarly, four fifths of the respondents included at least one British person among their closest friends. Of course, most also belonged to wider social networks which included a mixture of British people, other foreign nationals or expatriates. These might be individuals living in Manchester, or elsewhere in the UK or friends originally met in another country.

Turning to their romantic partnerships, nearly a quarter had formed these while in the UK with a long term partner who was neither British nor an expatriate. If we include those who were previously involved in several short-term romantic relationships both with foreigners and British partners this figure increases to just over a third. Moreover, a further six respondents entered long-term partnerships with a British person when living in a third country when both were 'foreigners'. Another quarter of the respondents were involved in long term relationships with British partners while, as we have just seen, a further 10 per cent had formed such relationships when overseas. If we add those respondents who were previously involved in temporary relationships with local people and foreigners we find that nearly half the respondents had been or were in romantic partnerships involving British people. In total, therefore, 70 per cent of the sample were, or had been, involved in mostly long-term romantic partnerships with other foreigners or British people. Only 10 per cent were in permanent relationships with co-nationals.

Personal Transformations

We have seen that most respondents had moved beyond a purely aesthetic or banal cosmopolitanism. Rather, through their transnational relationships they explored each others' 'cultural models' (Delanty 2006, 37). This required a recognition and respect for differences and the need for 'critical mutual evaluation' (Turner 2006, 142). Arguably, these require and engender orientations which involve a qualitative leap we might refer to as 'social' cosmopolitanism. However, for skilled migrants, creating a new life and social milieu also provides opportunities to undertake a kind of self transformation. Thus, although all the respondents maintained regular contact with people at home – through mutual visits, emails, phone calls and so on – going abroad alone also placed them beyond the immediate and continuous social control of their native society. But as we have seen they were also rather distant from the host situation. Together these social situations provided a degree of social freedom and therefore the possibility of not just forging a new social milieu but also of constructing an alternative self and life path. Of course, as we saw earlier, some sociologists see individualization processes as endemic in the advanced societies so that social actors increasingly desire and expect to construct their own life course and identity. Indeed, this becomes a necessity as social institutions retreat and the rise of the world risk society compels us all to engage in continuous, reflexive self-monitoring (Beck and Beck-Gernsheim 2002). The difference in the case of skilled migrants is that they place themselves in a situation where they become dis-embedded from their original society virtually overnight and much more completely compared to the gradual processes of individualization experienced by those who remain at home. At the same time they become exposed to a multitude of experiences involving encounters with cultural 'others'.

The following accounts describe quite vividly this process of finding oneself in an outsider position and the personal liberation it may engender. Petra was trained in Berlin as a musicologist and in Manchester combined part-time university teaching with studying for her doctorate.

> Going abroad it's easier for you to try things out, because you leave your close circle of friends who expect you to be exactly like you've always been. And you can try new things, find out things and change things, perhaps be around people you have avoided before...Yes. You cut off strings. I mean that's the most obvious thing, you cut off strings...you're on your own feet and you have to do it yourself, there's no on else you can really rely on. And what's really hard is you have to establish your own new circle of friends and your new social life. And, yeah, it's liberating – it's definitely been for me.

Oscar had worked in Britain since 1993 teaching languages. But he began training to become a homeopathic practitioner and in 2003 set up his own clinic.

> I don't have the same pressures other Germans have...I sidestep that...my experience of England has been different...it gave me this position of being here slightly on the outside. And I feel you know, none of the measurements, if you like, totally apply to me...you are in this strange cultural middle position of not being judged by your own country because I don't live there, so I'm in a sense a bit the odd one out over there – you know there's always an excuse – well, he lives in England – and of course the same applies here...But at the moment it seems to me this sort of middle ground, neither here nor there...seems to give me some kind of strange sense of freedom.

Overall, nearly half the sample (48 per cent) described how by becoming exposed to so many different people and ways of thinking they had attained a degree of self development and autonomy that would have been less possible had they remained at home. Thus they pointed to one or more of the following ways in which their lives had changed: they had developed as a human being (10 per cent), gained self knowledge (15 per cent), were now more free to make their own choices (19 per cent) or had become much more capable of managing their own lives (28 per cent).

Marta's story offers a good illustration of self-development. She came from a bi-national family with a Spanish and a British parent but lived mostly in Spain before coming to the UK. She taught Spanish part-time but also worked in a restaurant. Talking of her relation with Spanish friends, she said:

> [...] yeah, I think it's changed quite a lot. Well my friends back home are people who have never really left our home town, they went to university...they got a job...they settled...I can't connect to that kind of life just because I've met

so many people since that have been living such different lives. It's sometimes difficult to connect with them.

Later, talking about her identity, she said:

You can just see that everything is very relative. The way in which people organize their lives. Because you've lived in different cities and in every different city people live in certain ways and assume its normal…I think it makes you feel very free. I can do what I want.

The End of the Cosmopolitanism Journey? Taking on the World

Middle class cosmopolitanism may involve not just transnational relationships and interculturality but also becoming more open to some aspects of the wider world and its problems. Certainly most of the respondents (83 per cent) claimed that living abroad had helped propel them in this direction or had started them along this path. Moreover, as the following quotes illustrate, it was other people rather than media exposure, consumerism or travel which had awoken and/or shaped this world openness.

Christos is Greek and runs his own small business in information technology. Asked about his identity he said:

Yeah, I have, changed, I have been meeting people from many different places and that has shaped my views on the world, you know I am much more aware of what the world is now.

Asked whether and how living abroad had changed her, Petra replied:

The network of the world becomes more obvious…You broaden your horizon and once you let in one country you let in others.

When asked whether living in France and Britain had altered her identity, Elvira commented:

I think I'm much less narrow-minded than I used to be…you learn to see the value of all different cultures. Like with my African friends – 'oh, don't worry, we'll sort it out tomorrow'…and I think that's a very important aspect of their culture that I've learned to appreciate.

Sylvie is French but spent much of her childhood in Martinique where her parents had strong family connections. She came to Britain to study when she was eighteen but later lived in Venezuela for three years. At the time of the interview she was a French language teacher. Talking about how living in different places had changed her, she replied:

> […] because you get to meet loads of different people from different backgrounds, and you know people that might not be able to speak English but are intelligent. It's not thinking like other people…The reason why I very much liked my experience in Venezuela was because I was coming from a rich and developed country and I came across very, very poor people who had no means whatsoever…So I became more aware of poverty…But at the same time it's difficult to try and help the world unless you go there. And that's why I love interpreting – to actually be able to help people on a global basis.

I think Sylvie's narrative provides an example of perhaps the most difficult dimension of middle-class cosmopolitanism: moving from world openness to assuming moral responsibility for distant unknown others. There were around 15 respondents who had either made this jump towards ethical responsibility or who were in the process of doing so. It appeared to be micro relationships based on mutual liking that had triggered this wider moral concern. Sometimes, these relations involved people from other countries who the respondents had befriended. Massimiliano's example illustrates this. But alternatively, it might be a fellow national who conveyed their private sense of concern and moral responsibility to their fellow national following their own experience of forging a close relationship with a foreign person.

An Italian anthropologist in his early thirties, Massimiliano, came to Manchester in 1998 to begin his doctorate studies but this had involved spending some time in Namibia.

> I feel loyalty to the places I've been and I've worked in…Yes, I have strong links with the place I did my research, the people I worked with (in Namibia)…I went back already two times after I finished my research and I'm going back again…I feel very strongly attached to it, emotionally. Because of the human side of it – I left behind a lot of good friends and feel for the things they had to go through.

Finally, Edna was from Norway and after completing her degree in Manchester she was working in a clinic. She observed:

> In Norway the information about other countries is very good but I personally know some cultures better because of my overseas friends – so I know more personally. She continued: I might go abroad and work in Zimbabwe later because of my contact with a close Norwegian friend who has been there and all the things she described.

Concluding Thoughts

Of course, individuals may develop one or more cosmopolitan orientations without moving overseas. Nevertheless, and especially for certain kinds of skilled migrants, living abroad involves a sharp discontinuity with a previous life and this is likely to trigger influences which either initiate their movement along a cosmopolitan trajectory or which intensifies and propels them further in this direction. Here, several inextricably linked processes are going on simultaneously. First, the individualization processes that are said to be unfolding generally in the advanced societies may be hugely intensified because of the relative social vacuum into which skilled migrants place themselves by going abroad. Giddens' (1991, 113) concept of 'fateful moments' is useful here although he did not include migration in his list of these events (marriage, moving house and so). Fateful moments place the individual at 'a crossroads in his existence' and force him/her to confront new 'moral/existential criteria' (203). But, second, the experiences reported by the Manchester respondents strongly suggest that living abroad also propels skilled migrants towards constructing post-national relationships. Yet, third, through these relationships with other foreigners as well as some locals they became exposed to a much greater extent than would be possible or likely at home to a range of different and new cultural stimuli requiring mutual recognition and intercultural negotiation. This, in turn, led not only to increased confidence, a sense of autonomy and the ability to reflect critically on their own culture and society but also to greater world openness and even, in some cases, the ability to feel a degree of ethical commitment towards distant unknown others.

A 'strong' form of cosmopolitanism – one that contains a capacity to evolve far beyond a banal version – is probably most likely to occur where individuals undergo a clear break with established social ties and constraints and so are able to distance themselves more convincingly and comfortably from their early ethnic/national backgrounds. Yet, in partly escaping from the overriding dominance of one set of social affiliations and in discovering greater self autonomy they are nevertheless simultaneously propelled towards a new and much broader set of commitments and dependencies. Though these provide and indeed demand scope for a much broader and more urbane set of cultural references they also bring their own social and moral responsibilities – ones that perhaps contain a potential to ultimately encompass all humanity.

References

Beck, U. (2004), 'Cosmopolitical Realism: on the Distinction Between Cosmopolitanism in Philosophy and the Social Sciences', *Global Networks* 4:2, 131–56.
— and Beck-Gernsheim, E. (2002), *Individualization* (London: Sage).

Cheah, P. and Robbins, B. (eds) (1998), *Cosmopolitics: Thinking and Feeling Beyond the Nation State* (Minneapolis: University of Minnesota Press).

Delanty, G. (2006), 'The Cosmopolitan Imagination: Critical Cosmopolitanism and Social Theory', *British Journal of Sociology* 57:1, 25–48.

Featherstone, M. (ed.) (1990), *Global Culture: Nationalism, Globalization and Modernity* (London: Sage).

Giddens, A. (1991), *Modernity and Self-Identity: Self and Society in the Late Modern Age* (Cambridge: Polity Press).

Hannerz, U. (1990), 'Cosmopolitans and Locals in World Culture', in Featherston (ed.).

Hollinger, D.A. (2002), 'Not Universalists, not Pluralists: The New Cosmopolitans Find their Way', in Vertovec and Cohen (eds).

Kennedy, P. (2005), 'Joining, Constructing and Benefiting from the Global Workplace: Transnational Professionals in the Building-Design Industry', *Sociological Review* 53:1, 172–97.

King, R. and Ruiz-Gelices, E. (2003), 'International Student Migration and the European "Year Abroad": Effects on European Identity and Subsequent Migration Behaviour', *International Journal of Population Geography* 9:3, 229–52.

Recchi, E. (2006), 'From Migrants to Movers: Citizenship and Mobility in the European Union', in Smith and Favell (eds).

Sassen, S. (2000), *Cities in a World Economy* (Thousand Oaks, CA: Pine Forge).

Schutz, A. (1964), *Collected Papers Volume II: Studies in Social Theory* (The Hague: Martinus Nijhoff).

Sklair, L. (2001), *The Transnational Capitalist Class* (London: Blackwell).

Smith, M.P. and Favell, A. (eds) (2006), *The Human Face of Global Mobility* (New Brunswick, NJ: Transaction Publishers).

Szerszynski, B. and Urry, J. (2002), 'Cultures of Cosmopolitanism', *The Sociological Review* 50:4, 461–81.

— (2006), 'Visuality, Mobility and the Cosmopolitan: Inhabiting the World from Afar', *British Journal of Sociology*, 57:1, 113–32.

Turner, B.S. (2006), 'Classical Sociology and Cosmopolitanism: a Critical Defence of the Social', *British Journal of Sociology* 57:1, 133–52.

Urry, J. (2000), *Sociology Beyond Societies* (London: Routledge).

Vertovec, S. and Cohen, R. (eds) (2002), *Conceiving Cosmopolitanism – Theory, Context and Practice* (Oxford and New York: Oxford University Press).

Waldinger, R. and Fitzgerald, D. (2004), 'Transnationalism in Question', *American Journal of Sociology* 109, 1177–95.

Chapter 2
Ethnic Groups Unbound: A Case Study of the Social Organization of Cosmopolitanism

Mark-Anthony Falzon

The association of ethnic groups with cosmopolitanism seems to be fraught with internal contradictions. It is hard to reconcile communitarianism and universalism, spatial boundedness and multilocality, organized culture and an eclectic and open disposition. And yet, even the most cursory of looks at contemporary reality reveals a burgeoning number of ethnic and other groups claiming some sort of cosmopolitan status. In this chapter I shall argue: First, that there is no necessary contradiction between ethnicity and 'world citizenship'; second, that the dialectic between opposing models of social and spatial organization is what cosmopolitanism *in practice* is all about; and third, that this dialectic often takes place within the boundaries of ethnic groups. I shall be looking at the case of Sindhis, a diasporic Indian group.[1] Before I do so, however, I wish to make some general points.

It is clear that we are dealing here with what Robbins (1998) calls an 'actually-existing' cosmopolitanism – an empirical/ethnographic instance rather than a theoretical concept, that is. To my mind, one of the reasons why there is a real and urgent need to look at these practical instances is that scholars have tended to privilege cosmopolitanism in its philosophical sense at the expense of more vernacular types which seem to be open to the accusation of banality. However, quite apart from the fact that this distinction is uncomfortably reminiscent of otherwise-obsolete high:low culture dichotomies, there are important reasons why cosmopolitanism in practice matters. First, all cosmopolitanisms are to some extent actually-existing in that they are located within some historical and geographical framework; thus, as Stuart Hall (2008) argues, even the towering universalistic political projects of Kant turn out to be 'harnessed back' to a very specific ideological and cultural movement, namely the Western Enlightenment. Second, actually-existing cosmopolitanisms deserve our primary scholarly attention, since their actual existence presumably means that they are actually consequential (as opposed to Utopias, which are just that). Third, to look at the maps and histories

---

1   Extensive discussions of many of the empirical materials of this chapter are to be found in Falzon (2005).

– and therefore the limits and limitations – of particular cosmopolitanisms is partly to absolve oneself of the nagging feeling that contemporary social science, in waxing lyrical about 'flows', 'fractals' and 'fluidity', is (once again, some might say) being the handmaiden of contemporary regimes of production, accumulation, and power – in our a case a neo-liberal 'globalizing' agenda in which the 'emphasis falls more on individualist aspirations and universalizing norms' (Pollock et al. 2000, 581). Related to this is the argument that looking at practical (mundane) cosmopolitanism will serve to redress the balance in favour of various groups for whom belonging everywhere (and therefore nowhere) is not a choice but a predicament. 'Elite' political models of world citizenship have their rightful place, but they do not explain everything. Finally, understanding the social organization of cosmopolitanism is very much about overcoming trite local-global dichotomies. Smith's work (2001) on 'agency-oriented' 'transnationalism from below' in contemporary cities constitutes an important point of reference here. This chapter seeks to do for people (ethnic groups) what Smith does for places (cities).

Talking about actually-existing cosmopolitanisms, however, raises the perennial spectre of definition. In this sense the difficulty that so preoccupied Weber is still with us. In a nutshell, if all cosmopolitanisms exist within, and therefore take on some of the characteristics of, specific histories and geographies, this very specificity seems to preclude us from generalizing in any useful way. Scholars of cosmopolitanism (notably Vertovec and Cohen 2002) have, quite successfully I think, sought to circumvent this problem by creating inclusive typologies – rather than exclusive definitions – of cosmopolitan *attributes* which the various empirical instances we observe to some extent share. In this chapter, 'Sindhiness' will be shown to display the following attributes:

- a worldwide distribution;
- a problematic relation to the nation-state;
- an attitude or disposition which means that Sindhis, to quote Vertovec and Cohen (2002, 13), can 'end up anywhere in the world and be in the same relation of familiarity and strangeness to the local culture, and feel partially adjusted everywhere';
- a marked competence at operating within translocal business networks;
- and, finally, kinship practices based on marriage alliances beyond the person's immediate locality and which therefore result in cosmopolitan genealogies.

It is important to stress that, taken individually, none of these attributes leads to cosmopolitanism. Given the ongoing inflation of the term (as has happened with 'diaspora' – see Brubaker 2005) for instance, it is clear that self-ascription alone cannot be indicative of a tangible cosmopolitanism. Equally, just as travel does not necessarily broaden one's horizons (as anyone who has enjoyed the dubious pleasure of tourist enclaves knows), worldwide distribution *per se* does not make the cosmopolitan grade. Taken in conjunction, however, these family resemblances mean that belonging to the Sindhi ethnic group constitutes a powerful and well-trodden trajectory into the (currently desirable) cosmopolitan way of engaging with the world – even if mitigated by factors such as caste, resources, location, occupation and level of education.

The Conquest of Space

> My home, I carry on my shoulders.
> – Krishin Rahi (Sindhi poet)

My fieldwork with Sindhis was conducted over two periods of several months each. In 1995–96 I worked in Malta and in 1999–2001 mostly in Mumbai and London. Most of my informants were highly mobile people who produced 'multi-sited' data about their lives. In the context of the participant observation paradigm, moving around also became an essential aspect of my field practice.

With respect to the cosmopolitan distribution of Sindhis, there are two important aspects to note. The first concerns the dynamics of this dispersal and its consequences in the contemporary world. The second derives from the special significance of a number of locations where Sindhis are found and the heightened sense of cosmopolitanism that these sites foster.

The key point here is that spatial unboundedness is a key element of Sindhi self-ascription. Sindhis, particularly but by no means exclusively *bhaibands* (see below), think of themselves primarily as a globally-dispersed, interconnected ethnic group. The conquest of geographical space is possibly the dominant trope of vernacular histories (which tend to have sub-titles like 'The Scattered Treasure' (Hiranandani 1980)), popular narratives, everyday discourse, and rhetoric. All of these commonly give 'examples' of world's end locations where Sindhis ply their trade – the Falklands, Alaska, Antarctica, and so forth. One popular theory is that the Phoenicians were in fact Sindhis (Malkani 1984, 153), while a more ambitious one maintains that 'research indicates there must have been Sindhvarkis in the ports where Ulysses called in the course of his 30 year Odyssey' (Buxani in Panjwani 1987, 94). On our part we needn't go back that far, but we certainly need to trace the historical production of such ideas.

Between 1843 and 1947 Sind was a province of British India. It became part of the newly formed nation-state of Pakistan with the Independence of India and the Partition of the country in 1947. When the British conquered and annexed Sind to their Indian possessions in 1843, the province had for several hundred years been ruled by a series of Muslim dynasties and the population was mainly Muslim. The people of this chapter, the Hindus of Sind, were involved in commerce, either as small-time village *banias* (traders) or urban merchants. A small number, mostly pertaining to the *amil* caste, served as administrators to the Muslim royalty and aristocracy, and later to the British.

Well before the British period, specific groups of urban-based merchants had been involved in regional trade networks. The moneylenders of the northern town of Shikarpur, for instance, were renowned all over central Asia, particularly during the Durrani Empire period in the eighteenth century (see Markovits 2000), as long-ranging dealers in *hundis* (promissory notes). The towns of the fertile plains of the south, on their part, had tight knit groups of merchants that traded in various commodities in and around the Arabian Sea and Malabar Coast. The memoirs of one Seth Naomul Hotchand of Karachi (1804–78), albeit a masterclass of self-glorifying genealogy, give us a wonderful insight into the ways in which family firms set up networks and branches over a vast region (Hotchand 1915).

The British takeover incorporated these regional networks into an expanding universe. Clearly, the results were various. The Shikarpuri moneylending business, which by 1843 had in any case seen its best days, did not integrate in any consequential way into this new geography. The merchants of the south on the other hand, and in particular a mobile group known as *bhaibands* from the town of Hyderabad, explored the new opportunities presented by Empire. By the 1860s, pockets of *bhaiband* men were operating in places as far apart as Panama and Singapore (then the Straits Settlements). Their original line was the sale of Sindhi handicrafts for which there was a healthy demand, thanks in part to the great European exhibitions of the time. Due to these origins, Sindhi merchants are to this day often called 'Sindworkis'; in truth, by the 1870s they had diversified and were trading in a large number of commodities, notably tourist curios and souvenirs.

Sindworkis, then, were the first Sindhis to merit the description of a cosmopolitan (at least in a spatial sense) merchant group. The importance of Imperial and colonial projects – and of the informational, transport, and technological infrastructure which was their corollary – in the genesis of such mobilities cannot be overemphasized. So much so, that various South Asian merchant groups that today enjoy a worldwide distribution, experienced their first significant dispersals in the latter half of the nineteenth century. (Parekh (1994) has described these people, who followed the economic opportunities created by indenture and other projects of empire, as 'passenger Indians'.) In a matter of a decade or two, older *regional* networks became truly cosmopolitan. This historical convergence between Empire and spatial redefinition has been noted in various contexts. Diouf's (2000) work on the Senegalese Murids, for instance, shows how the French colonial context proved instrumental in creating a unified, centralized, and far-ranging diaspora of traders. It is not just that Empire fostered opportunities for travel. Perhaps more important was the proliferation of what we may call hotbeds of cosmopolitanism in the form of colonial harbour towns, route nodes, entrepôts, and even passenger ships themselves (aboard which these pioneers spent months on end). This was the experience of Sindhis in places like Gibraltar, Hong Kong, and Port of Spain – all examples of what Hall (2008) identifies as the 'market sites' within which cosmopolitanism especially thrives.

By the first decades of the twentieth century, therefore, the Hindus of Sind were largely composed of rural and small-town traders and moneylenders, a small and specialized caste of civil servants, and the high-profile Sindworki firms. The last group ran their transnational businesses from Hyderabad, based on a system of branches to which family members and/or employees were allocated. The events of Partition and its immediate aftermath changed all of this. In the exodus that followed, the various groups of Hindus followed a number of trajectories out of Sind. The small traders and civil servants moved to India and by 1951 36 per cent of them (around 250,000) were settled in Mumbai (then Bombay). The Sindworkis, on their part, tended to move permanently, and in many cases with their families, to the various countries in which their branches were located.

Since 1947, there have been two important forms of Sindhi mobility. The first involved people who initially settled in India but eventually (from the 1950s onwards) moved to the USA, Canada, Britain, and Australia. Interestingly *amils*, who tend to predominate in paid employment, are well represented in this loose group; a good number of them moved on the basis of their professional qualifications – medicine, engineering, and more recently information technology. To these we should add the thousands of Sindhis who have settled in the countries of the Gulf. In the 1970s and 1980s, for example, Sindhis dominated the textiles trade in Dubai (Weiner 1982). The second type of movement was what Boyarin (cited in Clifford 1994, 305) calls 'multiple experiences of rediasporization' and involved Sindworkis shifting their locations in response to political and/or economic changes. Sindhis settled in East Africa, some of them the descendants of the original Sindworki pioneers, were a case in point.

As a result of these movements, each of which belongs within a very specific set of historical circumstances (Empire, Partition, de-colonization, the rise of the oil-rich Gulf, Africanization and others), Sindhis today form a truly cosmopolitan ethnic group. As my informants were always keen on reminding me, 'Sindhis are everywhere'. The word 'everywhere' needs some qualification here in that most Sindhis, and especially those involved in business, are settled in cities and towns, which, as theorized by Simmel and others, imply the twin notions of 'strangeness' and alterity – and therefore, and perhaps paradoxically, of cosmopolitanism (see Sennett 2002).

Apart from these relatively large-scale population movements, there is a further form of Sindhi mobility. Transnational marriage involves a constant transaction of individuals across space which, albeit not as spectacular as Partition or the exodus from East Africa, is cumulatively very significant. It is also every bit as consequential, resulting in the cosmopolitan genealogies that so characterize Sindhi kinship. As is typical of South Asian societies, there is nothing 'essential' about the meaning of caste endogamy among Sindhis, and the notion has historically taken on various incarnations. From the late nineteenth to the mid-twentieth century the predominant operational notion of caste was one of regional/occupational types such as *bhaiband*, *amil* and Shikarpuri. Following Partition, the term has shifted somewhat and 'Sindhiness in general' is increasingly seen as an important form of caste. In this sense we can say that caste and ethnic group are converging, in a process known in the literature as the 'ethnicization' of caste (see Sharma 1999 for a concise discussion).

The upshots are that a biological idiom and its corollary, endogamy, unites Sindhis worldwide, and that marriages are accordingly arranged across vast distances. Whether at a marriage bureau in Mumbai or a kitty party in London, the world is the stage as far as Sindhi marriage matching is concerned. Women have much say over this type of dispersal, in two ways. First, as potential brides in a patrilocal universe, Sindhi girls are brought up to think that marriage quite often involves leaving one's natal country, a process over which increasingly the individual has a degree of choice. Second, the 'marriage market' (to borrow a term from my informants) is very much a woman's world through which 'aunties' travel, exchanging information. I emphasize this because an important element of cosmopolitanisms in practice must surely be their gendering. (I suspect that this topic will receive considerable scholarly attention in the near future.) Sindhis are therefore embedded in cosmopolitan genealogies that are actively manufactured, in significant measure by women, along communitarian lines. These include both the older caste meanings that are still with us (and indeed my research indicates that *bhaiband* genealogies and those of old Sindworki families are the most cosmopolitan of all), and the more recent notion of 'Sindhiness' as an operational endogamous group. In a marital take on 'cosmopolitan communitarianism' (Bellamy and Castiglione 1998), Sindhis marry out (geographically) by marrying in (socially).

The wide distribution in and the familiarity of Sindhis with 'the world' comes across in innumerable practical ways. To give one example, the magazine *BR International* (formerly *Bharat Ratna*) is published by the Harilela family of Hong Kong but draws on the services of a large number of correspondents from as many different localities to carry articles and gossip pages about the activities of Sindhis in these countries. It also covers matters of local interest such as a new airport or independence celebrations, which therefore become items of cosmopolitan interest. The gossip pages are particularly fascinating because they show Sindhis in their various countries celebrating weddings, family occasions, and national events; moreover, they are joined by Sindhis visiting from different countries. As the online blurb says, 'BR is the media organ of the worldwide Sindhi community. It affords easy access for regional communities to interact globally with their counterparts scattered around the world.'[2]

Doing Business with an Open Mind

> When with brahmins say 'Ram, Ram', when with mullahs say 'Allah, Allah'.
> – Sindhi proverb

---

2   www.bharatratna.com.

So far I have limited myself to discussing the geographical distribution of Sindhis and its spatial implications. In this sense 'cosmopolitan' comes close to its meaning in natural history, where it is used to denote a species which is broadly distributed and not limited to a single geographical and/or ecological region. Having a (world)wide range, however, also implies that the species is relatively adaptable and catholic in its choice of sustenance and habitat. Cosmopolitan species of butterflies, for example, often make use of a range of foodplants, in contrast to localized ones which often have very specialized requirements. By analogy, cosmopolitan human groups tend to cultivate models of culture which are adaptable and incorporative, at least up to a point. Sindhis are no exception, and in this section I shall discuss the incorporative aspects of Sindhi culture by focusing largely on narratives of *Sindhayat* ('Sindhiness'). The implication is that it is not the essentialist decision as to whether or not Sindhi culture is *really* incorporative that matters. If one can be pardoned for quoting 40-odd year old sources (Barth 1969), the emphasis will be on the boundary rather than the 'cultural stuff'. In this case, a boundary which is perceived, and actively constructed, as malleable – hence the cosmopolitan 'disposition'.

Religion is one such element of boundary dynamics. For Sindhis, the one key constant of their religious practice is its variability. Once, during a *janeo* (sacred thread ceremony) which was taking place in a temple in Mumbai, one guest told another, 'This is a typically Sindhi hotchpotch of different religions'. Sindhis are Nanakpanth Hindus, which means that both Hindu gods and the teachings of Guru Nanak (the first guru of Sikhism) hold an important place in their beliefs and rituals. Sindhi temples, for instance, combine Hindu *murtis* (statues) and the Guru Granth, the 'Sikh holy book'. Further, Sufi devotions have historically been common among Sindhis. In the South Asian context there is absolutely nothing extraordinary about this eclecticism. In the context of migration, however, and especially in locations where more monolithic and centralized notions of religion prevail, it lends itself to the idea that Sindhis are 'open minded' because of their stakes in Hinduism, Sikhism and Islam (in descending order). Further, Sindhis commonly involve themselves in local religious practices. In Catholic contexts, for instance, it is not unusual to find images of Jesus or the Blessed Virgin in their home shrines. Nothing could be more cosmopolitan-in-practice than the words of an informant who told me, 'I am proud to be a Sindhi but I follow only one religion – that of humanity'. The historical dynamics of such a disposition (which would also have to take into account contemporary discourses of Hinduism among South Asians) are beyond the scope of this chapter, but the point is that religion is serving to construct a boundary that lends itself to spatial unboundedness and an image of open interaction with the world. I should add that Sindhi gurus like Dada J.P. Vaswani and Dada Ishwar Balani are veritable jet setters who regularly do the rounds and exhort their followers to be open minded and incorporative.

A second select example is that of language. For historical-linguistic reasons, Sindhi enjoys a particularly rich sound inventory. Sindhis believe that this phonetic pedigree enables them to 'pick up' any language they may encounter anywhere in the world in a short space of time. As the late Gobind Malhi (a well-known writer) told me, 'Not even I can pronounce all of the 52 sounds, but somewhere in my veins they are there'. In this case, an ethnic group is constructing itself in biological and historical terms as being particularly adept at languages – a typically cosmopolitan 'open' disposition rooted in ethnic particularity.

The cosmopolitan organization of Sindhi ethnicity reaches its zenith in the group's involvement in business. Before embarking on a discussion of the specifics, however, I should make two general points. First, not all Sindhis are businesspeople. A good number of them, especially in India and the destinations that received the bulk of the post-Partition migration from India, are employed in the civil service, the professions, the service sector, etc. Individual choice, educational qualifications, caste, history of family migration and subsequent location of settlement – all of these are relevant factors with respect to occupation. However, the fact that self-employed business continues to occupy a majority of Sindhis, as well as the pre-Partition history of Sindhis as a trade diaspora, mean that they are primarily known, to themselves and outsiders, as traders; like other groups such as the Parsis and the Marwaris, they are sometimes popularly referred to as the 'Jews of India'. Business activity, then, has become one of the central modes of organization of *Sindhayat*. Second, that involvement in trade should hint at cosmopolitanism is an old idea. Simmel's (1950) trader is a traveller and a 'stranger', in the sense that s/he exists in an ambiguous relation of alterity and familiarity with a destination and its people and markets – the type of relation that characterizes cosmopolitans, in other words. Trade also positions its practitioners in the 'market sites' I referred to earlier. These convergences are especially real in the case of Sindhis.

Sindhis can be described as having a 'culture of exploration' as far as trade is concerned. The early Sindworkis, for instance, often started out simply by putting together some curios and handicrafts, boarding a passenger ship at Karachi, and scouting for opportunities along the way. It is for this reason that the names of ports of call along P&O routes come up so often in the papers of Sindhi businesses of the period. Since Partition, the development of the culture of travel, family visiting, and intense communication has meant that mobility and constant circulation (by men as well as women) foster a familiarity with 'the world'. The large-scale movement of Sindhi traders into the Caribbean with the rise of mass tourism in the region can be understood in this light, as can the rapid re-establishment elsewhere of the many Sindhi businesses that left Tangier as political circumstances shifted after 1956. My informants were invariably cosmopolitan in their outlook in that they were always ready to talk about business circumstances and opportunities in a large number of localities – even when they did not possess any profound knowledge of the various contexts. (Again, familiarity and strangeness.) I ought to emphasize that I am not saying that Sindhi businesses in general are constantly on the move. This would be totally inaccurate, given that a large number of Sindhis in various contexts run businesses the spatial continuity of which extends over several decades. And yet, because of the connections of these traders, and also because they see themselves as part of a cosmopolitan diaspora rather than a located group, the notion of mobility is never completely absent.

A second important element of Sindhi business is its high degree of corporacy across space. Business reputations, trust, creditworthiness, actual transactions – all of these are articulated translocally. In my research I came across a great many examples of Sindhis trading between themselves. Kinship of course provides an important connective medium. In contemporary forms, it is increasingly unusual to come across extended (joint) families running a unified set of operations and allocating the profits within the family. Much more common are smaller kinship units (such as nuclear families) that operate separately but collaboratively, as in import-export. Whether or not these are to be considered as effectively unified family ventures is a moot point. Beyond kinship, 'Sindhiness' constitutes another connective element, not least since its cosmopolitan nature implies some measure of social control across space. The dynamics of these various interactions are quite beyond the scope of this chapter (see Falzon 2005). The point is that, in episodic and ambiguous ways (as my informants liked to say, 'we are hardly one big happy family'), the worldwide distribution and connectivity of Sindhi kinship and ethnicity have an important counterpart in the business practices of the group.

Let us now look at some of the ways in which the cosmopolitan character of Sindhi business affects, in practice, its operations. The first thing to note is that the combination of geographical spread and networking fosters a familiarity with world markets and prices. This puts Sindhis in an excellent position to develop new product lines and locate the most advantageous sources, thus maximizing on price differentials. The formation of kinship networks across space means that middlemen are kept to a minimum. The readiness of Sindhis to move and set up shop elsewhere imparts a remarkable resilience and continuity to family business. Because they are 'strangers' and therefore not completely committed to locality, they are also more willing to operate in high risk, high profit circumstances; a number of Sindhis have made their money in conflict situations in Africa, for example. Mobility has its price, of course. Historically, specific business ventures have tended to come and go, and establishing oneself in a new market usually entails some flexibility with profit margins, at least initially. There are numerous instances of Sindhis entering new markets by operating on low profit margins. This includes the period following the mass migration of Partition, when thousands of small *banias* who moved to India from Sind sought, and often managed, to establish themselves as small traders in India; given the competition from 'native' traders, this was no mean feat, and the Sindhi practice of undercutting prices meant that they sometimes faced hostility.

The cosmopolitan character of Sindhi business emerges very clearly when one considers investment and consumption. Given the history of 're-diasporization' of Sindhi migration, as well as the spatial fickleness of the type of business just discussed, investment is bound to be a problematic issue – not least because many classical forms of investment, such as real estate and bank accounts, are very much embedded in local economies and jurisdictions. All mobile individuals/

groups have to come to terms with this problem, and many solve it by investing 'back home', whatever that may mean. With respect to Sindhis, there are four overlapping aspects to the issue. First, a substantial chunk of Sindhi wealth has historically gone into movable forms of investment. To say that diamonds are a Sindhi's best friend would partly be to replicate a caricature which often finds its way into vernacular histories, Bollywood films, and everyday discourse. It is a fact, however, that for Sindhis, and in particular for the wealthier and more mobile *bhaibands*, diamonds were, and to a lesser extent are, a favoured form of investment. Stories, some possibly apocryphal, circulate of Sindhis smuggling diamonds out of Africa in cans and flashlights, and no self-respecting *bhaiband* woman would contemplate going to a wedding not wearing a stone or two. In her work on women and gold in Northwest India, Ward describes jewellery as a 'bank belonging to women' (1997, 94). Gold and diamonds are perceived as objects of universal value, and thus convertible into cash anywhere in the world; surely this notion underlies Sindhi investment in jewellery. The second type of investment is, somewhat paradoxically, consumption. At first glance the two are diametrically opposed, but ostentatious consumption can be seen as a representation of one's wealth; the act of consumption transforms the person. This embodied value ('a person's worth') moves around with the individual and can be seen as a mobile form of collateral, especially in the case of businesspeople for whom creditworthiness is crucial. Weddings, which enjoy a high visibility, lend themselves particularly well to this idea. A third form of investment favoured by Sindhis involves what we might call localized investment in cosmopolitan sites. World cities, notably London, attract much Sindhi investment, notably in the form of real estate; institutions such as offshore banks and Swiss bank accounts constitute equally important 'sites'. Sindhis living in places which are thought to be particularly fickle (usually because of political instability) operate various measures to siphon money away to these sites. The meteoric rise of the ease of global capital flows of the late twentieth century has made these processes much more straightforward.

Mumbai represents the locus of the last form of Sindhi investment. A good number of families from all over the world own property in the city, preferably an apartment in the desirable northern and western suburbs. Besides, several institutions in Mumbai have benefited from overseas Sindhi wealth. Hospitals and colleges are the most prominent of these, some of which are associated with Sindhi families who own high-profile cosmopolitan businesses – Kishinchand Chellaram College and Hinduja Hospital are cases in point. There is a double ambiguity in all this. First, cosmopolitan wealth is being invested in local causes. Further, and perhaps more intriguingly, the meaning of investment in Mumbai is a cosmopolitan one. Given the construction of the city as the 'cultural heart' of the ethnic group, and the converging trajectories of travel that this implies, property and the endowment of institutions in Mumbai serve to establish reputations that are re-exported and become cosmopolitan.

Conclusion

At this point I wish to take stock by looking at what I earlier called 'dialectics between opposing models of social and spatial organization'. It is worth referring back to Diouf's (2000) work on Senegalese Murids. Murids constitute a successful trade diaspora and display many of the characteristics – such as linguistic proficiency and commercial networks – discussed in the present work. They are tightly organized primarily on the basis of ritual and location, and their cosmopolitanism is very much what Cohen (2003) calls an 'institution of stability-in-mobility'. The case of Sindhis is perhaps more complex. Until Partition, Hyderabadi *bhaibands* were a mobile group organized on the basis of caste and location. (It is worth noting that, with notable exceptions such as Rudner (1994) on the Nattukottai Chettiars, the literature on South Asia has tended to underestimate the importance of caste as a mode of stability-in-mobility (Falzon in prep.)).

As Sindhis re-organized themselves after the rupture of Partition, *Sindhayat* gained in importance as an organizing principle and, over the decades, a number of stabilizing devices came into the equation. One of these was location, as Mumbai (rather than Sind, which does however retain some nostalgic value as an ancestral homeland) came to be seen as the cultural heart of *Sindhayat*, the place where marriages are arranged, weddings celebrated, and profits invested in conspicuous ways. Every year in December, the hotels of Mumbai come alive with Sindhis travelling there from all over the world. Local narratives and reputations from wherever Sindhis are settled are transported to and re-exported from the city, becoming cosmopolitanized in the process (see Falzon 2003). A second organizing principle, ritual in nature, has been the post-Partition re-invention of the god Jhulelal, thought to be an avatar of Vishnu and the object of a localized devotion in pre-Partition Sind. Since the 1950s, Jhulelal has increasingly been seen – not in any passive way, but in large part due to the efforts of cultural entrepreneurs – as the *Sindhi* god, thus providing a centripetal force to an otherwise dispersed and invertebrate group. Hence the dialectics: Mumbai and 'the world is my home', Jhulelal and the 'religion of humanity'.

This ongoing dynamic is partly the result of an issue which all actually-existing cosmopolitanisms must face, namely that of a problematic relation with locality. To my mind, one reason why cosmopolitanisms are burgeoning is that contemporary processes are drawing more and more people into tricky legal, political, economic, and cultural relations with established models of location. The fact remains, however, that in spite of all the routes and rhizomes, a majority of groups still define themselves in terms of localities in which they claim some sort of historical continuity. In the contemporary world, states and the groups that 'belong' to them, nations, are probably the most important manifestations of such localized self-definition. Not surprisingly, cosmopolitans have always found themselves in awkward positions *vis-à-vis* formations like nation-states and city-states, and their requisite allegiances. The problematic leads to the internal dialectics I discuss above, the protagonists of which can sometimes get quite carried away. In the case of Sindhis, for example, a very few cultural entrepreneurs have gone so far as to suggest the recreation of an exclusively-Sindhi homeland, two of the nominations being the desert of Rajasthan and the Nicobar Islands (!)

Perhaps more interestingly, these colourful relations with locality can produce dividends. Historically, for instance, the strangeness/alterity factor may have helped Sindworki businesses in the sense that their worldwide connections, and therefore geographically-eclectic wares, ultimately made them stand out as purveyors of the exotic. Sindworki shops may have seemed strange and 'out of place', but it was precisely this characteristic which gave them the edge over less outward-looking local establishments. This comes close to what Vertovec and Cohen (2000, 7) call an 'aesthetic cosmopolitanism (based on) ... forms of consumption', and can be seen in the kimonos sold in Sindworki shops in Mediterranean harbour towns in the 1920s, or the incense sticks and 'ethnic' carvings that go down so well with customers today.

The problematic relation to locality as a factor which fosters what I have been calling the 'internal dialectics' of actually-existing cosmopolitanisms, cannot be seen in isolation. In the case of Sindhis a number of variables such as caste and divergent histories of mobility have left individuals and families *within* the ethnic group in very different structural positions. There are big differences between the 'old money' Sindworki families, with their webs of kinship stretching across the globe and reserves of mobile capital, small entrepreneurs who run textile businesses from small offices in Ahmedabad, and *amil* civil servants living in Mumbai. The structural differences also mean the production of different spatializing discourses and practices. On a global level, for instance, Sindhis have shown a marked reluctance to engage with local politics (generally by being on good terms with whoever is in power, irrespective of partisan alignments). On the other hand, Sindhis settled in India have readily involved themselves in Hindu nationalist politics, directly (as in the case of high-profile politicians like L.K. Advani), or indirectly (a significant number of Sindhis settled permanently in Mumbai cultivate close relations with the Shiv Sena). This involvement has a history and we find that the RSS (Rashtriya Swayamsevak Sangh, a vaguely para-military Hindu nationalist organization) enjoyed considerable support among *amil* civil servants in pre-Partition Sind. The ambiguity can partly be understood as a factor of the significance, to the ethnic group, of particular localities: for social, linguistic, historical, and political reasons, India and, say, Britain mean very different things to Sindhis.

It is crucial, therefore, to de-essentialize and de-homogenize ethnicities, not least cosmopolitan ones. Once cosmopolitanism is put into practice and embedded within actual social forms, it ceases to be normative and straightforward and develops a whole new dialectical dynamic which brings into play a host of variables. This complexity is behind the insistence of scholars like Vertovec and Cohen (2000) to think of cosmopolitanism as a form of imagination rather than an essential quality. For Clifford (1998), it is precisely this idea which gives cosmopolitanism (both as analytical concept and empirical practice) the edge over competing notions like multiculturalism. It is not as if Sindhis are condemned to be cosmopolitan; they may choose to organize themselves so, and quite often they do.

It sometimes happens that groups and/or individuals within groups become simultaneously more and less cosmopolitan. With Murids, successful and mobile traders with business stretching from Strasbourg to Chinatown in New York seek to enhance their chances to be buried in the hallowed ground of Touba in Senegal (Diouf 2000). With Sindhis, the traders that 'make it big' with respect to wealth, business networks, and transnational kinship connections, tend to engage in practices that seem antithetical to cosmopolitanism – 'pure' Brahminical lifestyles (see Bayly 1999), stricter endogamous practices, ostentatious investment in specific localities, etc. All this seems contradictory, but in this chapter I have argued that it is not. On the contrary, it is only by looking at its apparently non-cosmopolitan forms of organization that cosmopolitanism as a practical way of engaging with the world begins to make sense.

References

Archibugi, D., Held, D. and Köhler, M. (eds) (1998), *Re-Imagining Political Community* (Cambridge: Polity).
Barth, F. (1969), 'Introduction', in Barth (ed.).
— (ed.) (1969), *Ethnic Groups and Boundaries: The Social Organisation of Culture Difference.* (London: Allen & Unwin).
Bayly, S. (1999), *Caste, Society and Politics in India from the Eighteenth Century to the Modern Age (The New Cambridge History of India IV.3)* (Cambridge: Cambridge University Press).
Bellamy, R. and Castiglione, D. (1998), 'Between Cosmopolis and Community: Three Models of Rights and Democracy within the European Union', in Archibugi, Held and Köhler (eds).
Brubaker, R. (2005), 'The "Diaspora" Diaspora', *Ethnic & Racial Studies* 28:1, 1–19.
Cheah, P. and Robbins, B. (eds) (1998), *Cosmopolitics: Thinking and Feeling Beyond the Nation* (Minneapolis and London: University of Minnesota Press).
Clifford, J. (1994), 'Diasporas', *Cultural Anthropology* 9:3, 302–38.
— (1998), 'Mixed Feelings', in Cheah and Robbins (eds).
Cohen, A. (2003), *Custom and Politics in Urban Africa: A Study of Hausa Migrants in Yoruba Towns* (London: Routledge).
Diouf, M. (2000), 'The Senegalese Murid Trade Diaspora and the Making of a Vernacular Cosmopolitanism', *Public Culture* 12:3, 679–702.
Falzon, M.A. (2003), '"Bombay, Our Cultural Heart": Rethinking the Relation Between Homeland and Diaspora', *Ethnic & Racial Studies* 26:4, 662–83.
— (2005), *Cosmopolitan Connections: The Sindhi Diaspora, 1860–2000* (New Delhi: Oxford University Press).

— (in prep.), 'Caste and Space: Towards a Disembedding of Classical South Asian Categories'.

Hall, S. (2008), 'Conversation with Pnina Werbner', in Werbner (ed.).

Hiranandani, P. (1980), *Sindhis: The Scattered Treasure* (New Delhi: Manohar).

Hotchand, S.N. (1915), *A Forgotten Chapter of Indian History as Described in the Memoirs of Seth Naomi Hotchand, C.S.I., of Karachi 1804–1878* (Exeter: William Pollard).

Malkani, K.R. (1984), *The Sindh Story* (New Delhi: Allied Publishers Private).

Markovits, C. (2000), *The Global World of Indian Merchants 1750–1947: Traders of Sind from Bukhara to Panama* (Cambridge: Cambridge University Press).

Panjwani, R. (1987), *Sindhi ain Sindhyat* (Bombay: The Author).

Parekh, B. (1994), 'Some Reflections on the Hindu Diaspora', *New Community* 20:4, 603–20.

Pollock, S., Bhabha, H.K., Breckenridge, C.A. and Chakrabarty, D. (2000), 'Cosmopolitanisms', *Public Culture* 12:3, 577–89.

Robbins, B. (1998), 'Actually Existing Cosmopolitanism', in Cheah and Robbins (eds).

Rudner, D.W. (1994), *Caste and Capitalism in Colonial India: The Nattukottai Chettiars* (Berkeley: University of California Press).

Sennett, R. (2002), 'Cosmopolitanism and the Social Experience of Cities', in Vertovec and Cohen (eds).

Sharma, U. (1999), *Caste* (Buckingham and Philadelphia: Open University Press).

Simmel, G. (1950), 'The Stranger', in Wolff (ed.).

Smith, M.P. (2001), *Transnational Urbanism: Locating Globalization* (Oxford: Blackwell).

Vertovec, S. and Cohen, R. (2002), 'Introduction: Conceiving Cosmopolitanism' in S. Vertovec and R. Cohen (eds).

— (eds) (2002), *Conceiving Cosmopolitanism: Theory, Context, and Practice.* (Oxford: Oxford University Press).

Ward, H. (1997), *Worth its Weight: Gold, Women, and Value in North West India.* Unpublished Ph.D. thesis submitted to the Department of Social Anthropology, University of Cambridge.

Weiner, M. (1982), 'International Migration and Development: Indians in the Persian Gulf', *Population and Development Review* 8:1, 1–36.

Werbner, P. (ed.) (2008), *Anthropology and the New Cosmopolitanism: Rooted, Feminist and Vernacular Perspectives.* ASA Monograph No. 45 (Oxford: Berg).

Wolff, K.H. (ed.) (1950), *The Sociology of Georg Simmel* (Glencoe, Ill.: The Free Press).

Chapter 3

Looking at the Practice of UN Professionals: Strategies for Managing Differences and the Emergence of a Cosmopolitan Identity

Magdalena Nowicka and Ramin Kaweh

Cosmopolitanism is associated with an essentially moral view of the individual having allegiances to the wider world. This cosmopolitan world-openness does not easily fit with the territorially-bounded sociality of nation-states, and so a classical cosmopolitan would be someone who crosses borders and is ready to expose to new people, to appreciate their cultures, and to respect them independently of their national, ethnic or religious affiliations. Traditionally, it became associated with the revolt of the intellectual elites against the immediately given and closed world of particularistic attachments and low culture of the masses (Delanty 2006, 26), this view having roots in European colonialism and the Enlightenment. During the colonial age, travel was perceived as the key to self-enhancement and the attainment of a sophisticated, worldly outlook (Belk 1997). Christoph Martin Wieland, one of the most influential German intellectuals of the Enlightenment, attributed cosmopolitan qualities to people who grew wise through experience and reflection (Kleingeld 1999, 509). Georg Foster, a well-known anthropologist in Germany and elsewhere in the second half of the eighteenth century, a traveller himself, defined a cosmopolitan as someone who values cultural pluralism he encounters (Kleingeld 1999, 518). The perception of cosmopolitanism as a quality of socially and intellectually privileged and geographically mobile elites has prevailed until today. We may think of Castell's information-rich financial elites freed from local and national bindings (Castell 1996), Sklair's transnational capitalist class acting beyond national borders and alliances (Sklair 2001), Kanter's business cosmopolitans who know how to use local resources globally (Kanter 1995), Hannerz's foreign correspondents who desire to foster their audiences' experience of being at home in the world (Hannerz 2004) or artistic *avant gardes* and their transcending cultures beyond the local (Werbner 2008).

The idea of cosmopolitanism as a domain of geographically mobile, educational and financial elites has invoked criticism for describing a neo-liberal capitalist class or the elites' way of symbolic construction of an exclusive social world and hegemonic positions (Calhoun 2003a; Jones 2007). Yet these charges have too often been underpinned by the implicit assumption that mobile, financial elites are capable of an intellectual form of inclusive thinking and of acting irrespectively of their actual life situation, as well as by conflating geographical mobility and wealth with worldly outlooks. On the other hand, this stance also posits that cosmopolitanism contains hidden assumptions about the ranking of cultures, in which a mobile elite consumer, familiar with the languages and able to converse about world history and art, stands higher than the local, immobile majorities (Werbner 2008; Castells 1996). Yet the study of elite or professional international migration is peripheral to the main questions of migration studies (with exception of Favell 2003; Kennedy 2004; Beaverstock 2005); hence, we know little about the transnational life, identities, and motives of highly skilled mobile professionals. Some results suggest that young mobile professionals are often driven by international idealism or spirit of adventure, change and discovery, when they move abroad. Their cosmopolitanism remains, nonetheless, implicit. Indeed, authors assigning cosmopolitan qualities to these groups have paid little attention to their actual experiences and self-identifications.

On the other hand, cosmopolitan competence has been shown to exist among middle-class and working-class groups who bridge boundaries between other cultures and races (Werbner 1999; 2006; Lamont and Aksartova 2002; Kennedy this volume). Non-elite and also non-Western migrant groups prove to constitute trans-local and trans-ethnic collective spaces that transcend cultural boundaries and parochial lifestyles (Werbner 2008). Therefore, the research question which opens up this paper is not whether some groups are 'truly' cosmopolitan while others are not, but which kind of cosmopolitanism characterizes these groups. Thus, while sympathizing with the critics of the class bias of cosmopolitanism, we rather ask what are the actual experiences of such mobile 'elites' (in terms of their privileged access to information, few financial restrictions, and a high level of professional education). Do transnational mobile professionals 'embrace the culture of the other or receive the other's culture unconditionally' (Featherstone 2002, 13) during their travel? What are the particular social conditions in which this openness may come to display? Are they perhaps 'aesthetic cosmopolitans' who may have a great knowledge about non-Western cultures and their value yet who considers himself superior to them? Do they contest given classifications – for example that of a nation and national culture – and how they possibly constitute new symbolic boundaries between themselves and the others?

The UN professionals we studied display a general readiness to travel and to meet new people and cultures. Yet, we know from our own research and experience,[1] that these mobile professionals often suffer from time shortages, language barriers, extreme stress and physical diseases, which may lead to contradictions in the way they embrace 'others'.[2] We thus ask whether there are

---

1   Both authors were staff members in the UN-family organizations.

2   In this chapter, we use the terms 'the others' and 'the locals' interchangeably to refer to any people who our respondents consider 'different' from themselves during the period of settlement abroad. We are aware of the conceptual problems relating to both terms and the question whether 'otherness' is cultural and rooted in place (Gupta and Ferguson 1997).

limits to cosmopolitanism in practice, and what these limits are. By exploring how UN professionals encounter new people and places in particular contexts we look at their cosmopolitan identities in the making. By this we also mean how cosmopolitan ideas that are ingrained in the UN institutional environment lend value to their experience of the unfamiliar environments.

We recognize that cosmopolitanism has been a feature of everyday social and political life for a very long time both as a conscious avowal to identity as well as a more latent stance (Rumford 2005, 4). Studying the self-identifications and practices of people particularly exposed to such institutionalized cosmopolitanism helps us, thus, to address the question how such cosmopolitan ideas are employed by individuals to make sense of reality and manage encounters with culturally different others. Thereby, we ought not to forget that while geographical mobility might increase individuals' propensity for developing cosmopolitan outlooks, this is not its necessary condition. In this way, we attempt to challenge the elite bias of cosmopolitanism.

We draw on the results of two complementary studies to make our point. The first study consists of in-depth problem oriented interviews with 13 individuals employed in an international organization, which is a part of the UN system, conducted between February 2003 and September 2004 and analysed with the paradigm of the Grounded Theory (Strauss and Corbin 1990; Glaser 1978, 1998, 2001). Its aim was to make an explanatory contribution to our knowledge of daily practices of highly-skilled professional individuals in respect of how they make use and construct different spaces such as home, town or a cultural space (Nowicka 2006; 2007; 2008). This study revealed some aspects of cosmopolitanism, yet its strong focus on daily practices left the questions of self-definition open. In this respect, we support our argument on the results of a second study that consists of an online survey carried out in November and December 2006. A total of more than 270 people responded to the survey, out of which 171 respondents were professionals and staff working in the UN organizations.[3] The aim of the survey was to draw a general pattern of UN professionals in terms of their background,

---

Our decision is driven by our empirical results: the interviewees expect that each locality and its population are somehow different. They compare new places and new people with those familiar to them. They discover differences related to various factors, such as weather, political situation, religion or habits of people populating this locality. Culture appears here as an abstract category, while 'otherness' can be explained by referring to a number of factors; some of these strategies of managing the differences root the 'otherness' in place, other de-territorialize it (comp. Nowicka 2006, 187ff; forthcoming).

3　In total professionals and staff from 45 different international organizations responded, including: Office of the United Nations High Commissioner for Human Rights (20 per cent), United Nations (12 per cent), United Nations Development Programme (8 per cent), as well as International Labour Office, World Bank, UNICEF, United Nations Conference on Trade and Development, Food and Agriculture Organization, World Health Organization, Organization for Security and Co-operation in Europe. Responses from non-UN organizations (15 in total) included, among others, World Wide Fund for Nature,

their views of themselves and their self-identifications. In addition to collecting quantitative data, in terms of citizenships, languages and countries of origin, work and travel, it especially intended to analyse, in qualitative terms, the self-perception and self-description of the respondents *vis-à-vis* their allegiances and personal identity, with some open and neutral questions.

We first describe the conditions for the development of a cosmopolitan identity by sketching the features of the UN-family of organizations. We go on to present a silhouette of the typical professional depicted in our studies; we then focus in more detail on the self-identifications we surveyed. Irrespectively of their variety, we do not hesitate to call them cosmopolitan. They include explicit references to cosmopolitanism as well as statements on commitments to humanity, multiple, post-national affiliations or openness towards different people and their cultures. In the next step, we confront these self-identifications with personal stories of everyday life in a foreign country. Through these narratives, we demonstrate the paradoxes and ambivalences of cosmopolitanism in everyday life practice. Finally, this leads us to ask how these international professionals enact their cosmopolitan identities in particular social contexts. Cosmopolitanism emerges here as a strategy for making sense of everyday life tensions in unfamiliar environments and as a moral horizon lending value to the experience abroad.

The UN and its Professionals

Cosmopolitanism cannot be understood without reference to social, cultural, political and economic features (Calhoun 2003b, 17; Szerszynski and Urry 2002; 2006; Škrbiš et al. 2004). We presume that international organizations, and in particular the UN, are more likely to enforce cosmopolitan outlooks and practices than other contexts. A privileged occupational status and access to information, higher education as prerequisite of employment, and wealth can facilitate a kind of inhabitation of the world as an apparent whole. The immersion in an organization which operates in many countries and whose mission includes the protection and promotion of human rights and sustainable development provides a fruitful ground for cosmopolitan outlooks. Geographical mobility, imposed by the UN's mission, is considered a factor enforcing cosmopolitan outlooks. As cosmopolitan competence involves curiosity about places, people and cultures, the capacity to consume many places, and the willingness to appreciate some of its elements and readiness to take risks by virtues of encountering the 'other' (Szerszynski and Urry 2002, 470). In our studies, we are especially sensitive to such multiple conditions that shape individuals' values and practices.

The mission, role and responsibilities of the United Nations have substantially widened over the recent decades in attempts to eradicate poverty and hunger, to

International Committee of the Red Cross, the World Conservation Union, European Union Planning Team in Kosovo and the World Economic Forum.

prevent war and ease strife and to rectify injustices. The growing role of the UN has generated new conventions, treaties and regulations on issues ranging from terrorism and security to migration and refugees, crime, trade, human rights, and environment protection (Gareis and Varwick 2005). The cosmopolitan idea that human well-being is not defined by geographical and cultural location, that national, ethnic or gendered boundaries should not determine the limits of rights or responsibilities for the satisfaction of basic human needs, and that all human beings require equal respect and concern, finds direct expression in the legal and institutional initiatives of the UN (Held 2002). Cosmopolitan principles are part of the working creed of officials in the UN agencies (Held 2001, 10). At the same time, many critics have questioned the performance of the United Nations organizations (e.g. Shawn 2006) as well as the social and economic impact the development policies have on the populations of countries who avail themselves of financial assistance from these institutions (Randeria 2003; 2007). Also confidence in the UN shifts from country to country, strongly depending on the nature of UN's operations; it is especially poor in many Middle Eastern states, where only one in ten citizens supports the UN presence (Norris 2006). In response to these critics, the UN organizations undertook internal reforms to improve its impact and effectiveness; these actions range from the High Level Panel on the UN System-wide Coherence and changes in leadership, to increasing the involvement of anthropologists and local experts in policy work (Mosse and Lewis 2005).

None of these developments remains unnoticed by the UN's professionals and staff we researched. While, according to our interviews and the survey, they feel proud of belonging to the UN-family and of having a chance to work for the improvement of living conditions of people, they are aware of suspicious or hostile attitudes towards them in some of the host countries where they often stand as representatives of American imperialism. Cosmopolitanism is available to them not only as an abstract idea but translates into a particular mission and work programme. Yet it also constitutes a challenge in everyday life when their cultural background and multiple belongings might be an obstacle to the achievement of their professional aims or, simply, to meaningfully relating to others.

The nature of the UN's mission necessitates a particular organizational structure: a network of local offices worldwide and global distance communication structures. The professionals and staff of the UN come from more than 190 states. Geographical mobility belongs to the daily life of the UN professionals – having worked in Europe or the United States they have a chance to work next in Africa, Asia or Latin America. Changing work assignments involves a different scope of responsibilities, a new environment, new colleagues, and new destination countries. The UN's policy on 'mobility' actually practised in some of the organizations, such as the World Bank and the United Nations High Commissioner of Refugees, and implemented as a general rule in others (starting 2008), considers mobility (between geographical locations and departments) a desirable feature enabling exchange of knowledge and, therefore, improving the quality of work (Nowicka 2006, 156).

These specific conditions are reflected in the composition of our samples. The survey encompassed 171 UN professionals from 54 different countries, and we conducted interviews with 13 individuals from 11 countries. Twenty-four per cent responded that they carry now two different citizenships. At the time when we conducted our studies, and with regard to the location of workplace, people were based in almost 40 countries in all continents. The interviewees had lived for at least six months in average in five countries in their lifetime. Eighty-five per cent of all survey respondents had lived in at least three different countries, and almost every fourth person had lived in at least seven countries. Almost two thirds of the survey respondents speak at least two languages as a native speaker; every fourth speaks at least three, 10 per cent speaks four, and 3 per cent five languages. The same proportions were found in an earlier study (comp. Nowicka 2006). Every fourth respondent has close family members (parents and siblings) dispersed over at least two countries. Some 20 per cent of all respondents had friends coming from eleven or more counties; 13 per cent said that their friends live in more than 20 countries.

We conducted interviews with people aged 31 to 63 and in average around 40 years old. The survey respondents were generally younger (80 per cent between 26 and 40 years old). Regarding the interviews, six women and seven men were interviewed; nine people among them were married, two lived in a partnership, one was widowed and one single. Ten people had children. Concerning the survey, out of the 171 individuals, 65 per cent were women, and 35 per cent men; 74 per cent of them were in a relationship and 65 per cent had children.

We found out that the professionals we studied undertook a position in an international organization for several reasons. Despite their diverse ethnic and national backgrounds, we could identify a certain generational divide between our interviewees: those born in the early 1950s (who entered the organization as young university graduates in the 1970s) were often driven by idealistic reasons; they were interested in the issues of development and desired to help people. They also wanted to experience new people and their cultures from a position of someone who is geographically and emotionally close to them. Younger people turned out to be more pragmatic about their employment – they aspired to a prestigious job or simply grabbed a chance. Many of them studied abroad and searched for international employment opportunities for the sake of their own career development. Despite being first migrants in their families, they considered resettlement, frequent travel and bilingualism self-evident. Notwithstanding these differences, common to all our informants is a certain curiosity and intrinsic interest in distant places, people and cultures.

Cosmopolitan Self-Identifications

The respondents to the survey were asked to state who they are. We could order the 138 received answers according to three categories: individualist self-description, geographical bonds, and relation to the world and others. Most of the answers included elements of all three categories.

A half of all respondents provided some kind of self-description of their character, their roles as an individual or their personality, for example 'I am a 35 year old woman' or 'I am a loving mother, spouse, daughter and friend', 'I am in public relations, very open-minded and dynamic person'. Some 20 people simply wrote their name, and 15 wrote 'me' or 'myself' as a first association. Almost one third of all respondents identifies strongly with their profession (e.g. 'Human rights lawyer'). Women mentioned their gender (some 16 per cent of all answers) ('woman', 'mother', 'a professional woman'), only in few answers, a 'male' identity was declared. These self-descriptions point towards a particular expression of cosmopolitanism that places the individuals at the centre of social relations with the rest of the world, and which assigns to the individuals capabilities to decide upon own belonging (Rapport and Stade 2007).

Thirty two respondents identified with a nation-state, a continent, a city or a region (e.g. 'I would say I am an American', 'Indian Malaysian woman'). However, these identifications also included 'transnational' or 'international' elements, for example references to the current place of residence (different from their natal country): 'I am an Acadian (French Canadian) living in New York', 'A Californian girl living in Europe', 'German that grew in Bolivia' or 'International employee from the American continent living in French-speaking Switzerland'. Many stress their multicultural upbringing and past migration ('German-Canadian', 'Canadian citizen born in Denmark, raised in Iran, with Russian heritage'). From those referring to a continent, a majority are European. Few mentioned a particular town (e.g. 'An international red-haired girl from Geneva!'). Such narratives of trans-national and trans-ethnic belonging across new, complex social spaces expose a kind of cosmopolitanism typical to migrants who are capable of disengaging themselves from their social and cultural positions (Nida-Rümelin 2007, 229) and are able to question national and ethnic ascriptions (Rapport and Stade 2007).

Seventeen respondents describe themselves as a 'citizen of the world' or 'cosmopolitan'; 14 mentioned 'human', for example 'a concerned human being', 'a lucky human being', 'I would say I am a true cosmopolitan!'. Thus, they recall universal principles and values (Lamont and Aksartova 2002) that include readiness to help people irrespectively of their origin or belonging. Some of these general ideas were followed by further specification, for example 'A "citizen of the world", with an important European, Judeo/Christian cultural heritage' or 'I am a citizen of the world but firmly grounded in the culture I was born into'. This suggests that despite universalistic self-identifications our respondents retain their localized rooted identity (Werbner 2006, 497). Some reflect upon their roots, considering them as a certain kind of limitation:

would like to say world citizen ... and feel like one in many ways, but I guess I see
my limitations, which would make me a western European, even a Scandinavian
at the base ... (Survey respondent 127)

Fourteen statements include wishes or aims, which combine elements of a
mission of the employing organization and personal, cosmopolitan moral horizons.
The respondents feel committed 'to working to serve the community', 'striving to
protect human rights across borders' or they are 'always there to help people who
are in need', they describe themselves as 'human being working for a better world
with worldcentric governance and a reduction in the power of national, ethnic and
tribal identities'.

Over 20 self-descriptions explicitly involve categories of world-openness
which reflect the specific lifestyles and the character of the work carried on by the
respondents, in particular, with regards to their encounters with new people and
cultures. Five respondents explicitly state that they feel 'comfortable pretty much
everywhere' or that their 'home can be anywhere', and they 'live in the world'.
Ten describe themselves as 'very open to and very interested in other cultures'. A
further five relate to learning processes and a development of their identity, which
includes their 'upbringing, the interactions with others from different cultures,
places and religions'.

One answer drew our attention for including all these elements:

> I am a woman, who has lived in different parts of the world, who relates and enjoys
> different cultures, and has a cultural mix between the Latin and the European
> world. I am a person who is open to 'the other'. This probably stems from my
> education (in a large, religious family, of dual origin). I was encouraged to focus
> on others as opposed to myself ("love your neighbor as yourself") which I have
> translated into an interest for different cultures, development and gender issues,
> etc. I think spirituality (in the broadest sense) and relationships (family, friends)
> are more important than things such as career advancement (which I believe is my
> Haitian/African/people person side) but am very much a pragmatic/reasonable
> person (which I consider my Western legacy). This description sounds a bit too
> nice and perfect which is why I must add that this interest in 'the other' comes
> with many challenges, frustrations, misunderstandings and disappointments.
> But hey, that's life! (Survey respondent 26)

This woman reflects both on how she grew up to become open to the other and on
the difficulties of orientations and practices that can be described as cosmopolitan.
Our interviews, which focused stronger on motives for international employment
and geographical mobility, suggest that these people are not born cosmopolitan but
learn how to be them or they become more open and develop more cosmopolitan
outlooks in the course of their international career. We will return to this issue later.
The above quotation also suggests that encountering the 'other' might involve
more than a universalistic ideal to which one aspires. With this supposition we

want to suggest a more differentiated picture of cosmopolitanism as something that is more than the rhetoric of common human nature and universal principles of inclusion (Lamont and Aksartova 2002). It is the daily practice of overcoming misunderstandings and the frustrations inherent to encounters with new people that make someone a cosmopolitan.

Regulated Exposure

While involvement in the UN can enhance cosmopolitan outlooks and practices of the professionals, several elements of this institutional environment might challenge their cosmopolitan aspirations in everyday. In this section, we draw a picture of how the UN professionals we interviewed encounter 'others' and their cultures in one's place of residence other than their natal one.[4] This picture is full of contradictions: next to a general strategy of regulating exposure to otherness, we can also identify moments of openness and struggles for meaningful engagements with the locals. We point both to the limits of cosmopolitanism while also attempting to challenge an over-simplified image of the transnational professional as a consumer and a tourist (Hannerz 1990; Lash and Urry 1994).

Our informants stay in one location for a couple of years before moving to another country. As one of them puts it, they 'put down roots, uproot and start all over again' (Survey respondent 46). They move with their immediate families, who offer them emotional nearness; thus, they may not feel compelled to find new friends. We expect language to limit active participation in local activities. Most of the individuals interviewed currently live in a country in which the official spoken language is not their native language, and where the possibility of socializing depends on how widely English is spoken. The specific conditions of employment involve an extensive support of an international organization towards re-settlers on how to make the process of moving household and family less frustrating and less time-consuming. This includes advising on schooling for children, spouse career, housing, and child and elderly care. Voluntary staff networks provide guidance on living conditions, cultural customs, and religious beliefs and practice on the host

---

4   Transnationally mobile professionals are involved in different situations: they resettle to third countries but they also travel to many destinations where they stay between one week and three months at once over a longer period. They develop complex relationships to these destinations and their populations. They also feel rooted in their natal cultures and places of their birth and youth. Some administrative cities, like Brussels or Washington DC, where expatriate communities are large, create unique environments and the international professionals develop distinct relationships to them (comp. Nowicka 2006, 150–76). The situation described in the current paper includes elements of moving to an administrative city regarding the shape of interviewees' social networks, as well as of short-term frequent travels to multiple destinations; therefore, it is a representative example for discussing a nature of encounter with new people and places.

country, and they mediate between the new settlers and families of staff members already residing in the locality. All this might lead to a certain dependency from the organization and its staff members, which obviously quarrels with the desire to engage with locals and their culture.

The international professionals we studied are highly motivated to discover new people and places and to understand their lives, desires and problems for professional reasons. Being in place, meeting people and seeing how the international aid projects influence their lives lets the studied professionals feel satisfied with own efforts and see the sense of their support (Nowicka 2006, 105ff; 2008). Another reason is a curiosity for 'otherness'. They expect to find great diversity in the surrounding world, yet, as Diego explains, they also find similarity and universal rules and structures:

> Two things that are surprising when you move across ... at least my own experience moving across these very different countries has been that on the one hand how similar they are and on the other hand that as similar as they appear to be on ninety five percent of the issues how different they can be on the other five percent. So that's the very interesting thing. Yes, they are different, yes, they are not as different one thinks they are, 'cause on most things they tend to be quite similar but for those small percentages that are different, differences are big.

On the other hand, Diego is convinced that if countries were completely different, it would be more difficult (for him) 'to make an adjustment' when resettling. Serious differences between countries could 'put [his] family and [his] world up side down', he notices. Further, he reveals:

> I think, what is happening today is that you are able to go to countries as diverse as this [Saudi Arabia and Slovenia] and if you do not want to be exposed to any of these differences, if you are not someone to deal with them, there are ways to completely shut them off ... you could completely avoid the local ... you are able to almost consciously decide how much exposure do I really want to have to local things.

How do international professionals 'regulate their exposure' to the locals and the localities? We looked closer at their foreign language skills, social networks, use of schooling, housing and shopping opportunities and spare time activities. We noticed certain mechanisms, which our interviewees more or less consciously use to minimize or maximize the number and duration of encounters with the locals.

As the interviews reveal, hardly any of our informants know even some basics of the host country's language. The interviewees do not consider it a barrier because they do not necessarily need to know the local language: Ann, for example, notices that she never actually comes into direct contact with the locals, because someone translates everything for her: in business these are professional interpreters, in personal issues she is assisted by her colleagues. The other interviewees tell the same sort of story: they 'manage the situation'. They learn the basics of the language, as Steven did, and they are able to understand a simple conversation. Alternatively, they do not see any need to learn it: as Martin points out, 'everybody speaks enough English for you to survive'.

Missing language skills are also one of the reasons why the interviewees' social networks are very international. They do include the locals but the interviewees stress that no one tries to get closer to someone simply because this person is a local. Friendships are a matter of 'chemistry between people' (Interview with Lenka), and this is the case when two people share similar interests and problems. Usually, these are other international professionals and expatriates, who face similar challenges in a foreign country. Lenka notices, 'somehow foreigners stick together'. Many interviewees receive regular visits from their old friends:

> I run a guest house, I am booked solid, all my guest room is full, all the coming summer and it was like this the whole last summer so we are never alone ... (Interview with Ann)

In countries where armed conflicts, terror attacks or high criminality are common, they reside in Western compounds, which offer them security and a certain living standard. Houses and flats rented to foreigners are usually fully furnished, which is convenient for those, who move for few years to a country. In Eastern Europe, they live in quite luxurious and expensive areas, inhabited by many foreigners. They can afford such housing, and they prefer it because of short distance to facilities like international schools and kindergartens, or fitness and golf clubs.

International schools attended by the interviewees' children are a common platform for meeting new people:

> To get to know people and to make acquaintances, that is not a problem, that is very easy, very quickly through the school actually ... in the first two days of school, the school has already arranged for some ladies to show my wife around the city. (Interview with Diego)

Despite the fact that the local elites also visit such schools Tolga believes that their different life situations are a barrier to integration. She suspects that the expatriates are more in need of people or friends than the locals who are settled. Most of the interviewees feel unsatisfied with the developments of their social networks because they miss a greater diversity between people:

> ... we get to meet some new people but it tends to be always the same group, you know, the UN, some of the embassies ... but it is a closed circle and there are not too many locals in it. Then I have nice friends here in the office and that's very nice. But it is not what you would call a big circle or a diverse circle. (Interview with Ann)

Expatriate communities offer a friendly environment, certain familiarity and support for new settlers. However, the interviewees claim to feel alienation and estrangement if their social networks and activities are unintentionally restricted to this single environment.

Restricted social networks as well as missing language skills decide upon the uses that the interviewees' make of their spare time. The interviewees' hobbies are individualized: they do indoor and outdoor sports that do not require them to coordinate with others, for example power walking, biking or weight training and aerobics. Martin, who used to play in a music band when he was a student, now plays a piano at home. A favourite hobby of many informants is to be at home: to spend time together with the family, do some work in the garden, cook together, take care of the household. Several informants are interested in arts and regularly attend exhibitions or visit interesting architectural sites.

One-day or weekend trips are very popular among the interviewees. When they have visitors, they show them around the country and its most popular cultural sites. Families with small children make daily tours to amusement parks. Some are very conscious about the limited time they have to discover the attractions and particularities of their new country of residence and try to see as much of it as possible. Less reflectively, the interviewees decide to immerse from time to time in international environments like global cities and typical tourist sites. They enjoy short distances in Europe to discover neighbouring countries; some take a plane to go shopping in London or Paris, or attend a particularly interesting event in any European capital, for example a theatre play. Residents in Africa and Asia visit national parks to admire a distinct nature. Thus, they often behave like tourists, whom Hannerz (1990) contrasted with cosmopolitans: they consume places; they get to know few locals; they try out 'exotic' dishes. They remain at the surface, which stays in contradiction to their own self-descriptions. However, this picture of a superficial consumer needs to be revised when we look at how they travel: often, they choose to go by train where they strike up conversation with the other, local, passengers. The general practice of a tourist includes thus moments of openness and readiness to engage with otherness.

The interviewees show a great degree of flexibility in adapting to their environments. Our interview partners may avoid speaking a local language by shopping in supermarkets, where they take food or other products from a shelf not having to know their names or to ask a salesclerk. 'I manage in a taxi and in a shop, and after all the shops here are mostly supermarkets anyway', says Ann. They also choose to go to opera or to concerts instead of theatre:

> we go to the cinema a lot, we go to the opera a lot because ... these are very easy things, very accessible because in opera the language doesn't matter, music of course or concerts the language doesn't matter and then the cinema is mostly in English anyway, for the most part and it has only subtitles so we are not excluded from any of these. (Interview with Ann)

This is a different kind of flexibility that contrasts with the flexible one of navigating local culture which has typically been ascribed to cosmopolitans (Hannerz 1990; Molz 2006): the interviewees do not adapt to local habits by extending their cultural repertoire; rather, they resign from some activities, or embed them in familiar transnational networks and de-localized infrastructures.

Despite their aspirations to engage in encounters with 'others', they may often find themselves in a situation when they cannot expose themselves to 'local things'. They are aware of the danger of 'missing an opportunity' offered by an overseas assignment (Thompson and Tambyah 1999); yet they are confronted with many constraints. Missing language skills are the most obvious; however, also in countries and cities where English is widely spoken, our interview partners experience serious barriers to local involvement (Nowicka 2006, 155ff). These relate to the immersion in their employing organization and its structures, a site where they socialize with other foreigners, and even find their life partners. They tend to become friends with foreigners despite that in many countries, especially in the USA, they live in neighbourhoods inhabited 90 per cent by locals. They suffer from time shortages. Long working hours (up to 14 hours a day, including commuting time) and frequent business travels leave them little time for socializing outside of the immediate family.

Moreover, their families and friends are dispersed across many countries. They travel regularly to visit them because telephone conversations and email correspondence does not allow a degree of intimacy necessary to sustain relationships (Nowicka 2008). Many live in binational partnerships and they divide their scarce time to visit both families in two or more countries and offer their children a possibility to learn the culture of their grandparents. They face a dilemma, whether to go abroad to meet old friends and family members or to spend more time in a locality where they can make new friends.

Physical constrains such as diverse digestive system diseases may also lead to an unintended closure towards the locals and their culture. They are quite common in many countries and they disable travellers who may need to take several precautions to avoid them; these include taking medications and avoiding certain foods and drinks which the locals eat daily. Frequent travellers are making themselves fit to travel, which can be considered a part of a general cosmopolitan competence (Molz 2006). However, there is another side to securing their own safety: someone who, for the sake of his wealth, eats in expensive restaurants and never uses a bus or walks on the streets in places with high criminality is indeed much detached from the locals, who may lack means of such protection or develop alternative competence to cope with the risks at daily basis. We can term this a 'human limit' to cosmopolitanism – moments, in which people reach a physical or emotional limit of experiencing 'otherness' by direct, physical encounters.

However, also in this case we can identify some moments of cosmopolitan openness. For example, extreme conditions may also enforce direct encounters with local lifestyles. Atanas, another interviewee, recalls his travels to Kazakhstan, where he could reach the UN project site only by horse; he slept in tents for weeks without running water and a toilet. These primitive conditions brought him closer to the locals, he learned from them and became a bit like them, in respect of personal hygiene. In this sense, he was forced to open himself and to 'fit' into this particular local condition (Molz 2006). He is convinced that such 'authentic' experiences helped him to understand the needs and motivations of the locals. Reiner, who lived several years in Africa, soon became a local himself: poor schooling opportunities forced him to teach his children at home; bad roads and no facilities made him focus his social life on home. Despite the fact that he remained a Western expatriate his way of living has changed to become more like that of the locals, except that he could opt to return to the United States or to Europe at any time.

Concluding, we can say that the availability of international schools and kindergartens, English-language and subtitled films in cinemas, impersonal sites like supermarkets or fitness centres, and universally accessibly music in concert halls across the world causes a kind of laziness among our interviewees who often prefer the comfort of familiar facilities over the stress of discovering new people and places. Yet we also argue that one needs to be sensitive to the nature of their involvement in local issues. We gave examples for what we termed moments of cosmopolitan openness. Also, we ought not to forget that our interviewees often have a surprisingly broad knowledge of the history of the country where they work and reside. On the job, they meet country officials, they know the problems of the local economy, they have a good sense of social problems, and they are up-to-date with the country's political situation. They have access to knowledge not available to most of the locals. They acquire it not from television programmes, not during private chats with friends, but during official meetings, when talking to politicians and experts, reading reports, or attending conferences. All this is part of their business obligations but also a way of fighting negative stereotypes of international elites.

In this sense, their cosmopolitan practice may take a specific form. Differences that our interviewees wanted to discover are as much exciting as they are stressful. The routine of a frequent traveller and a notorious re-settler includes strategies of self-protection from 'too much' cultural difference. These moments of closure have less to do with the elite distinction of their own group *vis-á-vis* others than with the protection of their own family from too frequent or sudden changes of lifestyle. Our informants do take an effort to get to know the localities in which they live, and they also consume them; they are partly experts and partly tourists in these countries. They often observe rather than participate in local life. On the other hand, they are reflexive about the challenges and constraints of life in an unfamiliar environment; so they may choose to consciously act accordingly to the ideal of the knowledgeable cosmopolitan (Kleingeld 1999, 518), visit another museum to learn about the history, art and culture of the place, instead of watching television at home, even if this is a practice they would share with most of the locals in order to better 'fit in'.

Narratives of Social Learning

The stories of daily life in an unfamiliar environment put a different light on the cosmopolitan self-identification of the studied professionals. They are silent about the tensions and disillusionments in a foreign environment. Only when they speak of diseases and physical tiredness, we can feel how challenging their way of life is. We can see in the dissatisfaction with their friends' cycles or in how they adapt their hobbies that they struggle for meaningful connection with the locals, and we can recognize the moments of doubts if this struggle can ever be successful, when they ask: '[am I] so courageous or foolhardy?' (Survey respondent 46). They also feel the pressure of proving to be knowledgeable experts sensitive to local particularities, and they are aware of their exceptional economic, political and social status. This particular experience distinguishes them from the 'others': as Reiner says, 'travels have spoiled' him because he gets exceptional insights into diverse cultures; but he has also discovered that he 'no longer [has] much in common with his friends or relatives'. Similarly, the survey respondents describe themselves as people of 'exceptional cultural interests and many languages', unlike 'narrow-minded people "who have never left their little corner of the world"' (Survey respondent 36). This might indeed be a hint to the hierarchical thinking of particular lifestyles and attitudes, and it certainly reflects the extent to which cosmopolitan values such as world openness have been institutionalized and became desirable and highly valued.

Our interviewees feel they no longer 'remain at the surface' but 'become insiders' (Interview with Reiner) when they travel and meet local people personally. Dominant narratives are those of enrichment, rewarding encounters, growing wise and knowledgeable. They are proud of the learning process that they are a part of. For example, they pick up 'enriching' elements of foreign languages, even if they do not speak them fluently:

> I give you an example: in the Polish language, I would drop the 'pan' and 'pani' and just use the first name but still remain with the formal address; English doesn't have it, but some other language do, like German, you use 'Du' and 'Sie' – and this would keep the formality but it also offers more room for having something in common, which doesn't exist when you call everybody 'Mr' and 'Mrs'. So you adapt your own behaviour to what you think is enriching and experiencing relation, you know, experience in different culture behaviour ... (Interview with Cecile)

As another respondent notices, 'with each new language we take on whole new facets to our "selves"'. They reflect upon new banal habits or activities that they practice because they live abroad, and which seem a bit odd to them:

> ... I would never eat Swiss chocolate in India, and while in CH, would never touch anything else. Lived in CH for three years, never been to an Indian

restaurant; but in India, I would never have fondue or flamenkuch.[5] (Survey respondent 11)

They also translate such daily consumption of 'otherness' (Molz 2007) in more general ideas of the self as being 'a composite' of diverse elements from different cultures:

> ... often people ask me: where are you from, and I say: I am from the middle of the Atlantic, you know, you take, you learn from both sides and you try to integrate that in your own life and it puts you a little bit into the middle ... (Interview with Cecile)

They grow different through encounters overseas, and they gain new perspectives on themselves, their background and country; as Cecile says, she can see Europe 'through slightly different eyes' because she had lived many years in the United States, Asia and Africa. But some people may also believe having discovered more universal patterns across the world:

> ... while the countries are culturally very different, they have developed very, very differently, if you look beyond the obvious what you see and understand cause and effect relationships, many of these cause and effect relationships are replicable everywhere. I think this makes a lot of the essence of the work we all are doing, that the kind of understand, learn to see the essential of the problem and then to see to what extent this essential can be addressed in the context of the particular situation. (Interview with Cecile)

Some are convinced of having gained knowledge on human basic qualities, which are universal. What makes people different are their social positions; what unites them is their education and sense of humour, says Atanas.

Our informants are equipped with a basic disposition for working in an international environment: they have a general idea of cultural diversity across the world, and they are convinced that this diversity is valuable and should be appreciated. They have explicit desires for encountering this 'abstract diversity' but they rarely battle for coming together with concrete people. Rather, the majority is driven by quite pragmatic reasons. Employment in an international organization is an important step in their professional careers; often, they simply use opportunities that open up to them. They embody a readiness to frequent mobility and resettlement, yet, migration rarely is the primary reason for undertaking international assignments. Often, they develop a need to meet their clients or recipients of their services, first, in the course of the projects in which they participate. Irrespectively of their motives, they move abroad and they

---

5   Flammkuchen (also Flammenkuchen), a Tarte Flambee, an Alsace specialty made from a very think layer of pastry topped with chopped onions, bacon and sour cream.

become more exposed to foreign cultures and locals than their old friends and families.

Perhaps because of these ambivalences, they seem to develop pragmatic attitudes without falling into a moral dilemma: they take the best out of it, which is learning. They embrace the 'other', who they conceive of as the 'local', which helps them to undergo a personal transformation. These encounters are meaningful experiences insofar as they contribute to becoming a wiser, perhaps a better person. The value of the encounters with the 'other' lies in becoming a more reflective, a more conscious person who can see things in perspective, compare, and detect hidden patterns and universal principles while being sensitive to the particularities of each context.

As many of our interviewees notice, the world has become more alike. The astonishing similarity enforces their belief in universal, human values and qualities that allow a peaceful togetherness. Yet, there is a certain paradox entailed in this position. If particularities resulting from specific conditions in places are largely irrelevant to the possibility of socialization, our cosmopolitans are disappointed to meet little diversity to which respect they aspire to embrace; but in search for this disappearing diversity, they praise the contrasting, the exotic differences between people and cultures. In this sense, we can critically argue that their cosmopolitan quests include elements of modern, Western bourgeois voyages across foreign territories and cultures (Belk 1997; Veer 2002).[6]

Conclusion

These results from our studies lead us to engage with the notion of elite cosmopolitanism. On the one hand, the cosmopolitanism of international professionals appears as an aspiration embedded in their social positions and in the institutional context of the United Nations. It involves elements of individualism and universalism and a competence to question and re-establish one's own collective belongings. We have found the rhetoric of universalism as well as narratives of self-transformation and social learning that are to be seen as characteristic of elite travellers who value diversity. These narratives of encounters point to a social distance between mobile and immobile individuals, as well as to those who have a privileged access to information and the others but these are free of hierarchical understandings. Yet, the patterns of social involvement are still marked by the interviewees' economic and social status (Werbner 1999, 19; Falzon this volume), in particular, that delineated by a mobile and international lifestyle. But, then, we also find indications of a trans-national and trans-ethnic cosmopolitanism

---

6 Hannerz distinguishes cosmopolitans from locals and tourists. While locals remain content in their parochial ways of life, tourists are also provincial because they lack self-reflection and intellectual aspirations. Cosmopolitans are willing to explore and experience transnational diversity and reflect upon it (Hannerz 1990).

resulting from multiple ties and emergent spaces of cultural difference and shared transcendent world view.

On the other hand, cosmopolitanism emerges here as a constant effort that our interviewees and respondents need to make in everyday life to pursue their identities. We speak of an effort, because our informants need to overcome what we proposed to term 'human limits' to the cosmopolitan ethos. The circumstances such as time shortages, lack of language skills, physical weakness, or, even, the fear for their own life, and the desire to protect one's own family and its 'small world' – they all impose on individuals a great limitation to their cosmopolitan aspirations. We may thus perceive cosmopolitanism as a way of giving sense to some daily struggles in an unfamiliar environment, as a strategy for manoeuvring between different pressures: between the expectations placed towards them by the critics of international aid organizations – who demand them to know and to understand the locals – and the temporality of the stay and limited access to this knowledge and to the locals; between the general ideal of meaningful involvements in local communities and the desire to sustain globally dispersed ties with friends and family; between the demands of the global economy and the international aid system, and finding own position within it and the wish to take time to engage with the 'others'; between the 'small world' of one's own immediate family and the need to get to know new people and their cultures; between the anxiety of being hurt or misunderstood by culturally different 'others' and the willingness to respect every human being. Cosmopolitanism gives sense to these daily struggles as a value of learning and self-development. It helps one to appreciate every experience of difference as contributing to one's personal transformation also giving one a moral horizon to overcome the difficulties and the stress of resettlement.

References

Anghel, R. et al. (eds) (2008), *The Making of World Society. Perspectives from Transnational Research* (Bielefeld: transcript).

Beaverstock, J. (2005), 'Transnational Elites in the City: British Highly-Skilled Inter-Company Transferees in New York City's Financial District', *Journal of Ethnic and Migration Studies* 31(2), 245–68.

Belk. R.W. (1997), 'Been there, Done that, Bought the Souvenirs. Of Journeys and Boundary Crossing', in D. Turley (ed.).

Calhoun, C. (2003a), 'The Class Consciousness of Frequent Travelers: Towards a Critique of Actually Existing Cosmopolitanism', *The South Atlantic Quarterly* 101:4, 869–97.

— (2003b), *Social Solidarity as a Problem for Cosmopolitan Democracy, paper presented for the conference on 'Identities, Affiliations, and Allegiances'*, Yale University, October 3–4, 2003.

Castells, M. (1996), *The Rise of the Network Society* (Oxford: Blackwell).

Cohen, R. and Vertovec, S. (eds) (2002), *Conceiving Cosmopolitanism. Theory, Context and Practice* (Oxford: Oxford University Press).

Delanty, G. (2006), 'The Cosmopolitan Imagination: Critical Cosmopolitanism and Social Theory', *The British Journal of Sociology* 57:1, 25–47.

Favell, A. (2003), 'Eurostars and Eurocities: Towards a Sociology of Free Moving Professionals in Western Europe', Center for Comparative Immigration Studies Working Paper 971 (San Diego: University of California, San Diego).

Featherstone, M. (2002), 'Cosmopolis: An Introduction', *Theory, Culture and Society* 19:1–2, 1–16.

Gareis, S.B. and Varwick, J. (2005), *The United Nations. An Introduction* (Houndmills: Palgrave Macmillian).

Glaser, B. (1978), *Theoretical Sensibility* (Mill Valley, CA: Sociology Press).

— (1998), *Doing Grounded Theory. Issues and Discussions* (Mill Valley, CA: Sociology Press).

— (2001), *The Grounded Theory Perspective: Conceptualization Contrasted with Description* (Mill Valley, CA: Sociology Press).

Gupta, A. and Ferguson, J. (eds) (1997), *Culture, Power, Place – Explorations in Critical Anthropology* (Durham: Duke University Press).

Hannerz, U. (1990), 'Cosmopolitans and Locals in a World Culture', *Theory, Culture & Society* 7:2, 237–51.

— (2004), *Foreign News. Exploring the World of Foreign Correspondents* (Chicago: The University of Chicago Press).

Held, D. (2001), 'Globalization, Corporate Practice and Cosmopolitan Social Standards', paper presented at the conference 'Globalisierung und Sozialstandards', 30–31 March 2001, Feldafing/Starnberger See.

— (2002), 'Law of States, Law of Peoples', *Legal Theory* 8:2, 1–44.

Jones, P. (2007), 'Cosmopolitanism and Europe: Describing Elites or Challenging Inequalities', in C. Rumford (ed.).

Kanter, R.M. (1995), *World Class: Thriving Locally in the Global Economy* (New York: Simon & Schuster).

Kennedy, P. (2004), 'Making Global Society: Friendship Networks among Transnational Professionals in the Building Design Industry', *Global Networks* 4:2, 157–79.

Kleingeld, P. (1999), 'Six Varieties of Cosmopolitanism in Late Eighteenth-Century Germany', *Journal of the History of Ideas* 60:3, 505–24.

Lamont, M. and Aksartova, S. (2002), 'Ordinary Cosmopolitanism. Strategies for Bridging Racial Boundaries among Working-Class Men', *Theory, Culture & Society* 19:4, 1–25.

Lash, S. and Urry, J. (1994), *Economies of Signs and Space* (London: Sage).

Molz, J.G. (2006), 'Cosmopolitan Bodies: Fit to Travel and Travelling to Fit', *Body & Society* 12:1, 1–21.

— (2007), 'Eating Difference: The Cosmopolitan Mobilities of Culinary Tourism', *Space and Culture* 10:77, 77–93.

Mosse, D. and Lewis, D. (eds) (2005), *The Aid Effect: Giving and Governing in International Development* (London: Pluto Press).

Nida-Rümelin, J. (2007), 'Zur Philosophie des Kosmopolitismus', *Zeitschrift für Internationale Beziehungen* 13:2, 227–34.

Norris, P. (2006), 'Confidence in the United Nations: Cosmopolitan and Nationalistic Attitudes', paper presented at the World Values Conference 'Society, Politics and Values: 1981–2006', 3–4 November 2006, Istanbul.

Nowicka, M. (2006), *Transnational Professionals and Their Cosmopolitan Universes* (Frankfurt a.M. and New York: Campus).

— (2008), '"Do You Really Talk about Emotions on the Phone...?" Content of Distance Communication as a Structuring Moment of the Modern World Society', in: R. Anghel et al. (eds).

— forthcoming, 'Heterogeneity, Borders and Thresholds – How Mobile Transnational Professionals Order the World', *Journal of Borderland Studies*.

Randeria, S. (2003) 'Cunning States and Unaccountable International Institutions: Social Movements and the Rights of Local Communities to Common Property Resources', *European Journal of Sociology* 16:1, 27–60.

—(2006) 'Global Designs and Local Lifeworlds: Colonial Legacies of Conservation, Disenfranchisement and Environmental Governance in Postcolonial India', *Interventions: International Journal of Postcolonial Studies* 9:1, 12–30.

Rapport, N. and Stade, R. (2007), 'A Cosmopolitan Turn – or Return?', *Social Anthropology* 15:2, 223–35.

Rumford, C. (ed) (2007), *Cosmopolitanism and Europe* (Liverpool: Liverpool University Press).

Shawn, E. (2007), *The U.N. Exposed: How the United Nations Sabotages America's Security* (New York: Sentinel Books).

Sklair, L. (2001), *The Transnational Capitalist Class* (Oxford: Blackwell).

Škrbiš, Z. et al. (2004), 'Locating Cosmopolitanism: Between Humanist Ideal and Grounded Social Category', *Theory, Culture & Society* 21:6, 115–36.

Strauss, A. and Corbin, J. (1996), *Grounded Theory: Grundlagen Qualitativer Sozialforschung* (Wienheim: Beltz Psychologie Verlags Union).

Szerszynski, B. and Urry, J. (2002), 'Cultures of Cosmopolitanism', *Sociological Review* 50:4, 461–81.

Thompson, C. and Tambyah, S.K. (1999), 'Trying to be a Cosmopolitan', *The Journal of Consumer Research* 26:3, 214–41.

Turley, D. (ed) (1997), *Consumer Research. Postcards from the Edge* (London and New York: Routledge).

Veer, P. van der (2002), 'Colonial Cosmopolitanism', in R. Cohen and S. Vertovec (eds).

Werbner, P. (1999), 'Global Pathways. Working Class Cosmopolitanism and the Creation of Transnational Ethnic Worlds', *Social Anthropology* 7:1, 17–35.

— (2006), 'Vernacular Cosmopolitanism', *Theory, Culture & Society* 23:2–3, 496–8.

— (2008), 'The Cosmopolitan Encounter: Social Anthropology and the Kindness of Strangers', in P. Werbner (ed).

— (ed) (2008), *Anthropology and the New Cosmopolitanism. Rooted, Feminist and Vernacular Perspectives* (Oxford: Berg).

PART II
Memories

Chapter 4

Cosmopolitan Openings and Closures in Post-Yugoslav Antinationalism

Stef Jansen

A recent article calls for more precise operationalizations of cosmopolitanism beyond the 'vague and diffuse' notions that define it 'principally as an attitude of "openness" toward others cultures [sic]' (Škrbiš, Kendall and Woodward 2004, 127). The spelling mistake in this sentence may well have arisen during the editing process, beyond the control of the authors, and, in any case, as a non-native speaker of English working in Manchester, it cannot be my intention to engage in yet another diatribe on the Holy Apostrophe. But let us hypothetically assume that it is a consequence of a discussion between editors and authors on whether it should be 'other cultures' or 'others' cultures'. That issue opens up a wealth of anthropological debate on the concept of culture itself, and particularly on the question whether it should be thought of as a discrete whole that persons 'have' through collective rooting in place (e.g. Gupta and Ferguson 1997). This pertains to cosmopolitanism, for if the latter is usually conceptualized as a disposition of openness towards otherness, implicitly or explicitly, that otherness is virtually always seen as 'cultural'. But how is the cultural defined in cosmopolitanism? Which grammar of difference underlies its openness? Historically, cosmopolitanism has not been thought of as a generalized open disposition towards *any* difference (cf. Harris 1927; Introduction to this volume), but rather, the otherness that is considered relevant to its openness is almost invariably conceived of through *localized* notions of culture. Thus cosmopolitanism has been seen mainly in conjunction with mobility between places and with meetings of localized cultural patterns, e.g. through migration, tourism, media, trade or consumption. In contemporary terms, then, cosmopolitanism's most frequent categorical *hostile* Other – that is the Other against which it is closed and against which it defines itself – is a discourse that homogenizes and fixes culture in place: nationalism (Lamont and Aksartova 2002, 2). This chapter investigates how 1990s post-Yugoslav evocations of cosmopolitanism projected openness in opposition to hegemonizing nationalisms, and which closures were encapsulated within this process.

Cosmopolitanism in Post-Yugoslav Antinationalism

The post-Yugoslav wars of the 1990s fulfilled the dream of nationally homogenized homelands for some, but their violent establishment also involved massive physical displacement and a sense of social, political, economic and emotional dislocation for many who stayed put (Jansen 1998). It was against this background, shortly after the wars in Bosnia-Herzegovina and Croatia, that I carried out ethnographic research (1996–98) amongst antinationalist activists in the capitals that housed the governments most responsible for the post-Yugoslav wars, Beograd (Serbia) and Zagreb (Croatia) – in that order.[1] In addition to participating in institutional sites of activism (antinationalist NGOs, media, associations of intellectuals, etc) I also traced everyday practices of resistance, channelling solidarity, care, outrage and indignation. Committed to a critique of nationalism myself, my explicit aim was to learn from such resistance in the immediate context of war-infected nationalist homogenization. While I would not proclaim myself a 'cosmopolitan', this chapter engages in a parallel exercise: it explores how cosmopolitanism may function as a resource, not in the salons, business class cabins and senior common rooms of Western elites, but in contexts where nationalist war had rendered any breaking of the national ranks a sure sign of treason and disloyalty, and a possible ground for harassment and abuse.

In the 1990s Serbia and Croatia violence against national Others was banalized and war criminals were widely celebrated as national heroes. Individuals were continually interpellated in national terms – demanding that they prove themselves to be true nationals, for example, by fighting on the front, using the sanctioned vocabulary, voting for the right party, reproducing the right story lines in front of the neighbours, and, perhaps most importantly, by refraining from dissent. 'Speaking out' in words and deeds, antinationalism reclaimed public space through demonstrations, solidarity actions and publications. The very terminology of cosmopolitanism functioned as a rhetorical resource in these struggles to value certain forms of belonging over others. From a nationalist perspective it stood for the dangers of rootless disloyalty that threatened national unity and authenticity, whereas in antinationalism it could signpost a desirable alternative organization of social life. I myself was often interrogated on my sense of belonging and loyalty to localized national groups, and in response to my confusing, perhaps seemingly evasive replies I was sometimes categorized as 'a real cosmopolitan' (*pravi kozmopolit*) or 'a citizen of the world' (*građanin sv(ij)eta*). Clearly, this could be meant as an insult or as a compliment, but even when positively deployed, cosmopolitanism was rarely developed into a programme. In fact, in over ten years of ethnographic engagement with the post-Yugoslav states, by far the most frequent way in which I have heard the term used is in marked contrast to any kind

---

1   For detailed ethnographic evidence and analysis, see Jansen (2005a). I also rely on insights from later ethnographic research on post-Yugoslav transformations of home and hope. All names in this text are pseudonyms, all translations are mine.

of manifesto: through decidedly non-revolutionary reference to a past 'normality' that has abruptly and brutally come to an end.

With some exceptions (e.g. feminist activism), antinationalist evocations of cosmopolitanism were thus remarkably 'conservative', in the literal sense of the term:[2] particularly on the everyday level, there was a strong preoccupation with continuity. Counteracting the amnesia and emancipatory discourse of Serbian and Croatian nationalism, which had almost monopolized rhetoric concerning change and renewal, antinationalism evoked continuities of individuality and responsibility. It entailed a refusal to relinquish an alternative narrative of the past and tended to centre around a sense of generalized mourning. Usually, such memory work recalled the time when one had lived 'normally' (Spasić 2003; Jansen 2008). In Beograd and Zagreb (and, famously so, in Sarajevo) one dimension of this remembered normality was a 'cosmopolitan' city life. Here, rather than tracing the historical veracity of such mourning, I analyse it as retrospective self-positioning, holding up images of previous 'open' lives as a critical mirror to evaluate current predicaments of closure. This leads me to question the dominant presumption, regardless of whether one detects empirical evidence of 'cosmopolitanization', or if one conceives of it as an ideal to aspire to, that, in our day and age, the prevalence of cosmopolitanism is growing. In stark contrast, post-Yugoslav antinationalism contained a deep mourning for a cosmopolitan openness that was, at least retrospectively, associated with *yesterday*'s lives.[3] This chapter critically analyses the mechanisms underlying such laments of closure and the antinationalist yearnings for the speedy 're-opening' of life.

From Party-led Paradox to Politicized Primordialism

> I have always thought of myself as a Croat, but that didn't ... I mean, I myself have been married to a Beograđanka. A Serb. It never crossed my mind that that was something problematic ... You went to the coast, and you met people from Serbia all the time. When I was younger, particularly during summers, we always used to hang out with girls from Beograd. (Vedran Ivanišević, about 50, academic, Zagreb)

---

2   Many felt there had been too little change and activism aimed to bring about desirable forms of it, but from an antinationalist perspective, most changes so far had been either catastrophic (nationalist homogenization, xenophobia, violence, isolation etc) or pointless (ceremonial national euphoria, cosmetic democratic changes, etc). The 1990s were thus seen as a missed opportunity and even the improvements that had occurred had carried too terrible a price.

3   Also on life 'after' cosmopolitanism, see Ors (2002) on post-Ottoman Istanbul. See also much writing, scholarly and novelistic, on Bombay (e.g. Appadurai 2000).

Before, it wasn't like this at all. Beograd was a very cosmopolitan city and
people didn't care about nationality at all. (Sonja Bjelica, about 30, old human
rights activist, Beograd)

In the late 1990s, antinationalist activists in Beograd and Zagreb often
conveyed the shock they had experienced at the initial realization that nationalism
had 'invaded' their lives. Many felt caught unaware not only by the nationalism
of their presumed 'enemies', but also by its sudden rise in their own 'majority'
context, removed from military violence. In those capital cities, nationally diverse
for centuries, they recalled with horror the sudden nationalist urge to understand
and organize social reality through exclusive, discrete national categories. Let me
first briefly refract such narratives against the political organization of the former
Yugoslav state.

My informants were aware that, in fact, nationality had been a key variable in
the political organization of the Yugoslav socialist configuration. After the massive
inter-national violence of World War Two, the Communist Party's concentration of
security and military matters in the federal government, the suppression of those
suspected of loyalty to the losing World War II sides, and a pro-Yugoslav emphasis
on co-operative, socialist recovery excluded *political* forms of nationalism from
legitimate expression. However, in doing so, far from ignoring national affiliation,
the government deployed policies of national balance and compromise. Locating
itself strategically between the two Cold War camps, it created a federation of
more-or-less nationally defined republics and strongly emphasized and proclaimed
the equality of all national groups and of all citizens.[4] Constitutional changes and
power struggles within the Yugoslav League of Communists – itself organized on a
republican basis – actually made it not only possible but also politically expedient
to imagine communities in national terms, albeit in a contradictory way on at least
two levels. Firstly, through increasing decentralization, republican Party elites
consolidated institutional national power bases (especially after 1974), and the use
of nationality 'keys' that governed appointment and allocation policies in areas
officially recognized as nationally 'mixed' entrenched nationality as a central
parameter of competition. Secondly, after a brief dalliance with attempts to replace
the various nationalisms with a Yugoslav one, legitimacy was sought through a
celebration of the co-existence of national cultures, made possible through the
museumification of public assertions of nationality in the realm of folklore. Hence,
the Yugoslav system of *Brotherhood and Unity* deployed certain (now common)
multicultural policies in a socialist framework.

The first round of multi-party elections in Yugoslavia, held on the republican
level in 1990, brought victories for parties who concurred that any 'transition to
democracy' necessarily had to be national. Their shared, if ultimately conflicting
commitment to national interests therefore broke the Yugoslav taboo on political
nationalism. This process took shape partly through an entrenchment of the

---

4   For an overview, see for example Dyker and Vejvoda (1996).

national-cum-republican power bases that had grown in the former state. Yet, the new governments dealt with the Yugoslav legacy in diverging ways: for example, the Serbian leadership, headed by Slobodan Milošević, relied on a strategic mix of incorporative Yugoslavism and Serbian nationalism, while its Croatian counterpart, under the helm of Franjo Tuđman, emphasized national liberation from what was represented as a Serbian-dominated Yugoslav past. The war that opposed those two political projects, fought in Croatia, thus confronted local Serbian and Serbo-Montenegrin forces who claimed to 'defend Yugoslavia' with Croatian ones who came to see this 'foreign aggression' as a foundational 'Motherland War'.

The post-Yugoslav nationalisms can be understood as discourses of universalized primordialism, positing nationality, in the ethnic sense, as the ultimate ground for identification – over and above all other lines of differentiation, such as gender, class, age, locality, citizenship, etc. – and thus as the legitimate basis for political interests and claims to territorial sovereignty. This required a disambiguation of reality, past and present, into a theatre with discrete, opposed national groups as the only relevant political subjects. Such representations of national bodies as bounded and internally homogenous have successfully permeated many local and foreign views of the conflicts. The competing post-Yugoslav nationalisms then portrayed themselves as the embodiment of rightful claims to inclusion within the 'family of nations' – conceptualized, as in the dominant discourse of the 'international community', as a mosaic composed of discrete units (Malkki 1994). While there were some markedly vicious fights in the South-East European part of the family, the 1990s wars thus included a reflection rather than an aberration of a now globally dominant nationalist worldview.

During my research in the mid-to-late 1990s, retrospective representations of nationality in Yugoslavia were then differentially integrated into practice. The dominant narrative followed nationalist discourses in their claim that they had finally allowed the true national belonging of their peoples to emerge from under the lid of Yugoslav communist oppression. Antinationalist narratives, of course, expressed indignation at such representations and at the politics waged on this basis. As the quotations above show, many argued that, while national competition may have governed the political level in Yugoslavia, it had not been important in their lives at all. Yet the emphasis on the sudden interpellation by nationalism was not uniform. In the next section, I disentangle two threads in the antinationalist mourning for cosmopolitan openness with regard to nationality. Firstly, I take a lead from Mr Ivanišević's reassertion of 'open' Yugoslav co-existence in the face of current segregation. Then I elaborate on Ms Bjelica's exclamation, which 'opened up' the status of nationality itself. Importantly, such representations were not experienced as mutually exclusive – and such contradictions will allow us to highlight tensions in cosmopolitan discourse itself.

Open Boundaries in a Mosaic/Opening up Nationality in a Mess

A first understanding of nationality in previous lives that could be summoned to legitimize an antinationalist stance, was to place it in peaceful, interactive co-existence in Yugoslavia. This approach largely reflected the mosaic model of national belonging: it started from boundaries and from the very notion of people with various nationalities existing alongside each other. Unlike the Serbian and Croatian nationalisms of the 1990s, this antinationalist deployment of the mosaic-model stressed harmonious inter-national relations across 'open' boundaries. Mournings of cosmopolitanism such as Mr Ivanišević's thus reasserted the value of openness over *segregation*, over closed borders and boundaries between people of different nationalities. Without necessarily recalling Yugoslavia as a faultless political formation, its (possibility of) mixing was celebrated. As in conceptualizations of cosmopolitanism, bodily or imagined mobility was an important factor here. The previous crossing of national boundaries could be associated with travel to visit relatives or on holidays, neighbourly and work relations, as well as a wider sense of a diverse Yugoslav 'home'. This partly reflected the celebration of Yugoslav unity and diversity in education and propaganda, but more frequently, 1990s antinationalism evoked Yugoslavness through popular culture, sports and consumption.

Many antinationalist recollections emphasized the absence of conflict between local, regional, national, Yugoslav, European and global belonging. Republics and Yugoslavia were often referred to in overlapping terms: at some points 'we' and 'here' meant Croatia or Serbia, and at other points it referred to the whole Yugoslav area. In the 1990s, even people who had never felt a sense of belonging to Yugoslavia still often worked implicitly on the basis of a concentric model with their own republic as the core, then the other post-Yugoslav republics and only then 'abroad'. In over a decade I have never heard anyone refer to citizens from other post-Yugoslav states as 'foreigners', except ironically. Hence many imagined Yugoslavness as a discursive space with a distinct, diverse, open (and only sometimes explicitly 'Yugoslavist') character. This was usually a rather diffuse experiential point of reference that seemed only special in retrospect, in the face of nationalist segregation.[5] In the largely segregated context of the 1990s, antinationalism thus often included a yearning for the open channels of interaction between people of different nationalities, and much activist energy was invested in the maintenance, or (re)creation, of links across the new post-Yugoslav state borders as well as across boundaries within (drastically reduced) local co-existence. Like liberal multiculturalism, this cosmopolitan strategy relied on a universalist cultural grid that allowed for equal recognition of and harmonious relations between existing particularistic differences.

---

5   Vast amounts of journalistic, autobiographical and essayistic work documents this process in people's everyday lives. For some examples by women writers during the wars, and an analysis of Yugoslav senses of 'home' in more detail, see Jansen (1998).

Importantly, recalling a Yugoslavia of open boundaries was neither a sufficient nor a necessary dimension of antinationalist discursive practice. Yugoslavism often functioned as a thinly disguised incorporative Serbian nationalism (deployed as such by the Milošević government), and evidence of past good international relations could be integrated into a discourse of former naïveté and betrayal. Perhaps precisely for this reason, a second manner in which antinationalism deployed mournings of cosmopolitanism was by undercutting the status of nationality itself (Jansen 2005a, Chapter 3). Rather than segregation *per se*, this strategy aimed to undo nationalist discursive closure by breaking open the status of nationality. It problematized the notion of a national mosaic, even a harmonious one, itself, and presented instead a much messier picture of belonging.

In a poststructuralist reading we may consider nationalist discourses as modes of representation that articulate certain elements ('differential positions') into moments ('differential positions insofar as they appear articulated within a discourse') (Laclau and Mouffe 1985, 113). A key question is which differences are accorded significance by hegemonizing discourses and which are not. Laclau and Mouffe understand the social as a struggle for hegemony between various discourses that aim to establish their particular articulation of elements into moments as an implicit body of consensual knowledge. No articulation can ever be completely successful and erase antagonism: elements never turn into perfect moments fully deriving their meaning out of the discourse in which they are articulated (Laclau and Mouffe 1985, 7, 106). In this way, post-Yugoslav antinationalism can be analysed as a struggle against the drive for closure embodied by nationalist hegemonic projects, retrospectively opening up nationality as an element in a messy universe of belonging.

Hence, while nationality had been articulated into an important moment of Yugoslav politics, and while its everyday importance in rural areas has been ethnographically demonstrated (e.g. Lockwood 1975) and analysed within interactions between local, national-religious and supranational identification (Bringa 1995), some post-Yugoslav antinationalist narrations of nationality radically disagreed. In contrast to dominant nationalist representations of the private persistence of nationality under Yugoslav oppression, and out of tune with their own anti-segregation discourse of open national boundaries in a mosaic, many of my urban informants argued that nationality had been of minor relevance in their everyday lives. In Beograd it was sometimes implied, *à la* Sonja Bjelica, that it had not been an issue for anyone at all, whereas in the Croatian capital most, regardless of national background, felt that while nationality had been a minor issue for them, it had been a more important factor for many others. To different degrees, then, antinationalism relied on soothing anecdotes illustrating a previous age of innocence in contrast to the post-Yugoslav environment, where nationalism had achieved such a level of closure through articulation of nationality into a, no, *the*, moment. Nationalist retrospective disambiguation – reorganizing the past around nationality categories only – was thus resisted through dissenting idealizations that reflected self-censorship of the opposite variety, aiming to break open nationality itself through 'retrospective ambiguation'.

Antinationalism remembered such open mundane discursive practice as removed from the level of politics and thus narrated the past in terms that matched the contradictions of the official Yugoslav discourse on nationality. Emphasizing the shocking newness of nationalism, such exaggerated recollections of the irrelevance of nationality did not effectively deny the previous existence of national lines of differentiation, but they undercut their status by pointing out that their meaning had been relative to context (cf. Jansen 2005b). Rather than a precise and consistent representation of past experience, this provided a mode of resistance on account of remembered multi-layered and ambiguous realities of people's 'messy' sense of belonging. In a context where national categories had been elevated to issues of life and death, antinationalism stubbornly recalled nationality as one element only amongst many differentiating factors in the mundane context. Rather than adding to the clamour of voices on nationality *per se* – a topic that already saturated the public sphere – the more common way of doing this was through emphasizing the relevance of these *other* differences. Let us now trace such lines of division beyond the national.

After Cosmopolitanism: Waking Up in the Isolated, Suffocated City

In their 1992 documentary *Geto*, film-makers Mladen Matičević and Ivan Markov have the narrator deplore the loss of an icon from Beograd's subcultural scene, SKC (Student Cultural Centre). He blames the Milošević government for:

> destroy[ing] the places where we used to meet. The worst case is SKC ... That place had to suffer ... They knew that rock'n'roll and exhibitions can teach kids to say 'no' tomorrow ... Instead of urban types, the main positions are now occupied by shepherds ... SKC has become a village cultural centre filled with flute players, amateurs from Užice [town in South-West Serbia] and dubious diarists, instead of Cave [Nick, Australian singer], the Brejkers [Partibrejkers, a Beograd rock band] and Šerbedžija [Rade, a mainly Zagreb-based actor]. Of course, kids don't go there anymore, except for a piss.

In this context, many urbanites attempted to maintain some continuity of their 'normal lives'. As I would learn during my frequent visits to their Beograd flat, my friends Nataša and Aleksandar, a lecturer and an NGO-worker, had experienced a socio-economic catastrophe since 1990. Yet they framed their predicament primarily as a *cultural* disaster, mourning the open, cosmopolitan lives they felt robbed of. In defiance to what they called the 'primitivism' around them, they attended events and discussed developments in the world of fine arts, social theory, film and popular music. And despite the imposed isolation, they maintained a network of friends abroad and their slow, unreliable internet connection provided a crucial opening to 'the World'. Aleksandar and Nataša had travelled widely before the wars and continued to do so whenever the scarce occasions arose through NGO and academic projects. Notwithstanding financial restrictions, they returned from these trips with bags full of books, reflecting the household policy of sacrificing socio-economic comfort for intellectual and aesthetic stimulation. Regular theatre and film goers, they also circled their agenda dates for lectures, concerts and DJ sets, and exhibitions. Such discursive practices of distinction also structured their everyday lives in other ways. For example, whenever their reduced budget allowed them, they chose to eat food stuffs that had cultural capital attached to them, such as Asian vegetarian products, often imported via Western states.

Meanwhile in Zagreb, a 1997 controversy broke out about the reasons for the electoral success of the ruling Croatian nationalist party (HDZ) in the countryside and its loss of appeal in the cities. Armed with nationality statistics, the pro-government daily *Vjesnik* argued that HDZ performance was weaker in cities exclusively because non-Croats there voted for the opposition. In contrast, the oppositional Zagreb weekly *Tjednik* described the urban population as 'younger, better educated, more tolerant, with a mind of their own, better informed and intellectually curious'. Then it argued:

> A population with an urban sensibility, an upbringing and the habits of a citizen's home – and they do not only live in cities – will find it hard to live with the HDZ's decrees of Croathood ... and the medieval state-building mystique ... For those with the city in their heads it is not enough to have lunch and a blanket, but they also want quality schooling, they want to live decently, do their job, listen to classical music, jazz or rock and travel abroad. (*Tjednik* 25/04/97: 28)

Due to propaganda and social control in small-scale communities, *Tjednik* continued, rural folk were conformist and 'afraid of any dissonant decision'. This was then embedded in an evolutionist approach ('All that which the city thinks today, the village will think in ten or fifteen years, not before that'), which, in contrast to *Vjesnik*'s articulation of nationality as a moment, relied on an alternative articulation around the urbanity/rurality division.

If the discourse of cosmopolitan openness, as we have seen, was evoked in resistance to the exclusionist hardening of nationality boundaries, these vignettes indicate it could also be deployed against other forms of closure. Antinationalist narratives reconstructed a Yugoslav past in which nationality had been only one amongst many lines of division, and they evoked a range of such alternative differences (party membership, gender, age ...). Yet there was an overwhelming tendency to specify that the most important distinction in those days had been that between cities and villages, between citizens and peasants, between open, nationally heterogeneous, modern, urban life and closed, nationally homogenous, backward, rural life (cf. Brown 2001). Elsewhere I have investigated this urban-centric discourse, organized around the concept of 'culturedness', through a detailed ethnographic analysis of balkanist distinction in a domesticated modernization format (Jansen 2005a, Chapter 2; 2005c). Here, my more schematic argument will be two-pronged, exploring how remembered cosmopolitan openness was deployed, firstly, against *isolation* from the outside world, and, secondly, against *suffocation* by 'primitivism'.

Membership of 'the World' vs. Isolation

Lamont and Aksartova (2002, 2) argue that the 'opposition of nationalism to cosmopolitanism conveys the fundamental tension between moral obligations to one's local origins and group memberships, on the one hand, and to the rest of the world, on the other'. Yet post-Yugoslav antinationalism actually emphasized the reassertion of the very links between the 'local' and the 'global', both of which were understood in a particular way. This was exemplified in a central slogan of the 'Winter Protest' against the Milošević government that brought up to hundreds of thousands of people onto the streets for months at the turn of 1996 and 1997.[6] In Beograd, the student section was invariably headed by a gigantic banner saying *Beograd je svet* (Beograd is the World). This message conveyed at once the city's worldliness and the desire to end isolation from 'the World' (Jansen 2000). The 'local' was thus the city, and, while the demonstrators waved state flags from around the globe (as well as for example Ferrari and rainbow flags), the frequent references to 'world standards' and to 'how things are done in the world' left no doubt which 'world' was meant here: the very world that the Milošević government tended to defy and that had imposed sanctions on Serbia – the liberal democracies of the West.

Resentment at isolation was widespread far beyond antinationalist activism, and it could convey different things to different people. In fact, isolation had come to be seen increasingly not simply as a symptom of the losses suffered during the 1990s, but as a *reason* for them. Complaints about Serbia being closed off from 'the World' were commonplace and a similar, if much less prominent, discourse pervaded dissatisfaction in Croatia under Tuđman. In such laments, remembered cosmopolitanism functioned as a yearning for openness towards 'the World', with a prominent place reserved for travel, whether through bodily movement or through flows of ideas and goods. Particularly in Serbia, the contrast between current visa restrictions and the previous freedom to cross borders with the Yugoslav passport structured many narratives of loss in everyday life. People also frequently argued that popular culture in Yugoslavia had been on a par with 'the World', in marked contrast to neighbouring Eastern European states under the Soviet umbrella. Hence, the mourned 'openness' with regard to 'the World' had two mutually constitutive

---

6   Sparked by the government's refusal to accept local election results, these demonstrations were not antinationalist *per se*: while some protesters did blame Milošević's nationalism for the wars, others reviled him for losing them (hence, for his failure to *complete* the nationalist project) (Jansen 2000, 2001).

dimensions: on the one hand, it referred to the fact that flows from 'the World' had relatively freely entered everyday lives in Yugoslavia, and on the other, it conveyed a sense of legitimate 'membership' of that World. In addition to better socio-economic standards and travel abroad, people thus often recalled sporting performances and events (the Sarajevo Olympics, Yugoslav basket or ski-jump medals, etc.) which had, as it were, put Yugoslavia *on the map*. Such narratives resonate with what Dević calls Yugoslav 'urban cosmopolitan lifestyles' (1997, 131), pervaded by an ethos that, while based on the anti-fascist World War Two legacy, grew to be staunchly individualist and centred around western-inspired consumption patterns. Therefore, in those 1990s mournings of cosmopolitanism, Yugoslavia's significance was related less to its socialism than to the remembered comparative Western-ness of the mundane lives people had led in it.

Antinationalism blamed the loss of these cosmopolitan lives on nationalist policies. And with nationalism emphasizing cultural authenticity and particularism, the antinationalist universalist emphasis on re-establishing social, material and moral links between the lives of citizens in Serbia and Croatia and 'the World' was in fact overwhelmingly pro-Western in outlook. With few exceptions (e.g. some feminist, anarchist and other alter-globalist initiatives) there was hardly any antinationalist opposition to, or even critical reflection on, integration processes into NATO or the EU.[7] Membership of Western-dominated power blocs was seen as the self-evident manner to break isolation and to finally take up one's place in 'the World' again. The much larger non-Western part of the globe was usually ignored. The Yugoslav government's important role in the Non-Aligned Movement, for example, was almost only referred to either ironically or in order to specifically emphasize Tito's stature as a global politician who had put Yugoslavia on the map in the eyes of the West.

In the 1990s, then, replacing isolation with an openness to 'the World' often came to mean catching up with the West. With the nationalist governments waging a relentless campaign of harassment and abuse against 'domestic traitors and foreign mercenaries', Western funding and pro-European discourses of legitimacy were crucial to organized antinationalist opposition (cf. Chen Xiaomei 1996). For example, much activism was made possible through funding by the Open Society Foundation, which derives its name from the early Popperian notion that truly democratic systems should always provide room for dissent. Like Popper's political thought, the Foundation ended up promoting a strongly pro-Western, liberal model of openness. And if, in principle, such 'European-ness' (Jansen 2002) was accessible to all post-Yugoslavs by default, with the real-existing political configurations of Europe unfavourably inclined, many, particularly in Serbia, came to accept that there was some way ahead before their societies could ascend to their rightful European-ness. In this context, Western-led and -funded

---

7   Opposition to these processes was seen as the exclusive domain of ultranationalist parties.

institutions functioned as important channels for the creation and reproduction of a pro-Western elite in postsocialist Europe.

In addition to a variety of small groups working on shoestring budgets, post-Yugoslav antinationalism worked through sophisticated institutions for campaigning, education, publishing and conferences, largely Western-funded and steeped in liberal-democratic discourses of legitimacy (cf. Bruno 1998). These organizational vectors of antinationalism permitted some persons to accumulate different kinds of capital: salaries, kudos, contacts, travel opportunities, media space, and so on. Some activists themselves denounced the elitist, cliquish dimensions of certain dissident circles and, paraphrasing a much more lucrative post-Yugoslav industry, some individuals who had channelled such engagements into economic privilege were referred to as 'anti-war profiteers'. However, for most, the possible material rewards were much less obvious than the risks of harassment, exclusion and abuse that came with the decision to speak up against injustice done to others.

Post-Yugoslav nationalisms keenly pointed out the *red bourgeoisie* background of some antinationalist activists to underpin their policies of intimidation. Such nationalist representations of communist nostalgics turned capitalist mercenaries, failed to add that this class was also prominent in the new nationalist elites, alongside the offspring of anti-Yugoslav families. Moreover, the social differentiation underlying antinationalist activism was actually more complicated. Writing on NGO work in Croatia, Stubbs (1997) suggests that the engagements of local and foreign professionals culminated in the formation of a globalized professional middle class, mainly around cultural and social capital. Many activists, now in mature middle-age, were highly educated and well-travelled, and their previous status had also been guaranteed more by cultural than by economic capital, reflecting to a certain extent Bourdieu's dominated fraction of the dominant class (1979, 321ff). Efforts by the Open Society Foundation and other Western organizations to create a vanguard of 'leaders' of the transformation of Eastern Europe were thus integrated into internal hierarchies of social distinction (Spasić 2006). And it was precisely an open, 'cosmopolitan' disposition that these persons themselves tended to see as setting them apart from those implicated most clearly in the nationalist order (ruling politicians, war profiteers and their supporters). In what follows, we take a closer look at this and at the closures of its own it entailed.

Open City Lives versus Suffocation by Primitivism

In his analysis of the 'decosmopolitanization' of Bombay, Appadurai (2000, 628) states that until the 1970s Bombay was 'well-managed' and, despite its explosive population growth, 'a civic model for India'. Mentioning housing, employment and basic services, he then recalls that trains previously

... seemed to be able to move people around with some dignity and reliability and at a relatively low cost. The same was true of the city's buses, bicycles, and trams ... People actually observed the etiquette of queuing in most public contexts, and buses always stopped at bus stops rather than fifty feet before or after them (as in most of India today). Sometime in the 1970s all this began to change and a malignant city began to emerge from beneath the surface of the cosmopolitan ethos of the prior period. (Appadurai 2000, 629)

It is only after deploring the end of dignified public transport and queuing manners, seen as signposts of a 'cosmopolitan ethos', that Appadurai moves on to discuss the politics of the ultranationalist Hindu party Shiv Sena. In this section, I trace a similar tendency to associate cosmopolitanism with certain practical aspects of 'modern civilization' in post-Yugoslav antinationalist mournings of previous lives, now suffocated by 'primitivism'.

Let me start with an example from the Beograd weekly *Vreme*, which has over the years critically documented war crimes, corruption and nationalist euphoria, and served as a prominent voice in an urban discourse of resentment at the loss of cosmopolitan city life. In 1997, under the large title *They Hate Beograd*, *Vreme* juxtaposed a photograph of a government limousine with one of a crowd struggling to climb on an already packed city bus. The accompanying text linked such contrasts to isolation as well as to the rural closure of the city:

They travel from their houses in Požarevac, Kolašin, Vranje to work and back by helicopter or Mercedes. Meanwhile, Beograd citizens suffer like cattle in dilapidated city transport. The federal government has not approved the import of buses from Berlin, a present to this city. They hate *Beograđani* and they hate this city. (*Vreme* 16 August 1997)

Laments about the state of city transport, followed by references to the humiliating conditions that made 'cultured behaviour' a challenge for even the most upstanding citizen, were rife in both Zagreb and Beograd. Like Appadurai, people framed this as a key symptom of the loss of a wider 'ethos', blamed on the city's political-economic and cultural occupation by peasant newcomers who had imposed primitive nationalism. Such resentment at the suffocation of an open, cosmopolitan city life was prominent amongst broad layers of urbanites. For example, the only large street protest in Croatia against the Tuđman government occurred not with regard to displacement, war crimes, neo-fascist revivalism or even corruption, but on the occasion of the 1997 clampdown on *Radio 101*. Under the slogan *Možete nam uzeti sve, ali Stojedinicu ne!* (You can take everything from us, but not *101*!), Zagreb folk decided to take to the streets in numbers on this and on no other occasion, representing the station as a bastion of Zagreb's urban spirit. Its announced closure was experienced as one step too far in the city's closure under peasant primitivism.

Radicalizing early sociological analyses of urban life (e.g. Wirth 1938), many believed that by virtue of its heterogeneity and size the city was per definition politically 'open' too. Parallel to the abovementioned Zagreb example from *Tjednik*, the oppositional vote in the central Beograd boroughs was also put down to the fact that they were inhabited by educated people whose families had lived there for generations. The sociologist Sreten Vujović (1992, 63) argued that these autochthons supported policies of 'modernity, democracy and the future' as opposed to the regime-voting 'workers, clerks, non- or less educated, often half-illiterate newcomers in Beograd's extended suburbs'. Moreover, he stated that 'all great cultures are born in cities' and that 'world history is actually the history of urban people' (Vujović 1992, 62). Eat your heart out, hunters-gatherers of the world... Asserting that 'the only real distinction in modern times was: peasant/citizen, or even better: cosmopolitan versus provincial' (Vujović 1992; cf. Bogdanović 1993; Kangrga 1997), antinationalism thus inverted the moral evaluation of nationalist representations of rural purity and authenticity. Heterogeneity, condemned by nationalism as promiscuity, was celebrated and contrasted with the suffocating and unchanging backwardness of village primitivism, now imposed onto the city by peasant newcomers.

Cosmopolitan dispositions have long been associated with cities (Featherstone 2002, 1). Often this is based on the Kantian notion of hospitality – cities as spaces allowing the reception and mutual recognition of Others (Derrida 1999; Dikeç 2002). Yet, post-Yugoslav antinationalism relied on a *memory* of cosmopolitan city life and was rather hostile to the other that was actually arriving in its cities now: this other, namely, was not defined nationally but rather with reference to their attributed national*ist* political profile and (lack of) cultural competence. And they were destroying cosmopolitanism. Conditioned by long-standing social patterns in the region, by the influence of socialist development policies, and by the nationalism it opposed, antinationalism thus came to define an ideal of urbanity (Buden 1996, 50) as pro-Western or European (vs. Balkan), educated (vs. illiterate), autonomous-individualist (vs. conformist-collectivist), gender equal (vs. patriarchal), tolerant (vs. exclusivist), peaceful (vs. violent), heterogeneous (vs. homogenous), sophisticated (vs. boorish), connected (vs. isolated), welcoming towards otherness (vs. xenophobic), going forward (vs. standing still), etc. This entire series could then be subsumed in a dichotomy, embedded in an evolutionist paradigm, that opposed the openness of past city life to its current village-like suffocation. Note that the past was thus remembered as modern (cf. Ors 2002), and the current predicament was conceived of as a relapse into pre- or anti-modern primitivism.

In response, the 1996 and 1997 Beograd demonstrations deployed city-space as a terrain of resistance and articulated their political subject around urbanites, robbed of their cosmopolitan lives (Jansen 2001). An important mode of self-recognition amongst the protesters crystallized around educated sophistication and etiquette, coming up for air after having been suffocated by primitivism for years. Slogans, chants and stories in the crowds insisted that the spirit of the city had finally risen to show 'the World' that Serbia did not only consist of primitives (Jansen 2000). Amongst younger persons, these assertions of distinction, reintegrating their Beograd into 'the World', attached considerable importance to active engagement and conversational fluency in popular culture. Some recalled the city's status as the 'second clubbing city in Europe after London', and many cherished the resilient coolness of its nightlife, expressing satisfaction at Western magazine features reaffirming that the Beograd beat had refused to die during the dark 1990s (cf. Collin 2001; Gordy 1999).

Such urban resentment at the loss of cool modernity, as well as defiant assertions of its resilience, could be integrated directly into cosmopolitan attempts to 'mess up' nationality's status as *the* moment. For example, many men referred to their military service in the former Yugoslav army, which, with its policy of nationally heterogeneous groups of recruits, served as a primary experience of inter-republican contact for many. Conscripts from Zagreb and Beograd, it was then argued had always socialized more with each other than they had with rural soldiers from their own republic (and thus, more probably of the same nationality). They were, as one thirty-something man remarked, rock'n'roll kids, regardless of nationality.[8] Urbanity/rurality could also crosscut nationality in other ways, as exemplified by the story of Biljana Nušić, a literature student from a Serbian Zagreb family who had fled to Beograd and with whom I volunteered in a refugee organization. Biljana patently distanced her own Zagreb background from that of the other refugees, mostly hailing from around Knin – the centre of aggressive Serbian nationalism when Croatia proclaimed its independence in 1991. She recalled the euphoria, the flag and gun waving and the nationalist songs there as 'typically peasant' and attached more blame to those fellow-Serbs than to most Croats when assessing her own fate. In Croatian nationalism, of course, such assertions distorted the dichotomy between barbarian Serbs and civilized Croats (Buden 1996, 92), particularly when juxtaposed with stereotypical images of the focus of Zagreb urban resentment: Croats from Herzegovina (a proverbially 'backward' area in Bosnia-Herzegovina). Many Zagreb people complained that their city had been overrun by a powerful 'Herzegovinian lobby' within the elite, consisting of hard-line nationalists, warlords and business tycoons, as well as by the cultural 'degradation' they had brought with them. This was reflected in graffiti that appeared in Zagreb only shortly after the war that had seen massive violence between Serbs on the one hand and Croats (including Herzegovinian Croats) on the other:

VRATITE NAM NAŠE SRBE, EVO VAM NATRAG VAŠI HERCEGOVCI
(GIVE US BACK OUR SERBS, YOU CAN HAVE YOUR HERZEGOVINIANS BACK).

---

8   Not coincidentally, the story line of the first big budget post-Yugoslav cinematic co-production, Rajko Grlić's 2006 *Karaula*, focuses on the rock'n'roll friendship between a Croatian recruit from the city of Split and a Serbian one from Beograd, set off against a faceless harmonica-playing peasant soldier.

When mourning previous cosmopolitan 'normal lives', post-Yugoslav antinationalism thus tended to organize itself around the articulation not of nationality but of urbanity/rurality.

Conclusion

If cosmopolitanism can be considered a 'moral commitment to universals' and analysed in terms of grounded, particular 'cultural repertoires of universalisms' that confront nationalist particularism (Lamont and Aksartova 2002, 4–5), what was the grammar of difference underlying its post-Yugoslav antinationalist avatar? Antinationalism revalorized universalist understandings of humanity around the moral imperative to treat 'a person as a person', regardless of nationality (Ibid.). Such moral cosmopolitanism emphasized individual autonomy, integrity and responsibility, contrasted with the collectivist conformism of the hegemonizing nationalisms that had recently caused so much suffering and that continued to underlie widespread injustice. To this end, antinationalism relied heavily on strategies of continuity with remembered 'normal' cosmopolitan lives. Firstly, remembered cosmopolitan lives were deployed to resist nationalist closure by insisting on the previously open nature of national boundaries or by refusing to articulate nationality into a moment, doggedly insisting on its open character as an element of messy everyday life. In the latter representation, other-than-national differences were crucial to point out the relativity of nationality, and the most importatnt one in post-Yugoslav antinationalism was the contrast between isolating and suffocating peasant primitivism and worldly urban cosmopolitanism. Such evocations of past cosmopolitan lives allowed an assertion of continued attachment to open 'normality', both as membership of 'the World' and as a characteristic of an urban, modern sense of self. This was itself constituted through discursive practices of distinction that incorporated 'openness' as a defining self-ascribed characteristic. Such claims formed the basis for important activism against nationalism, but, particularly through its urban-centrism, the creation of antinationalist openings was premised on alternative closures. While it never led to anything like the sort of violence and discrimination that the nationalisms engaged in, to an important extent this alternative discursive closure, articulating the element of rurality/urbanity into a moment, supplanted that around nationality. Antinationalist openness, then, successfully welcomed certain differences, but it closed off others. As much universalist discourse, it thus ended up flattening the cultural-national difference it was programmatically open to, through emphasizing (in this case, urban) sameness across its boundaries.

References

Appadurai, A. (2000), 'Spectral Housing and Urban Cleansing: Notes on Millennial Mumbai', *Public Culture* 12, 627–51.

Bogdanović, B. (1993), *Die Stadt und der Tod* (Klagenfurt: Wieser Verlag).

Bourdieu, P. (1979), *La Distinction: Critique Sociale du Jugement* (Paris: Éditions de Minuit).

Bridger, S. and Pine, F. (eds) (1998), *Surviving Post-socialism* (London: Routledge).

Bringa, T. (1995), *Being Muslim the Bosnian Way: Identity and Community in a Central Bosnian Village* (Princeton: Princeton University Press).

Brown, K. (2001), 'Beyond Ethnicity: The Politics of Urban Nostalgia in Modern Macedonia', *Journal of Mediterranean Studies* 11:2, 417–42.

Bruno, M. (1998), 'Playing the Co-operation Game: Strategies around International Aid in Post-socialist Russia', in Bridger and Pine (eds).

Buden, B. (1996), *Barikade* (Zagreb: Bastard/Arkzin).

Chen Xiaomei (1996), *Occidentalism: a Theory of Counterdiscourse in Post-Maoist China* (Oxford: Oxford University Press).

Collin, M. (2001), *This is Serbia Calling: Rock'n'roll Radio and Belgrade's Underground Resistance* (London: Serpent's Tail).

Derrida, J. (1999), *Cosmopolites de Tous les Pays, Encore un Effort!* (Paris: Galilée).

Dević, A. (1997) 'Anti-war Initiatives and the Un-making of Civic Identities in the Former Yugoslav Republics', *Journal of Historical Sociology* 10:2, 127–56.

Dikeç, M. (2002), 'Pera, Peras, Poros: Longings for Spaces of Hospitality', *Theory, Culture & Society* 19:1–2, 227–47.

Dyker, D.A. and Vejvoda, I. (eds) (1996), *Yugoslavia and After* (Harlow: Longman).

Featherstone, M. (2002), 'Cosmopolis: An Introduction', *Theory, Culture & Society* 19:1–2, 1–16.

Golubović, Z., Spasić, I. and Pavićević, Đ. (eds) (2003), *Politika i Svakodnevni život: Srbija 1999–2002* (Beograd: Disput).

Gordy, E.D. (1999), *The Culture of Power in Serbia: Nationalism and the Destruction of Alternatives* (University Park: Penn State University Press).

Gupta, A. and Ferguson, J. (eds) (1997), *Culture, Power, Place: Explorations in Critical Anthropology* (Durham: Duke University Press).

Harris, H. (1927), 'The Greek Origins of the Idea of Cosmopolitanism', *International Journal of Ethics* 38:1, 1–10.

Jansen, S. (1998), 'Homeless at Home: Narrations of post-Yugoslav Identities', in Rapport and Dawson (eds).

— (2000), 'Victims, Rebels, Underdogs: Discursive Practices of Resistance in Serbian Protest', *Critique of Anthropology* 20:4, 393–420.

— (2001), 'The Streets of Beograd: Urban Space and Protest Identities in Serbia', *Political Geography* 20:1, 35–55.

— (2002), 'Svakodnevni Orijentalizam: Doživljaj "Balkana"/"Evrope" u Beogradu i Zagrebu', *Filozofija i društvo* 18, 33–72.

— (2005a), *Antinacionalizam: Etnografija Otpora u Zagrebu i Beogradu* (Beograd: XX Vek).

— (2005b), 'National Numbers in Context: Maps and Stats in Representations of the Post-Yugoslav Wars', *Identities: Global Studies in Culture and Power* 12:1, 45–68.

— (2005c), 'Who's Afraid of White Socks? Towards a Critical Understanding of Post-Yugoslav Urban Self-perceptions', *Ethnologia Balkanica* 9, 151–67.

— (2008), 'Troubled Locations: Return, the Life Course and Transformations of "Home" in Bosnia-Herzegovina', in S. Jansen and S. Löfving (eds) *Struggles for Home: Violence, Hope and the Movement of People* (Oxford: Berghahn), 43–64.

Kangrga, M. (1997) *Izvan Povijesnog Događanja: Dokumenti Jednog Vremena* (Split: Feral Tribune).

Laclau, E. and Mouffe. C. (1985), *Hegemony and Socialist Strategy: Towards a Radical Democratic Politics* (London: Verso).

Lamont, M. and Aksartova, S. (2002), 'Ordinary Cosmopolitanisms: Strategies for Bridging Racial Boundaries among Working-Class Men', *Theory, Culture & Society* 19:4, 1–25.

Lockwood, W. (1975), *European Moslems: Economy and Ethnicity in Western Bosnia* (New York: Academic Press).

Malkki, L. (1994), 'Citizens of Humanity: Internationalisms and the Imagined Community of Nations', *Diaspora* 3:1, 41–67.

Mimica, A. and Čolović, I. (eds) (1992), *Druga Srbija* (Beograd: Beogradski Krug).

Ors, I. (2002), 'Coffeehouses, Cosmopolitanism and Pluralizing Modernities in Istanbul', *Journal of Mediterranean Studies* 12:1, 119–45.

Rapport, N. and Dawson, A. (eds) (1998), *Migrants of Identity: Perceptions of "Home" in a World of Movement* (Oxford: Berg).

Škrbiš, Z., Kendall, G. and Woodward, I. (2004), 'Locating Cosmopolitanism: between Humanist Ideal and Grounded Social Category', *Theory, Culture & Society* 21:6, 115–36.

Spasić, I. (2003), 'Sećanje na Nedavnu Prošlost', in Golubović, Spasić and Pavićević (eds).

— (2006), 'Distinkcija na Domaći Način: Diskursi Statusnog Diferenciranja u Današnjoj Srbiji', in I. Spasić and M. Nemanjić (eds).

Spasić, I. and Nemanjić, M. (eds) (2006), *Nasleđe Pjera Burdijea: Pouke i Nadahnuća* (Beograd: Disput).

Stubbs, P. (1997) 'NGO Work with Forced Migrants in Croatia: Lineages of a Global Middle Class?', *International Peacekeeping* 4:4, 50–60.

Vujović, S. (1992), 'Drugi Beograd', in Mimica and Čolović (eds).

Wirth, L. (1938), 'Urbanism as a Way of Life', *American Journal of Sociology* 44:1, 1–24.

Chapter 5

Europe's Evolving Public Space: Cosmopolitan Engagements through the Lens of American Mass Culture

Rob Kroes

The United States, throughout what is commonly referred to as the 'American Century', has held cultural sway over those living within its imperial reach, particularly in the years following World War II. Among Europeans at the receiving end of its cultural radiance there has been a blend of intrigued fascination mixed in with cultural resistance, trying to make sense of America's cultural Otherness as measured by European standards, and to fathom the impact of American mass culture on Europe's cultural landscape. In fact the history of these European concerns predates the 'American century'. Words like Americanization were coined in Europe as early as the nineteenth century when America was still in the early stages of developing forms of mass culture to Americanize the many who had come as strangers to its shores. In the process Americans managed to develop a cultural vernacular that could speak to mass audiences rather than elite publics. And it did so with all the mastery it used in reaching mass markets for its mass-produced consumption commodities. In fact it never shrank from applying the logic of marketing to the production of cultural forms. From its early origins, it might be argued, American mass culture was both democratic and commercial, conceiving of its public as cultural consumers constituting a market. And it appealed to that market with all the force of its advertising wizardry, wrapping its products, whether economic commodities like cigarettes, or cultural products like film, in seductive narrative fantasies that were all equally evocative of an imaginary America, a dreamscape that had Americanized the immigrants before it would tempt foreign publics.[1]

The history of the European encounter with an American culture cast in this mould is one of European audiences, mostly the younger generations, appropriating these seductive dreams and making them their own, against parental strictures. Thus, particularly in the post-World War II years, when Europe had set out on its own course towards a culture of consumption, in many cases America provided them with the standards for emulation, providing each next generation

---

1 For the early history of the formation of American mass culture, I may refer the reader to Rydell and Kroes (2005).

of youngsters with a cultural vernacular redolent with American fantasies. In their quest for a cultural identity clearly their own these American ingredients served as alternatives in cultural struggles waged in every European national setting with cultural gate-keepers guarding the purity of the national identity. Thus a shared cultural vernacular could evolve that is meaningfully summarized in the quip that the only culture that Europeans have in common across national borders is American culture.

In this view we may conceive of this new cultural vernacular in terms of cosmopolitan memory. Replete as this cultural vernacular – or vernacular culture, for that matter – is with imagined Americas, it does put one in mind of Levy and Sznaider's view of cosmopolitan memory as independent of specific group carriers, acting *in loco parentis* so to speak, but rather as being mediated by films, television, the music industry, books, photographs, all being available for mass consumption. As they put it: 'Cosmopolitan memory thus implies some recognition of the history (and memories) of the Other', the Other in our case being an imagined, if not imaginary, America (Levy and Sznaider 2002, 103). This chapter will argue that European experiences and cultural habits are imbricated with patterns of American mass culture, particularly in the post-World War II era. America, in our case, is that 'Other' whose history and memories, as refracted in its mass cultural productions, are being increasingly acknowledged in European forms of cultural appropriation and resistance. To make my case, I'll be looking at the many ways in which American cultural transmissions, as so many semantic bits and pieces, have been filling Europe's public space. In other words, I'll be looking at the American 'signage' that has increasingly come to constitute the semantic environment of daily life in Europe.

Europe's Inner Contradictions: Nationalism vs. Cosmopolitanism

In current reflections on the ways in which Europe is changing if not evolving, two pairs of buzzwords emphasize the contradictory forces affecting Europe's changes. One pair of mass cultural productions are being increasingly acknowledged, cosmopolitanism and transnationalism, which focuses our attention on the many ways in which the political affiliations and cultural affinities of Europeans have transcended their conventional frames of reference, away from the nation and the nation-state. The other pair, nationalism and localism, stresses the enduring power of precisely such conventional forms of affiliation and self-identification. At the present point in time, with Europe engaged in the Promethean venture of framing a Constitution for the European Union following its last dramatic expansion of scale, hidebound forms of nationalism and localism are gaining strength. Public opinion in the member states of the Union is increasingly sceptical of the whole project, seeing it as a cultural and economic threat rather than as a promise of a better life for all involved. This may be temporary and transient, a moment's hesitation in the face of a daring leap into a future whose costs may outweigh its benefits. The current economic malaise in much of Europe may in fact lead many ruefully to look back at the days of national sovereignty and the sense of collective control of the national destiny that is now a nostalgic memory. There is a feeling of loss of direction which in many member states takes people to a renewed reflection on national identity and national culture. Even in countries like the Netherlands where Dutchness has most of the time been more of a 'given' – to use Daniel Boorstin's (1953) word to describe the consensual nature of America's political culture – and therefore hardly ever openly contested or argued, has recently become the topic of lively intellectual discussion. The triggers are as much domestic, to do with the increased multicultural nature of Dutch society, as they are European, if not global. Yet in the eyes of many the two are interrelated; the increased porousness of national borders is seen as due to the super-imposition of a 'Europe without borders'.

This hidebound view of what is wrong with Europe stands in opposition to views of European developments in the light of cosmopolitanism and transnationalism. German sociologist Ulrich Beck is among those who see transnationalism as the outcome of long-term processes ushering in a stage of Second Modernity; they are processes that have worked to erode the logic of the historical stage of First Modernity, centred on the bonding and bounding force of nationalism in the historical formation of the nation-state (Beck 2003a; 2003b). Nationalism as a historical project aimed at moulding nations conceived in terms of cultural and political homogeneity, speaking one national language, sharing one cultural identity. Its logic was inherently binary. At the same time as defining insiders, it defined outsiders. These could be strangers in the midst of the 'imagined community' of the nation, a living contradiction to the ideal-typical construction of the 'pure' nation, and therefore subject to a range of forms of exclusion, if not persecution,[2] or they could be literally outsiders, members of other nations, and therefore cultural, almost legitimate, 'others'. In our age of globalization this binary logic has been relentlessly eroded. Exposed to a worldwide flow of cultural expression, people everywhere have appropriated cultural codes alien to their homogenized national cultures. They have developed multiple identities, allowing them to move across a range of cultural affinities and affiliations. The communications revolution, most recently in the form of the World Wide Web, has made for a freedom of movement between a multitude of self-styled communities of taste and opinion, transcending national borders. A person's national identity is now only one among many options for meaningful affiliation with fellow human beings, triggered at some moments while remaining dormant, or latent, at others. One's local roots are now only one of the many signifiers of a person's sense of self. Beck calls this rooted cosmopolitanism. There is no cosmopolitanism without localism (Beck 2003a, 17).

As Beck also points out, much of this new cosmopolitanism is relatively unreflected, 'banal' (Beck 2003a, 21). Teenagers affiliating with a transnational

---

2   On these processes of exclusion and inclusion, as they relate to historical dramas of ethnic and cultural cleansing, see Bauman (1989).

youth culture, sharing cultural appetites with untold others dispersed across the globe, are simply consumers of mass culture, unaware of the existential joy of their transnational venture. Banal nationalism is being constantly eroded by the torrent of banal cosmopolitanism in the forms of mass culture that wash across the globe. It is banal *because* it is unreflected, never leading the new cosmopolitans to pause and ponder what happened to their sense of self. Yet, unaware as they may be of the intricate pattern of cultural vectors that guide their cultural consumption, collectively they have worked to cosmopolitanize the nation-state from within. Countries like France, Germany, Britain or the Netherlands are no longer nation-states but transnational states. Mass culture of course is only one of the forces of change. International migration, the formation of diasporic communities across the map of Europe, and the attendant rise of multi-culturalism have also changed the conventional paradigm of the nation-state. There is nothing banal here, in the sense of an unreflected cosmopolitanism taking root. Quite the contrary; the anguished consideration of the changed contours of nationhood and the citizenry is a clear reflection of the concern, shared by many, about what has happened to the idea of the nation. Yet, as Beck (2003b) argues in *Dissent*, the only way for the European project to go forward is for Europe to become a transnational state, a more defined and complex variant of what its component nations are already becoming.

Much as I agree with this vision of Europe's future, I am struck by the historical myopia in Beck's argument. As he presents his case, Europe's Second Modernity, its age of transnationalism and cosmopolitanism, evolves from Europe's First Modernity, an age whose central logic was that of the nation-state. This seems to deny the long historical experience of cosmopolitanism in Europe, of a view of the civilized life centring on what can only be described as European culture. No banal cosmopolitanism here, but the high-minded version of cultural elites producing and consuming a culture that was truly cosmopolitan, transcending the borders and bounds of the nation-state. It was always a rooted cosmopolitanism, with European trends and styles in the arts always being refracted through local appropriations, reflecting local tastes and manners. As Kant defined cosmopolitanism, it was always a way of combining the universal and the particular, *Nation und Weltbürger*, nation and world citizenship. This is the lasting and exhilarating promise of European history, in spite of the atrocities committed on European soil in the name of the homogenized nation, marching in lock-step, purging itself of unwanted 'others'. The vision of world citizenship, the transcending idea of humanity, has always had to be defended against the other half of Kant's dialectical pair, against the claims on behalf of the nation. In an astute discussion of the Nuremberg tribunal and the new legal principle of 'Crimes against humanity' which it introduced, Beck (2003b, 35) makes the following observation, worth quoting in full:

> It is at this point that cosmopolitan Europe generates a genuinely European inner contradiction, legally, morally, and politically. The traditions from which colonial, nationalist, and genocidal horror originated were clearly European. But

so were the new legal standards against which these acts were condemned and tried in the spotlight of world publicity. At this formative moment in its history, Europe mobilized its traditions to produce something historically new. It took the idea of recognition of the humanity of the Other and made it the foundation of an historically new counter-logic. It specifically designed this logic to counteract the ethnic perversion of the European tradition to which the nation-based form of European modernity had just shown itself so horribly liable. It was an attempt to distill a European antidote to Europe.

This is truly what the post-World War II project of building a new Europe has been all about, to draw on a long European tradition of high-minded cosmopolitanism, inclusive of cultural variety and cultural Others, and internalized by its citizens as a plurality of individual selves.

This is a daunting project. If it succeeds it may well serve as a model to the world, a rival to the American ideal of transnationalism, of constituting a nation of nations.[3] If they are rival models, they are at the same time of one kind. They are variations on larger ideals inspiring the idea of Western civilization and find their roots in truly European formative moments in history, in the Renaissance, the Reformation, and the Enlightenment. Larry Siedentop places the formative moment even earlier in time, coinciding with the rise of a Christian view of the universal equality of mankind *vis-à-vis* God. As he presents it, the formative moment consisted in universalizing a religious view that in Judaism was still highly particularist, claiming an exceptionalist relation between God and the people of Israel (Siedentop 2000, 190, 195, 198). This shared heritage inspired the first trans-Atlantic readings of what the terrorist attack of 9/11 signified. It was seen as an onslaught on the core values of a shared civilization. How ironic, if not tragic, then, that before long the United States and Europe parted ways in finding the proper response to the new threat of international terrorism. As for the United States, the first signs of its farewell to internationalism in foreign policy – to its Wilsonianism, if you wish – and to its pioneering role in designing the institutional and legal framework for peaceful inter-state relations in the world, had actually preceded 9/11. No longer did the Bush administration conceive of the United States as a *primus inter pares*, setting the guidelines for collective action while seeking legitimacy for action through treaties and UN resolutions. As the one hegemon on the world stage it now feels free from constraints set by its own Constitution or by international law in the pursuit of its national interest through policies that one can only describe as unilateralist. It may seem like a throwback

---

3   I remind the reader of high-minded calls made at the time of World War I by a young generation of intellectuals, such as Waldo Frank and Randolph Bourne, who brilliantly and paradoxically sought to express their cultural nationalism in a quest for American transnationalism, inspired by the heterogeneous, immigrant multitudes who composed the nation.

to the time of nation-state sovereignty, a stage in history that Europe is struggling to transcend.

The tragedy in these recent trends is all the more poignant for those who gratefully remember America's relatively disinterested role, following World War II, in the creation of a larger, self-conscious, European entity, if not identity. This entity, as the United States envisioned and sponsored it, was to be economic, political, and cultural (Lundestad 1986). As for the latter aspect, United States public diplomacy actively worked to disseminate its culture abroad, from its high-brow to low-brow varieties. In addition, though, under its own commercial steam, American mass culture successfully conquered foreign markets and formed cultural tastes and appetites abroad, Americanizing its publics in the process. Ironically, in this way as well America worked to create a larger European sense of self and of place, by providing Europeans with a shared cultural vernacular.

Europe's Evolving Public Space: Lost Cosmopolitan Europes, Liminal Europes

Where does Europe end? It is a question of immeasurably greater complexity than the question of where America ends. America as a national entity may extend from sea to shining sea, yet as we also know it projects an image of itself far beyond its national borders. People anywhere in the world can meaningfully connect themselves to inner constructs of what America represents and means to them. With the European Union explosively expanding, now having to digest the presence in its midst of new member states that until the end of the Cold War found themselves under the sway of the Soviet Union, the United States blithely leapfrogs across all the new political borderlines in Europe. Travellers venturing beyond the new eastern border of the European Union find prominent displays of MacDonald's golden arches in the Crimea, with a statue of Lenin in the background. It is the further extension of a visual presence of iconic images of American mass culture that have featured prominently in European countries during the Cold War. But it has always been a surface phenomenon overlaying the crackled face of Europe and its intricate pattern, in perpetual flux, of fault lines and cultural borderlands. Old Europes have vanished, remembered only by those who once lived in vibrant communities that are no more. Many Europes, many vibrant communities, have come to an end, leaving hardly a trace other than in the memory of scattered survivors. This suggests one answer to the question of where Europe ends. Many Europes have ended many times over, due to genocide, population transfers, ethnic cleansing, and internecine war. As in the movement of tectonic plates, historic forms of Europe have submerged, molten into oblivion.

But Europe ends in different ways as well. Looked at in a certain way the map of Europe offers a mosaic of borderlands, of invisible lines separating communities from each other. Regional communities, historically rooted, see their cohesion threatened by restless migration movements or more generally by the wider horizons brought by modernization and globalization. Diasporic communities, of Turks, Moroccans, Algerians, live among members of their host societies, on the margin, in cultural interstices, yet with a proto-cosmopolitan sense of the larger European space that they now inhabit, straddling national borders. Certain established Europes, as defined by those sharing a sense of cultural commonality, draw lines to include or exclude neighbours. They are all lines where certain Europes end and rub shoulders with new Europes struggling to emerge.

As I argued before, overlying all this is the idea at least of a larger Europe, offering a framework for meaningful identification to all denizens of the new, emerging Europe. It is a dream more than a reality at the moment. In a stunning collection of photographs, on show in the summer of 2004 in the *Kunsthal* (House of Arts) in Rotterdam, Dutch photographer Nicole Segers displayed pictures taken along the new eastern border of the European Union, from Finland all the way down to Bulgaria. They mostly are bleak pictures of people left astray by the turmoil of political change since the end of the Cold War. Segers, the photographer, was accompanied by a journalist friend, Irene van der Linde, who interviewed many of the people who found themselves without bearings. Many are now citizens of the European Union. In one conversation, a Bulgarian fisherman says: 'You feel it if you love someone and you feel it if someone loves you.' The fisherman takes a pause, like an actor on stage. Everyone sits in silence. 'In the case of Europe, I feel nothing.' After these words, all the fishermen at the table raise their glass. 'Nazdrave', they toast. 'Let us drink to this.' 'Welcome to the end of Europe' (van der Linde and Segers 2004, 388).

This end of Europe, where people do not have any feelings about the larger political community that now defines their citizenship, is not only to be found at the extreme eastern border of the Union. People all across Europe feel no meaningful affiliation with the 'New Europe', and are in anguished search for more meaningful frameworks to define their citizenship. In that sense there are many 'liminal Europes', situations where Europe dims into irrelevance as if it reaches its far borders. There are as yet few overarching emblems helping people to conceive of the larger Europe. There are no potent iconic images in the way that America has projected them onto the European canvass. In what follows I propose to contrast these two situations, the crackled pattern of liminal Europes and the presence across Europe of imaginary Americas.

American Iconography in Europe's Public Space: A Semiotic and Historical Reading

Many have been the discussions in Europe as to what exactly it was that America, seen as the harbinger of Europe's future, held in store. Germany had its *Amerikanismus* debate in the 1920s, France for over two centuries looked on in fascination and trepidation as modernity in its American guise unfolded. Intellectuals in many other countries contributed their views as they observed

the American scene.[4] Many travelled there and reported back to their various
home audiences; others stayed home trying to fathom the forms of reception and
appropriation of the American model, in culture, in economics, and in politics.
More often than not the form of these critical exchanges was one of triangulation.
Parties engaged in debate on how to structure the future in Europe's various nation-
states used America as a reference point to define their positions, either rejecting
the American model or promoting it for adoption. I have written extensively on
these processes of triangulation (see Kroes 2000). Here I propose to take a different
approach. I will look at the presence of iconographic representations of America
across Europe, exploring the ways in which it may have affected the sense of
European space among Europeans.

I must have been 12 or 13, in the early 1950s, when in my home town of
Haarlem in the Netherlands I stood enthralled by a huge picture along the
entire rear wall of a garage. As I remember it now, it was my first trance-like
transportation into a world that was unlike anything I had known so far. I stood
outside on the sidewalk looking in. Not surprisingly, given the fact that this garage
sold American cars, the picture on the wall was of a 1950s American car shown
in its full iconographic force as a carrier of dreams rather than as a mere means of
transportation. Cars in general, let alone their gigantic American versions, were a
distant dream to most Dutch people at the time. Yet what held my gaze was not
so much the car as the image of a boy, younger than I was at the time, who came
rushing from behind the car, his motion stopped, his contagious joy continuing.
He wore sneakers, blue jeans rolled up at the ankles, a T-shirt. His hairdo was
different than that of any of my friends, and so was his facial expression. Come
to think of it, there must have been a ball. The boy's rush must have been like
the exhilarating dash across a football field or a basketball court, surging ahead
of others. The very body language, although frozen into a still picture, seemed to
speak of a boisterous freedom. Everything about the boy radiated signals from a
distant, but enticing world.

This may have been my first confrontation with a wide-screen display of
the good life in America, of its energy, its exhilaration, its typical pursuits and
satisfactions. As I now think back on the moment, I am aware that my distant
exposure to America's dreamscape was not unlike an astronomer's, catching light
emitted aeons ago by distant stars. Metaphorically speaking America was aeons
away from Europe at the time, feverishly engaged as it was in the construction of
the consumers' republic and the pursuit of happiness that it incited. Beholding a
picture of America in a garage in Haarlem, I was exposed to a representation of
life in America in a rare reflection of public imagery that in America had become
ubiquitous. Nor was it all that recent there. Even at the depth of the Great Depression
the National Association of Manufacturers (N.A.M.) in typical boosterism had

---

4   For a survey of these European debates I may refer the reader to Kroes (1996). For
a survey of French views of American modernity, see my chapter on the subject in Kroes
(2000).

pasted similar images across the nation, advertising 'The American Way' in displays of happy families riding in their cars. Much of the jarring dissonance between these public displays and the miseries of collective life in 1930s' America still applied to Europe in the early 1950s. Those were still lean years. In Haarlem I stood beholding an image that had no visual referent in real life anywhere in Europe. Yet the image may have been equally seductive for Europeans as for Americans. Consumerism may have been a distant dream in postwar Europe, yet it was eagerly anticipated as Europeans were exposed to its American version, through advertising, photo-journalism, and Hollywood films.

Now, as images of America's culture of consumption began to fill Europe's public space, they exposed Europeans to views of the good life that Americans themselves were exposed to. To that extent they may have Americanized European dreams and longings. But isn't there also a way we might argue that Europe's exposure to American imagery may have worked to Europeanize Europe at the same time? There are several ways of going about answering this question. It has been said in jest that the only culture that Europeans had in common in the late twentieth century was American culture. Their exposure to forms of American mass culture transcended national borders in ways that no national varieties were ever able to rival. True, there was the occasional Italian or German hit song running up the charts in other European countries. There were still audiences across Europe for films made in one or another European country. There were the 1960s when England contributed to international youth culture, in areas such as music and fashion, often giving its own characteristic twist to American mass culture that had reached England in the years before. But the one continuing line throughout the latter half of the twentieth century was of an exposure of European publics to American mass culture.

The points of exposure were not necessarily only in public space. Much of the consumption of American mass culture took place in private settings when people watched television in their living rooms, or Hollywood movies in the quasi-private space of the darkened movie theatre. American popular music reached them via the radio or on records and once again made for a formation of audiences assembling in private places, such as homes or dance clubs. This private, or peer-group, consumption of American mass culture does not mean that larger virtual audiences did not emerge across Europe. Far from it. Shared repertoires, shared tastes, and shared cultural memories had formed that would make for quick and easy cultural exchange across national borders among Europe's younger generations. They could more readily compare notes on shared cultural preferences using American examples than varieties of mass culture produced in their own national settings.

One area in particular – properly called public space, outside private homes, outside gathering places for cultural consumption – has served across Europe as a site of exposure to American mass culture. Much as it is true that forms of American mass culture, transmitted via the entertainment industry, travel under commercial auspices – they are always economic commodities in addition to being cultural goods, to be sold before they are consumed – public space is the area where American mass culture most openly advertises itself, creating the demand if not the desire, for its consumption. In public space, including the press, we find the film posters advertising the latest Hollywood movies, or the dreamlike representations of an America where people smoke certain cigarettes, buy certain cars, cosmetics, clothes. They are literally advertisements, creating economic demand, while conveying imaginary Americas at the same time. They thus contributed to a European repertoire of an invented America, as a realm for reverie, filled with iconic heroes, setting standards of physical beauty, of taste, of proper behavior. If Europe to a certain extent became 'other-directed', much like America itself under the impact of its own commercial culture, Europe's significant Other had become America, as commercially constructed through advertising.

If we may conceive of this re-direction of Europe's gaze toward America as a sign of Europe's Americanization, it means an appropriation of American standards and tastes in addition to whatever cultural habits were already in place to direct people's individual quest for identity. Americanization is never a simple zero-sum game where people trade in their European clothes for every pair of blue jeans they acquire. It is more a matter of cultural syncretism, of an interweaving of bits of American culture into European cultural habits, where every borrowing of American cultural ingredients creatively changes their meaning and context. Certainly, Europe's cultural landscape has changed, but never in ways that would lead visiting Americans to mistake Europe for a simple replica of their own culture.

My larger point, though, is to pursue a paradox. As Henry James at one point astutely perceived, it is for Americans rather than Europeans to conceive of Europe as a whole, and to transcend Europe's patterns of cultural particularism. He meant to conceive of it as one cultural canvass of a scale commensurate with that of America as one large continental culture. His aphoristic insight certainly highlights a recurring rationale in the way that Americans have approached Europe, whether they are businessmen seeing Europe as one large market for their products, or post-World War II politicians pursuing a vision of European cooperation transcending Europe's divisive nationalisms. If we may rephrase James's remark as referring to an American inclination to project their mental scale of thought onto the map of Europe, that inclination in its own right may have had a cultural impact in Europeans as an eye-opening revision of their mental compass, inspiring a literal re-vision.

Whatever the precise message, the fact that American advertising appeared across European countries exposed travelling Europeans to commercial communication proceeding across national borders, addressing Europeans wherever they lived. More specifically, though, there is a genre of advertising that precisely confronts Europeans with the fantasy image of America as one, open space. If all American advertising conjures up fantasy versions of life in America, the particular fantasy of America as unbounded space, free of the confining boundaries set by European cultures to dreams of individual freedom, may well have activated the dream of a Europe as wide and open as America. The particular genre of advertising I am thinking of finds its perfect illustration in the myth of Marlboro Country and the Marlboro Man. The idea of tying the image of this particular brand of cigarette to the mythical lure of the American West goes back to the early 1960s and inspired an advertising iconography that has kept its appeal unto the present day (at least in those countries that have not banned cigarette advertising). Over time the photographic representation of the imaginary space of Marlboro Country expanded in size, filling Europe's public space with widescreen images of Western landscapes, lit by a setting sun, with rock formations glowing in deep red colour, with horses descending to their watering hole, and rugged-faced cowboys lighting up after the day's work had been done. This was a space for fantasy to roam, offering the transient escape into dreams of unbounded freedom, of being one's own free agent. It was hard not to see these images. They were often obtrusively placed, hanging over the crowds in railway stations, or adding gorgeous colour to some of Europe's grey public squares. I remember one prominently placed to the left of the steps leading up to Budapest's great, grey Museum of Art. The show opened right there. One couldn't miss it.

The formula was widely imitated. Other cigarette brands came up with their own variations on the theme, using different iconography, showing young couples in leisure time pursuits, or showing a jet set life style that one might vicariously share for the time it took to smoke a cigarette. In post-Cold War Poland a roadside poster showed a young couple, radiating joy, its text inviting the audience 'to have a taste of freedom'. The advertisement was for an American cigarette. But European cigarette makers as well adopted the approach, as in the French Gauloises campaign, using Parisian settings. The attractive, young males in the photographs have a casual informality about them – with jackets flung over their shoulders, or their feet up on the table of a roadside terrace – that is vaguely resonant of American styles of public behaviour. The over-all impression is summarily captured in the advertisements' affirmative statement: '*La liberté, toujours.*' Peter Stuyvesant cigarettes in the Netherlands used a more post-modern collage technique for conveying a similar message. They reduced the explicit markers of European dreams of America as open space, so central to the Marlboro approach, to mere echoes to trigger the same repertoire of fantasies. They showed young couples in the gathering places of an international leisure class, captioned in each case by the names of a hotel in Miami Beach, San Francisco, or other such places of *rendez-vous*. The central slogan, giving meaning to the jumble of text and visuals, reads: There are no borders. The advertising campaign was set up by a Dutch advertising agency as further testimony to the adoption by Europeans of American dreams and messages of unbounded space. The use of English in a campaign addressing a Dutch audience is increasingly common, and intended to give an international flavour to the message. Indeed, there are no borders.

In fact the commodified lure of open space has by now become so familiar that advertisers have begun to ironize their messages with an implied wink to an audience of initiates. One example of such an ironic twist is a commercial for an Italian travel agency, calling itself Marlboro Country Travels. Playing on the escapism of much modern tourism, where you have to lose yourself in the hope of finding yourself, it arranges travel to the United States while casting the destination in the image of Marlboro Country's fictional space. A large colour photograph, actually a montage, shows a 1950s gas pump, a nostalgic reminder of the romanticism of Route 66 ('Get your kicks on Route 66'), of Jack Kerouac's *On the Road*, or the exhilaration of road movies. As a backdrop the photograph offers a view of the American West, with a little cloud of dust at its centre trailing a diminutive SUV rolling off into the distance. The central slogan tells us: *'Fai il vuoto'* ('Go for the void'). It plays on the standard request at gas stations 'to fill'er up' (*'Fai il pieno'*). It beautifully captures the desire of modern travellers to empty themselves of their concerns and pre-occupations, to leave all their worries behind and take off into empty space.

A similar punning approach to advertising can be found all over Europe's public space nowadays. Freedom still is the central idea in these games, although it is given many ironic twists. There was a poster for Levi's 508 jeans, pasted all over the Netherlands in the mid-1990s.[5] The photograph showed a male torso, naked from the neck down to the pair of blue jeans. The iconography has a high degree of intertextuality, at least to an audience steeped in American mass culture. It is reminiscent of Bruce Springsteen's cover for his album 'Born in the USA', or of Andy Warhol's cover design for the Rolling Stones album 'Sticky Fingers'. Again, the poster uses a collage technique, offering a jumble of visual and textual ingredients. Surprisingly, given that this was an advertisement designed by a Dutch agency, in the lower left-hand corner we see a variation on Roosevelt's famous four freedoms. The first two sound pretty Rooseveltian, evoking the Freedoms of Speech and Expression, followed by the Freedom of Choice (not among Roosevelt's foursome, and sitting ambivalently astride the freedom of choice of people seen either as political citizens or as individual consumers). In fourth place, following the words Levi's 508 in bold face, is the Freedom of Movement. Again there is the political ring, expressive of a political longing that many in Eastern Europe may have felt during the years of the Cold War. Yet a pun is intended. The freedom of movement in this context is meant to refer to the greater movement offered by the baggier cut of the 508, a point visually illustrated by the unmistakable bulge of a male member in full erection, touched casually at the tip by the right hand of its master.

The list of further examples is endless. Advertising across Europe's public space has assumed common forms of address, common routines, and common themes (with many variations). Originating in America, it has now been appropriated by European advertising agencies and may be put in the service of American as well as European products. That in itself is a sign of a transnational integration of Europe's public space. But as I suggested before, the point of many of the stories advertisements tell refers precisely to space, to openness, to a dreamscape transcending Europe's checkered map. An international commercial culture has laid itself across public space in Europe, using an international language, often

---

5   I would like to thank Kate Delaney for calling this poster to my attention one rainy night in Amsterdam.

literally in snippets of English, and instilling cravings and desires now shared internationally. Has all this gone on without voices of protest and resistance rising in these same public spaces?

In fact there are many instances of such contestation, turning Europe's public space into yet another showcase of liminal Europes. Right at the heart of Europe, in its public space, we can see battle lines running as so many indications of groups pitting themselves against forces of globalization and its appropriation. If appropriation, however playfully and creatively done, is a form of acceptance, we can see many signs of rejection at the same time. On a highway outside Warsaw I saw a poster for ladies' lingerie, using the familiar techniques of drawing the spectator's gaze. It used the female body, shown here from the back, in reference (if not deference) to international ideals of female beauty. If such pictures are apt to draw the male gaze, they do so indirectly, through the male gaze as internalized by women. This is what they would like to look like in the eyes of men. The poster further used the appeal of English. The brand of lingerie was called 'Italian Fashion', throwing in the appeal of Italian fashion design for good measure. But evidently, such public display of the female body was not to everyone's taste in Poland. Someone had gotten out his or her spray can to write the Polish word '*Dość*' (meaning 'enough' or 'stop it') across the poster. If a he, he may have been a devout Catholic protesting against the desecration of public space, if a she, she may have been a feminist, objecting to the commodification of the female body. In another instance, in the Northern Italian city of Turin, my gaze was drawn to the base of an equestrian statue. On all four sides, another spray can artist had left these public messages: 'McDonald *bastardi*', '*Boycotta* McDonald', and more such. If the square had been turned into a liminal Europe, with Europeans putting up resistance at what they saw as foreign encroachments, it happened in a rather ironic, if not self-defeating way. If the point of the protest was to rise in defence of the European cultural heritage, it did not shrink from turning one emblem of that heritage, an equestrian statue, into a mere blackboard for messages of protest, desecrating what it meant to elevate.

In Europe's lasting encounter with American mass culture, many have been the voices expressing concern about its negative impact. Cultural guardians in Europe saw European standards of taste and cultural appreciation eroded by an American way with culture that aimed at a mass market, elevating the lowest common denominator of mass preferences to the main vector of cultural production. This history of cultural anti-Americanism in Europe has a long pedigree. In its earlier manifestations the critique of American mass culture was highly explicit and had to be. Many ominous trends of an evolving mass culture in Europe had to be shown to have originated in America, reaching Europe under clear American agency. An intellectual repertoire of Americanism and Americanization evolved in a continuing attempt at cultural resistance against the lures of a culture of consumption. Never mind that such cultural forms might have come to Europe autonomously, even in the absence of an American model. America served to give a name and a face to forces of cultural change that would otherwise have been anonymous and seemingly beyond control.

Today this European repertoire is alive and kicking. Yet, ironically, as a repertoire that has become common currency to the point of being an intellectual stereotype rather than an informed opinion, America nowadays is often a subtext, unspoken in European forms of cultural resistance. One example may serve to illustrate this. A political poster for the Socialist Party in Salzburg, in the run-up to the 1997 municipal elections in the city, shows us the determined face and the clenched fist of the party's candidate. He asked the voting public whether the younger generation would not be losers, and called on the electorate to 'fight, fight, and fight'. What for? 'In order to avoid that young people would get fed up with the future' ('*Damit unsere Jugend die Zukunft nicht satt wird*'). In a visual pun, at the poster's dead centre, the getting fed up is illustrated by the blurred image of a Hamburger flying by at high speed. Fast food indeed. The call for action is now clear. Austrians should try and fend off a future cast in an American vein. American culture is condensed into the single image of the Hamburger, as a culture centred on consumption rather than consummation. It is enough to trigger the larger repertoire of cultural anti-Americanism.

We may choose to see this poster as only a recent version of cultural guardianship that has always looked at the younger generation as a stalking horse, if not a Trojan horse, for American culture. In fact, historically, it has always been younger generations who, in rebellion against parental authority and cultural imposition, opted for the liberating potential of American mass culture. Yet interesting changes may have occurred in this pattern. Today young people as well, in their concern about forces of globalization, may target America as the central agency behind these global trends. They may smash the windows of a nearby McDonald's (and there is always a McDonald's nearby), they may deface equestrian statues in Turin, or may choose more creative and subtle forms of protest. Yet again America tends to be a mere subtext in their resistance against global cultural icons.

One more example may serve to illustrate this. I have a music video, a few years old, of a Basque group.[6] The video, in its own right, is an act of cultural emancipation. The lyrics are in the Basque language and the station broadcasting the video had all-Basque programming. This may suggest localism, if not cultural provincialism. Nothing would be farther from the truth. What we have here is a perfect example of 'glocalisation', to use Roland Robertson's (1994) neologism. The music used is ska, an ingredient of 'world music' hailing from the Caribbean and popularized through the British music industry. The format of the music video itself is part of global musical entertainment. Yet the message is local. What the video shows is a confusing blend of the traditional and the modern. The opening shot is of a man using a scythe to cut grass. The camera moves up and shows a modern, international-style, office block. A mobile phone rings, and the grass cutter answers the call. More images show modern life. We see an old man talking

---

6   < http://www.youtube.com/watch?v=gtUSaf62wO0> accessed 2 November 2006.

into a microphone strapped to his head, as if he were talking to himself. We see a group of young men on a flatbed lorry moving through traffic. They are working out in tandem on treadmill machines, yet in complete isolation, like a transported glimpse of an American gym. Then the protagonists of the video appear, with a rickety van, getting ready to sell the local variety of Basque fast food, a sausage on a roll. The very smell breaks the isolation of people caught in the alienating life of modernity. They all flock to the sausage stand to get a taste of true Basqueness. They come to life, spurred by the suggestion of authentic and traditional Basque life. The lyrics repeat the refrain: Down with Big Mac, Long live Big Benat (the name of the Basque delicacy).

The claim made in this video is on behalf of the authenticity of regional cultures struggling to survive in a world threatened by the homogenizing forces of globalization. Yet the medium of communication testifies to the impact of precisely those forces as much as it protests against them. There is much irony in all this, but most important is the fact that what is shown as modernity truly revives a long repertoire of European cultural anti-Americanism. America *is* modernity and the long history of European resistance to America is truly a story of resisting the onslaught of modernity on Europe's chequered map of regional and/or national cultures.

To watch this ambiguous proclamation of a regional culture's superiority and authenticity is to be reminded again of the irony of life in today's many liminal Europes, literally at the *limes*, the edge, of Europe's cultural sway. As one visit to Bilbao, the industrial city in the Basque country, will make clear, the Basqueness of the place is, if anything, an imposed and unduly homogenized reading. Under the impact of industrialization Bilbao, like so many other industrial centres, has drawn its work force from a large hinterland, forgetful of the integrity of local culture. If capitalism, as Joseph Schumpeter reminded us long ago, is a force of creative destruction, Bilbao testifies to the truth of this statement. People from all over Spain have migrated there and lived there for several generations, giving the place a multi-cultural tone, and eroding Basqueness from within its own territory. Following years of decline, the city has now revived. In addition to restoring its heritage of a residential and industrial architecture redolent of its past prowess, it also sought to reconnect itself to the contemporary modernity of cutting-edge architecture. By the river that runs through the city now stands one of Europe's great modern structures, a museum of art designed by the American architect Frank Gehry, and financed by Guggenheim money. With its wavy lines it evokes a local seafaring history and seems to mirror the river that connected Bilbao to the wider world. It is a modern rendition of a local history that lives on as collective memory. It seems to have sprouted from that store of memories, much as the creative genius who shaped it lives across the ocean's waters that wash the Basque coast at their eastern reach. If Bilbao seeks to reconnect itself to a cosmopolitanism it once reflected, its strivings stand at right angles to the efforts at freezing Basqueness in time. Whatever the peculiarities of this tension, its inherent logic makes Bilbao a microcosm of Europe's many internal contradictions.

The Ironic Recycling of American Mass Culture as a Form of European Cosmopolitanism

The analysis, semiotic and historical, of America's iconographic representations in Europe's public space suggests two general points. For one thing, American mass culture has managed to overlay the map of Europe with a cultural vernacular that, like a new language, allows of cultural exchanges and conversations across older dividing lines. Also, it allows Europeans ironically to subvert the inherent Americanness of the vernacular and to use it to produce commentaries on Americanization and globalization as they affect Europe. Thus, American mass culture was appropriated by Europeans first before it provided them with a new language that could then be reflected back upon its source and could once again project America as the cultural Other. This was the result in other words of a self-reflexive, self-conscious, and ironic appropriation of American mass culture by Europeans. This may remind us of a point made by Brian Turner who, in his stance about cosmopolitan virtue as irony, argues that 'the ability to respect others requires a certain distance from one's own culture, namely ironic distance'. He further argues that 'cosmopolitan virtue also requires self-reflexivity with respect to both our own cultural context and other cultural values', linking this to humanist traditions in Europe (Turner 2002, 55, 57). This takes us back to our earlier discussion of forms of cosmopolitanism in section II.

To the extent that the European appropriation of American mass culture has made for the formation of a European cultural vernacular this has led, inside European nations as well as across national borders, to forms of what Beck would call 'banal cosmopolitanism', in the sense of an unconscious and unreflexive engagement with American culture. But as I have argued, it has also led to a self-reflexive cosmopolitanism able to speak in a European voice, resonating with European publics, and, although not produced by cultural and intellectual elites, is not unlike the high-minded cosmopolitanism once advocated by the likes of Kant, Heine, Nietzsche, Zweig, Hesse, Hoffmannstal, to name only a few, who believed in Europe as a gospel and conceived of it as a realistic vision of the future. In a recent public address Ulrich Beck referred to this list of high-minded cosmopolitans calling them the realists, 'while those, who call themselves 'realists' do not understand the reality of Europe' (Beck 2006) What I have tried to do is to give forms of cosmopolitanism that are more than merely 'banal' their place in this reality of Europe.

References

Bauman, Z. (1989), *Modernity and the Holocaust* (Cambridge: Polity Press).
Beck, U. (2003a), 'Rooted Cosmopolitanism: Emerging from a Rivalry of Distinctions', in Beck, Sznaider and Winter (eds).
— (2003b), 'Understanding the Real Europe', *Dissent* 50, 32–8.

— (2006), 'Understanding the Real Europe: A Cosmopolitan Perspective', Annual Neale Wheeler Watson Lecture at the Nobel Museum, Stockholm, 1 June 2006.

—, Sznaider, N. and Winter, R. (eds) (2003), *Global America? The Cultural Consequences of Globalization* (Liverpool: Liverpool University Press).

Boorstin, D. (1953), *The Genius of American Politics* (Chicago: The University of Chicago Press).

Kroes, R. (1996), *If You've Seen One, You've Seen the Mall: Europeans and American Mass Culture* (Urbana/Chicago: The University of Illinois Press).

— (2000), *Them and Us: Questions of Citizenship in a Globalizing World* (Urbana/ Chicago: The University of Illinois Press).

Levy, D. and Sznaider, N. (2002), 'Memory Unbound: The Holocaust and the Formation of Cosmopolitan Memory', *European Journal of Social Theory* 5:1, 87–106.

Linde van der, I. and Segers, N. (2004), *Het Einde van Europa: Ontmoetingen Langs de Nieuwe Oostgrens* (The End of Europe: Encounters along the New Eastern Border) (Rotterdam: Lemniscaat).

Lundestad, G. (1986), 'Empire by Invitation? The United States and Western Europe, 1945–1952', *Journal of Peace Research* 23:3, 263–77.

Robertson, R. (1994), 'Globalisation or Glocalisation?', *The Journal of International Communication* 1:1, 33–52.

Rydell, R.W. and Kroes, R. (2005), *Buffalo Bill in Bologna: The Americanization of the World, 1869–1922* (Chicago: University of Chicago Press).

Siedentop, L. (2000), *Democracy in Europe* (London: Penguin Books).

Turner, B. (2002), 'Cosmopolitan Virtue, Globalization and Patriotism', *Theory, Culture & Society* 19:1-2, 45-63.

Chapter 6

Cosmopolitanization of Memory:
The Politics of Forgiveness and Restitution[1]

Ulrich Beck, Daniel Levy and Natan Sznaider

How do the political and cultural forms of collective memory change in the age of globalization? How can the national perspective and the conceptual horizon inherently determined by the nation-state be opened up towards a transnational and cosmopolitan space of memory transcending national borders? What does cosmopolitization of memory mean, and under which conditions does it become possible? This essay addresses those issues using the example of the correlation between forgiveness and restitution in terms of legal practices and a corresponding dissolution of boundaries in national policies. Our thesis is that the historical discourse about remembering the Holocaust is a prime example of a memory becoming cosmopolitan.

Through the lens of a historical examination, we will focus on the interplay between national and transnational cultures of memory and show that this gives rise to their highly conflictual internal cosmopolitization. We want to probe how this new 'cosmopolitan memory' takes on the historical discourse on the Holocaust while lending political and moral authority to the new human rights regime.

The ways the Holocaust is remembered have provided both the starting point and the model for a type of global politics observed in recent years that is characterized by discourses on guilt and forgiveness (Levy and Sznaider 2001, 2005). Having said that, the key role of the Holocaust does not imply that it is to be remembered as some time-transcending totality; after all, it is bound to become part of a greater whole as the new cosmopolitanism and its new ways of remembering leave their origins behind and assume a separate existence. The revolution of 1989, the overthrow of dictatorships, has produced new forms of guilt and penitence. The same is true of *Wiedergutmachung* (reparations), which is becoming universalized and detached from its origins in the historical context of the 1950s. In that process, forgiveness and guilt are becoming important pillars of cosmopolitan modernity.

The results of this are twofold: Not only does the transnational discourse determine the meaning, profile, and spatial extent of an all-European space of

---

1 This chapter is a modified version of the chapter 'Erinnerung und Vergebung in der Zweiten Moderne' published in *Entgrenzung und Entscheidung*, edited by Ulrich Beck and Christoph Lau, Suhrkamp, Frankfurt am Main 2004. Translation by Thorsten Möllebeck.

memory, it also determines the criteria for membership and participation in an emerging community of values based on human rights. It gives rise to material obligations to seek justice (i.e., restitution and compensation) for the victims of the past. It raises the question of moral inclusion and exclusion, while at the same time involving strategic wrangling over power: How and to whom is responsibility being ascribed under the conditions of increasingly permeable boundaries in general and the eastern enlargement of Europe in particular?

We develop our argument by presenting two case studies – the Polish struggle for the cosmopolitanization of memory in the discourse on Jedwabne and the German reparation (*Wiedergutmachung*) of the 1950s. In these investigations, we use the tools of historical and comparative analysis to interpret official public discourses in the form of parliamentary debates, bills, media texts and secondary historical literature in Germany, Poland and Israel.

The Holocaust as a Paradigmatic Case: Towards a Cosmopolitanization of Memory

The foundations for a cosmopolitan memory emerged out of the efforts to come to terms with the extermination of the Jews. The memory of the Holocaust creates and fosters an outlook on the world and on humankind that clearly distinguishes between victims and offenders, between good and evil. Auschwitz carries a clear moral message: We recognize 'evil' because we see it, and if we do not prevent it, it is only due to our own moral failure. Victims, as those of the Holocaust, have to be 'innocent'; there have never been 'guilty' victims. Also, Europe's extermination of the Jews is a national-global crime: In its planning and execution, it overrode national borders; Holocaust survivors scattered almost all over the world. This is what sets the Holocaust apart from other, 'national' crimes, which, as insane as they were, did not go beyond the framework of the nation-state.

But that is not all. Emphasizing specific historical events and embedding them in a 'moral' worldview produces the outlines of a history that considers itself as global. The Holocaust, this is empirically valid as well, is part of global history. In spite of the disagreement as to the causes of this, its consequences are noticeable now and everywhere. It is the memories of war and genocide that – under specific circumstances – transcend the national framework and dissolve its borders. At the same time, we have to address the history of the loss of transnational cultures which did not survive the national imperative – the principle of 'unmixing', violent expulsions, and ethnic cleansings.

In fact, Hannah Arendt was one of the first to try and approach the Holocaust from a sociological perspective. As early as 1950, she published a study in which she adumbrated her thesis about the 'senselessness' of the Holocaust; 'senseless' insofar as this phenomenon defied understanding in the conventional categories of law, morality, and politics. Due to this sheer senselessness, she was already insisting then that the Holocaust involved crimes for which there no longer was any appropriate punishment: What are the consequences of the Holocaust for international law? Where are the limits of law when we are talking about 'crimes against humanity'?

This also means that in Second Modernity, cultural memory can no longer be located territorially as was the case in First Modernity (Beck 2000; Beck and Bonß 2001). Not only was the crime itself transnational, but also the memory of it, and now Holocaust studies are beginning to become transnational. Among other things, this means that collective memories are oriented on new certitudes that may evade and ultimately perhaps even replace the nation-states' already alleviated friend-foe concepts.

The Holocaust has become the epitome of all evil; the struggle against such and similar crimes against humanity in the name of human rights has become the new credo of the 'civilized' world. This became particularly evident during the Kosovo conflict of 1999. The wars of the twentieth century have spawned the new category of stateless and thus rightless people. These could be robbed, humiliated and murdered, as no one guaranteed their rights. Rights – like the right not to be murdered or tortured – can no longer rest on abstract principles guaranteed by sovereign states. Rights manifest their potency, or the lack of it, negatively: What happens when they are violated? This is the paradigmatic role Holocaust remembrance plays for a global human rights policy.

After the Holocaust, the sovereign state can no longer be the sole basis of rights and justice. Conversely, this fact created the moral foundations for global institutions of justice. The UN conventions on universal human rights, the attempt to illegalize genocide, eventually the endeavour to prevent any future 'Holocausts' were all created as a negation, i.e. out of the experience of what must never happen again.

Human rights violations are becoming everyone's business. The language of human rights is changing the relationships between states that have power, but little legitimacy and human rights organizations that have little power, but much legitimacy. The rules of 'internal affairs', which had been the main criteria of sovereign states, must be re-interpreted. Inaction is becoming yet another kind of action, a token in the strategic power game of world politics (cf. Beck 2002): When should and can one intervene, who is allowed to and who is not? The model of de-territorialized power, as demonstrated by the globalized economy, is on its way to becoming a model for global politics.

Human rights disempower weak states that trample on human rights, and at the same time they empower powerful states to intervene in those states. Human rights limit the power that governments have over their citizens. They reverse the question of responsibility. The revolutionary bottom line is the idea that the governments are – potentially – the criminals. Therefore, conventions on human rights do not only liberate individuals from the absolute sovereign rule of dictators, but also of democratically elected governments. Up to 1945, international law had still favoured the power of governments *vis-à-vis* human rights.

Yet as far as the Holocaust is concerned, not only political contingencies contribute to the implementation of cosmopolitanism, which is developing into the ethical horizon of an increasing number of people and self-image of various life-worlds. It was the Americans who promoted the cosmopolitanization of the culture of remembrance, interpreting it as an event that had happened to 'the world' as a new, large-scale crime against humanity. The Americans did not consider World War Two as a specifically Jewish tragedy, and they did not categorize the victims of the Holocaust along ethnic and religious, but political lines (as Hannah Arendt had anticipated). They universalized the liberation to emphasize the triumph of good over evil. It was the historical embedding – Nazi Germany as the evil barbarian and the U.S. as the progressive liberator – which made this universalization possible. With the Universal Declaration of Human Rights and the Convention on the Prevention and Punishment of the Crime of Genocide of 1948, Holocaust remembrance began to be institutionalized politically and cosmopolitically, and to disengage from the national historical frame of reference of the Third Reich.

Through the use of images (as in the motion picture *Schindler's List* or the miniseries Holocaust), this Americanization also accomplished to visualize the crime in a way that invited emotional identification. Our approach maintains that mass media make an essential contribution towards conveying global morality, despite all critique of the 'instrumentalization' of the Holocaust. While this critique shows a strong normative commitment, it does not display the emotional aspect of cosmopolitanism. However, without the kind of emotionality generated by the mass media, any policy-making turns out to be ultimately impossible in an age of global individualization. Cosmopolitanism implies universal as well as local values that emotionally engage people. These values become a constituent part of personal identity, thus gaining political significance as well. Concrete historical events and cultural developments contribute toward implementing cosmopolitanism, which is developing into the ethical horizon of an increasing number of people and a self-image of various life-worlds. The new, transnational memory does not function erratically. War, destruction and disasters all contribute to shape it.

The Jews as Archetypical Cosmopolitans

The relevance of the Holocaust for our intention to outline the emerging cosmopolitan memory is not just a result of its iconic status. The memory of the Holocaust is tied to the fate and role of the Jews, not just as its victims, but also as modernity and cosmopolitanism personified. Cosmopolitanism has been an enemy concept not just since the emergence fascism, but as early as in the aggressive nationalism of, for example, Oswald Spengler. According to Spengler, Cosmopolitans are 'enthusiasts of world peace and international reconciliation ... the intellectual leaders of fellahdom' (1991, 781). Spengler's hate speech culminates in a declaration of war: 'The fate of a nation ... depends on in how far

[it] succeeds in rendering this phenomenon (i.e., the cosmopolitans) historically ineffectual' (1991, 782). Between the lines, 'eliminating' already shines through.

In the period before World War II, Jews were too universal to be particular, and too particular to be universal. They were living at the 'crossroad of the wide open spaces' (Lion Feuchtwanger). But there was a price to be paid for this. 'For almost half a century', Stefan Zweig wrote in his memoirs, 'I was educating my heart to beat in a cosmopolitan fashion, like that of a *citoyen du monde* – to no avail. On the very day I lost my passport, I discovered, at age 58, that losing your homeland (*Heimat*), you are losing more than just a fenced-in plot of earth' (Zweig 1988, 468). Their 'non-belonging' made the Jews the cosmopolitans of Europe, but also the defenceless victims of the Nazis. The European Jews were assimilated and orthodox, Jewish and not Jewish, national and cosmopolitan, all at the same time. There was just one thing they were not: an integral part of Europe's national societies.

European Jewry was calling into question the premises of homogeneity, which are always conceived of as shaped by and confined within the nation-state: 'The homogeneity of space and population, and the homogeneity of past and future' (Beck 2001, 22). The extermination of European Jewry was a fanatical attempt by ethno-national Germany to destroy the transnational Jewish cultures and societies in the heart of Europe. European Jewry represented everything that could threaten extreme nationalism: They were deemed to personify all things universal, rootless, international and abstract, as opposed to all things local, enrooted and concrete. Thus, a victim-oriented remembrance will also need to recognize the 'delocalization' of the victims.

Holocaust remembrance may develop along national lines, but it may also be guided by the cosmopolitan attitude personified by the victims. Such remembrance does not need to abandon national or ethnical structures; instead, it may emerge from them. The Jews had not been a part of the national world; their integration into the modern world of the nation-states had failed. To be able to evolve, Jewish communities were depending on the niches that the multi-ethnic variety of the large empires offered (cf. Diner 2003). It may be no coincidence that people like Raphael Lemkin, who coined the term 'genocide', Hersch Lauterpacht, who first codified the modern concept of human rights, or Hans Kelsen, a convert to Protestantism who revived the legal cosmopolitanism of the Roman Empire, were all so-called 'imperial Jews'. It was not until the advent of the modern concept of the nation-state that hitherto rather vaguely defined nationalities became ethnically homogenized. The unity of people and territory was a concept unknown to the Jewish religion. The transition towards a post-national, multi-ethnic society without territorially bound identities is nothing new to Jews, who have traditionally inhabited similar life-worlds. Thus, it is no coincidence that the concept of Diaspora has migrated from Jewish theology into transnational cultural studies. Neither time nor space unambiguously define what it means to be Jewish. This is what makes the crimes against Jewry and the Jews paradigmatic for a memory on its way to becoming cosmopolitan.

Identifying with the Victims of the Others

Cosmopolitanizing memory manifests itself in identifying with the victims of 'the Others'. For example, while Germany paid most attention to its 'own' victims – the victims of Nazi Germany – during the first post-war decade, the politics of memory focused on Germans as victims, rather than just perpetrators. In later years, in contrast, it was the development of emotional solidarity with the victims of the Others that laid the cornerstone for a cosmopolitan memory. Was this just an illusion? Had the defeat of Nazi Germany in 1945 really been a victory of the victims, as it appeared to be for many years?

The Holocaust when dealt together with World War II was related to all humans affected and as such universalized. At the same time, the crimes of the Germans and their collaborators are interpreted as a part of a brutal century – and in this way localized as a particular moment of the past. However, cosmopolitanizing memory is not about the uniqueness of the Holocaust, but about persecution and victimization as such. The particular victim experience of the Jews may, but does not have to be, universalized. The temporal aspect is crucial here. Regarding the future, a new discourse is opening up that categorizes the Holocaust among global-scale genocides and violations of human rights.

In sociological terms, the opening up of transnational spaces of memory has ambivalent consequences: In Germany it is now again possible to emphasize one's own experience of suffering, be it as a victim of aerial bombing or a victim of forced expulsions at the end of World War II. Whereas until recently these topics were associated with historical revisionism, they are now being embedded in a discourse that transgresses national boundaries. The boundaries that once kept the memory of specific suffering are breaking down under the aegis of a human-rights discourse claiming global validity. Thus, national and cosmopolitan legitimacies begin to interlock and to challenge each other due to an Europeanization of perspectives.

The particular and the universal, the cosmopolitan and the national are two sides of the same coin. In 1961, Eichmann's trial in Jerusalem gave the victims a chance to speak with worldwide attention. Unlike Nuremberg, the trial was not about 'crimes against humanity', but about crimes against the Jewish people. It was less about establishing historical truth than about the psychological and emotional truth of the victims, about healing their wounds. The testimony given at Eichmann's trial brought to light supposedly subjective testimonies. In the global age, this is no coincidence: It is all about bearing witness to the truth, individually. The victim speaks up and seeks recognition for their story. From a moral standpoint, the Nuremberg trials and Eichmann's trial are not a dichotomy which would oblige us to make a choice between universalism and particularism. In principle, Eichmann's trial combined both the desire for territorial independence and the universal message of the Diaspora. Put another way, it represented the Jews as cosmopolitans and as a nation – a tension, but not a contradiction. Quite possibly, the trial was also intended to provide the young nation with what is commonly called an identity, to strengthen Israel's claim to legitimacy, and to do justice to the widespread intuition that only Jews can defend Israel. On the other hand, another consequence of the trial was that victims could openly relate their experiences in a collective catharsis. Not only heroic strength was discussed, but also abysmal weakness.

Eichmann's trial resembles the truth commissions that were set up in some post-totalitarian countries decades later. The disaster of the Holocaust became the source for a world-conscience, by which we do not mean some globally homogenous conscience, but a 'local' conscience in which universal memories of the Holocaust combine with particular memories and manifest themselves in different places. The cosmopolitan implication of Holocaust remembrance enables other groups of victims to recognize themselves in the Jewish victims of the Holocaust.

This has tangible consequences for international politics, as well: In the last three decades, remembering the Holocaust as the 'crime against humanity' par excellence has essentially contributed to the emergence of new international institutions, for example, international courts. The expansion and institutionalization of international jurisdiction are indicative of a fundamental change. Just like the Nuremberg Trials had marked a moment of cosmopolitanism, which was albeit thwarted by the Cold War, new international tribunals are awaiting terrorists today. Thus, also war is being cosmopolitanized.

Justice beyond the Nation

Looking for the origins of this cosmopolitanism, we inevitably come upon the documents and proceedings of the Nuremberg Trials. This was the first significant event in international justice after World War II. It involved the creation of legal categories and procedures beyond the limits of national sovereignty that allowed casting the enormity of the systematic, state-run extermination of the Jews into the mould of legal terms and court procedures. Remarkably, it was this that may and must be identified as the central source of the new European cosmopolitanism.

Article 6 of the Charter of the International Military Tribunal contains three types of crimes – 'crimes against peace', 'war crimes' and 'crimes against humanity' – on the basis of which Nazi crimes and criminals were tried and sentenced. Interestingly, 'crimes against peace' and 'war crimes' presuppose the existence of national sovereignty, i.e. they comply with the national perspective, whereas the concept of 'crimes against humanity' attempts to capture the cosmopolitan perspective in legal categories. It may be no coincidence, therefore, that the prosecutors and judges at Nuremberg had little use for this historically new category. After all, it did not only introduce a new law or principle, but a whole new logic of law that completely departed from the previous logic of international law, which had been based on the nation-state.

And yet, it is the investigations into 'crimes against humanity' that Nuremberg is most remembered for today. In this respect, the political process at Nuremberg differs from subsequent trials. The Nuremberg trial itself hardly dealt with the extermination of the Jews. Nuremberg is considered as the starting point of a new level of civilization, on which the desire for revenge is making way for a new understanding of justice. Its denunciation as 'victor's justice' also still reverberates in today's controversies about international jurisdiction. However, this criticism tends to overlook that there may also be victim's justice. The sentences of Nuremberg as well as the future sentences of an international court might demonstrate that not a whole nation has incurred guilt, but that it is borne by individuals – which is why the concept of 'collective guilt' fails as an analytical instrument when it comes to accounting for historical injustice. This realization may have caused the suffering of the victims to be recognized in Nuremberg, and may do so again, to interrupt and end the cycle of retaliation.

In retrospect, Nuremberg is seen as the beginning of a development towards awareness for crimes against humanity. Article 6a of the London Charter defines them as 'murder, extermination, enslavement, deportation and other inhumane acts committed against any civilian population, before or during the war; or persecutions on political, racial or religious grounds in execution of or in connection with any crime within the jurisdiction of the Tribunal, whether or not in violation of domestic law of the country were perpetrated'. The wording 'before or during the war' clearly distinguishes crimes against humanity from war crimes. It establishes the accountability of individual perpetrators outside of national law, before the international community, before mankind. If a state is becoming a criminal state, individuals that serve it must envisage being tried and sentenced by an international court of justice. The wording 'any civilian population' suspends the national legal principle, according to which there is total responsibility for one's actions inside the national borders, but none outside, and replaces it with cosmopolitical accountability. This cosmopolitical legal principle protects the civilian population not only from violence committed by other, enemy states (which is contained in the concept of 'war crimes'), but also from the despotic violence of sovereign states against their own citizens. In this, it is much more radical and provocative, ultimately reversing the priorities: Cosmopolitical law overrides national law. Crimes against humanity may neither be legitimized by national law, nor can they be tried and sentenced by nation-states. In summary, the historical novelty of 'crimes against humanity' suspends the categories, the entire grammar of national legislation and jurisdiction.

Cosmopolitan Europe and Remembrance of the Holocaust: the Politics of Memory in Poland

After World War II, the concept of cosmopolitan Europe was inaugurated as the antithesis to nationalist Europe and the physical and moral havoc it had wreaked. With this in mind, British wartime Prime Minister Winston Churchill rhapsodized amidst the rubble of the ravaged continent in 1946: 'If Europe were once united ..., there would be no limit to the happiness, to the prosperity and the glory which its … four hundred million people would enjoy.' It was the charismatic statesmen of the Western democracies and, significantly, the people and groups from the ranks of the active resistance, who re-invented Europe across national trenches and mass graves by drawing on tradition. Cosmopolitan Europe is a project of the resistance. This is important to state, because two aspects converge in it: First, resistance was ignited not by the collapse of European values (that would be trivial), but rather by the experience that those values could be perverted or even were perverse in themselves; by the realization that totalitarian regimes have always rested on some idea about 'true human nature' to identify, exclude, transform or exterminate those who did not (or did not want to) conform to the ideal. Hence the second, that anti-humanism not humanism formed the point of departure.

However, if there no longer is any human substance that must be saved; this is where the sources of public protest and resistance, which reflect the conditions for sympathy and the defence of human dignity, gain importance. Cosmopolitan Europe is a Europe which is morally, politically, economically and historically struggling for reconciliation. The adjective cosmopolitan represents this openness, limited only by the criticism of ethnic nationalism that was struggling for the recognition of cultural diversity and differences.

Cosmopolitan Europe constitutes a European self-contradiction in moral, legal and political terms: The traditions that spawned the colonialist and nationalist horrors and the genocide were European – but so were the legal categories and ethical standards against which they were measured, identified as crimes against humanity, and tried before the world public. The victors could just as well have court-martialled and executed the responsible Nazi elite, as initially demanded by Stalin and Churchill. Or they could have put them before national judges and sentenced them according to national law (as was the case in Eichmann's trial in Jerusalem or the Auschwitz Trials in Germany). Instead, the European tradition to recognize the Other and the law based on this tradition were mobilized against the ethnic perversion of law.

There is yet another pattern of interpreting the Holocaust, and it is no coincidence, of course, that this narrative originated in Europe. It dissolves the concrete image of the Nazi perpetrators into abstract metaphors, according to which the true culprits are not human beings at all, but modernity, bureaucracy, or even Man. Such postmodern criticism of Enlightenment cites the Holocaust as evidence for the failure of modernity. Holocaust remembrance is becoming a monument to the omnipresent modernization of barbarity (cf. Levy and Sznaider 2001). European awareness of the negativity of modernity is not just some fashionable attitude, not an ideology of tragedy. Rather, it manifests the historically important realization that modernity has derailed from the tracks of the nation-state, mercilessly exploiting its own potential for moral, political, economical and technological catastrophe in a real-life laboratory, even without consideration for its own survival. The mass graves of the twentieth century – the world wars, the Holocaust, the atomic bombings of Hiroshima and Nagasaki, the Stalinist gulags and the genocides

– all bear witness to this. But there is also a poorly understood, uninterrupted link between the European pessimism about modernity and postmodernity, which perpetuates despair. To put it another way, there is a paradoxical coalition between national and postmodern Europe, because the theoreticians of postmodernity deny that the possibility – and the reality – of combating the horrors of European history with 'more Europe', i.e., with a radicalized, cosmopolitan Europe.

Europeanization means to struggle for institutional answers to the barbarity of European modernity – and to bid farewell to postmodernity, which ignores this fact. In this sense, cosmopolitan Europe is the institutionalized self-critique of the European way. This process is incomplete, and it can not be completed. It has only just initiated the sequence of Enlightenment, postmodernity and cosmopolitan modernity. Cosmopolitan Europe is an experimental version of Europe which is rooted in its history, breaking with its history, and drawing the strength to do so from its history. This makes it the locus of reflexive modernity, where the foundations, limits and guiding principles of national politics and society are all subject to renegotiation. The radically self-critical European memory of the Holocaust does not destroy the identity of Europe, it constitutes this very identity.

In the remembrance of the Holocaust, the break from the past is gaining influence on future developments. The task is to establish the forward-looking forms of memory of a cosmopolitan European self-critique against national war and founding myths. This also became evident in the context of the European Union's eastward expansion. In Eastern Europe, the political process of remembrance is primarily directed against Stalinist crimes, but they will have to confront the issue of collaboration with the Nazis as well.

A case study about Poland lends itself to illustrating this topic. Poland's relationship to its own past and the politics of remembering it have been determined by three different factors. The first and second factor is Polish victimhood under National Socialism and Stalinism, respectively. Thirdly, the allegation of Nazi collaboration has been made a subject of public dispute in recent years, the Jedwabne debate being a significant example.

On 10 July 10 2001, the Jews returned to Jedwabne – where they had been rounded up and murdered by their Polish neighbours exactly 60 years before (cf. Gross 2001). Now they were back. They had come to mourn the victims in the company of Poland's post-communist political elite led by President Aleksander Kwaśniewski. For Poland, World War II turned out to be more traumatic and to have graver consequences than for many other nations it affected. For Poland, there can be no escaping the fact that Auschwitz, Majdanek, Belzec, Chelmno and Treblinka are places in Poland. Poland and the Holocaust 'belong together'. After the war, Poland lay devastated and plundered, its elites had been murdered, the West had betrayed it to Stalin. The only thing left to Poland was its ethnic homogeneity. This ethnic homogeneity was accompanied by a consciousness of innocent victimhood. Now, the Jews once murdered by their Polish neighbours, are suddenly turning things upside down.

The ethnic memories of Poles and Jews have always gone separate ways. For non-Jewish ethnic Poles, World War II was the war in which millions of them had been murdered by the Nazis and another few millions had been deported and murdered by the Soviets. The Warsaw Rising is not to be confused with the uprising of the Warsaw Ghetto of 1943. It was a separate uprising in 1944, in which hundreds of thousands of Poles met their death. Despite having a common citizenship, Poles and Jews had experienced different wars.

After Jedwabne, this attitude is no longer possible. The cosmopolitan portion of Polish society wants to face this past. It wants to open Poland towards Europe, and this implies confronting one's own history, de-glorifying it, apologizing to the victims and recognizing being a perpetrator. Polish President Kwaśniewski realized this. In contrast to his political rivals, he sought to Europeanize Poland. This is why he apologized to the Jews of Jedwabne in Poland's name: 'For this crime we should beg the souls of the dead and their families for forgiveness. This is why today, as a citizen and as the president of the Republic of Poland, I beg pardon. I beg pardon in my own name and in the name of those Poles whose conscience is shattered by that crime ...'

Despite all opposition, a part of Polish society has understood that remembering the Holocaust within the framework of an all-European space of memory has created new imperatives with far-reaching political consequences. Establishing recognition for this cosmopolitan community of values is becoming the horizon of action for the state. In Poland and elsewhere, opposition is coming from circles that are trying to understand (or to contextualize as the historians call it): Is Jedwabne not in the area that had been occupied by the Soviet Union between 1939 and 1941; and haven't the Jews always been known to collaborate with the Soviets against the Polish people? This is the thesis held by some, and not only Polish, historians. Wasn't Jedwabne an understandable act of revenge against the communist Jews? It can be as simple as that if one refuses to escape from the provinciality supported by national historians (cf. Henning 2001). And as the global world now recognizes, victimhood no longer absolves from the guilt of the perpetrator. One can be both a victim and a perpetrator at the same time. The 'Jedwabne deniers' refuse to accept this truth. Instead, they seek to preserve the guilt of both the Nazis and the Jews, as well as the innocence of the Poles. Thus, they are disconnecting themselves from Europe. It is no wonder, therefore, that this attitude has found its apologists in Germany as well, where both Jewish and German guilt are concepts with a long history, which one does not want to abandon.

The Polish president understood that the globalization of this norm, which involves the cosmopolitanization of Holocaust remembrance, has become an integral part of European politics. In this universalized form, it serves to Europeans – including the Poles – to redefine themselves. Of course, this cannot happen without resistance; in particular, the Catholic Church is finding this difficult to come to terms with.

The global politics and discourse about guilt and forgiveness, which we have seen in recent years, are indicative of a new historical awareness detaching itself from the boundaries of the nation-state. In the past, being prepared to forgive and pay reparations has often been understood as a sign of weakness and an obstacle to *realpolitik*. This is also true of the Polish opposition to acknowledging the crimes in Jedwabne. However, the fact that people feel the need to protest against the danger of forgiveness at all, points to its increasing normative and political power. Collective memory of guilt – once the exclusive domain of West German post-war society – is more and more becoming a factor in international politics. This may explain the discontent of some German observers with Jedwabne. The Holocaust is no longer just a German, but a European problem. We are witnessing the emergence of a new European memory which is remembering Europe's past as that of a 'dark continent'. Still, the question remains: Who can forgive, who can ask for forgiveness?

The Politics of Forgiveness: the German Reparation of the 1950s

But does this discourse of forgiveness not ignore the real victims of the catastrophe? May the victims not preserve their right to be unforgiving, instead of becoming the bearers of some new human-rights policy? Indeed, the records of the Nuremberg trial also formed one of the most important sources for a historiography of the Holocaust that centred on the perpetrator (cf. Hilberg 1961). It renders the victims irrelevant and lets them appear (if at all) only indirectly, through the perpetrators' perspective.

Ultimately, we face a classical dilemma of modernity, which the politics of forgiveness must find an answer to. This is where Derrida's theory of forgiveness starts off – with the self-incrimination of humanity that is contained in the concept of 'crimes against humanity'. He argues outside the realm of sovereignty and outside the constraints of political logic. 'Only the unforgivable can be forgiven.' For him, the politics of forgiveness is at the same time global and metaphysical. We are all of the same kind and of the same value; we are created as humans and humanity. In this sense, 'crimes against humanity' presupposes the existence and forgiveness of the one God who makes humanity possible. In this sense, forgiveness cannot be thought of as a system of counter-trade; it is apolitical. Here, too, the concrete victims are absent from the scene.

Can the Jews forgive the Holocaust at all? It is the survivors who do not attempt to reconcile the irrationality of evil with the omnipotence of love. The victims want to preserve their right to unforgiveness. Of course, this does not mean that 'reconciliation' is becoming impossible to achieve, especially at a time when the number of survivors is getting smaller all the time. But it does raise the question about the limitations of reconciliation, about which awareness needs to be raised. Global messianism is not the issue, but concrete people in most diverse political settings. At the same time, the limitations of Holocaust remembrance when it comes to establishing global morality need to be pointed out. This prevents conflating the differences between the extermination of the Jews, other genocides, and political crimes.

The example of the so-called *Wiedergutmachung* illustrates the inherent cosmopolitan potential of this procedure. In several respects, the German reparation payments of the 1950s have become a precedent, and increasingly also a reference for a transnational rhetoric calling for a politics of forgiveness and a corresponding jurisdiction. Elazar Barkan (2000), for example, analyses this development in terms of a new 'guilt of nations'. He describes a new international morality which is characterized not only by accusations against others, but also by a preparedness of nations to recognize their own guilt. The national catastrophe of the Holocaust is removed from its historical context and spelled out anew under global conditions. Whenever these days victims challenge perpetrators to admit their guilt and this admission manifests itself in material reparations, it is the Holocaust and *Wiedergutmachung*, the Jewish and German memories, that provide the model for the institutional framework of this global phenomenon.

The trend towards restitution over recent years does not rest on the assumption of any universal legal idea, but rather on some lowest common denominator that also acknowledges local, particularistic idiosyncrasies. The discourse of restitution is the result of cross-cultural negotiation with the Other, which also involves redefining the dichotomy between the local and the global and the antagonism of universalism and particularism. Yet, there is no abstract, universal sense of justice behind this; rather, mutual recognition forms the basis of reconciliation and the very foundations for common experience and memories. In other words, we are not talking about some universal morality the thinkers of the Enlightenment had envisaged. Instead, we are witnessing the global genesis of standards and conditions of reconciliation that are only just emerging from the acceptance of and the dialogue with the Local. Often, there is an *ad hoc* concept of justice emerging from concrete negotiations, in which particularistic local claims are being merged with universal expectations, and which also factor in a globalized culture of human rights.

The symbolic value of restitution should not be underestimated. Money does not only provide concrete assistance to former victims. The abstract universality of money is also the precondition for establishing non-personal relations. With money, liabilities can be made anonymous and transformed into services. In this sense, money furthers the idea of human equality, since inequality can then only be based on individual qualities. Therefore, money allows former victims and perpetrators to enter the same phenomenological space and open their identities for each other, i.e. cosmopolitanize them. For former victims, material restitution is also a strategy for giving meaning to past suffering. As anthropological literature (e.g., Mauss 1990) in particular emphasizes, the material exchange of goods entails obligations. The money being exchanged in material restitution cannot be separated from the giver. This is precisely the connection between 'moral cosmopolitanism' and 'economic cosmopolitanism'. Thus far, this nexus has hardly been examined within this context. Not rarely, political controversies revolving around historical guilt and responsibilities assume that these concepts are primarily about authentic intentions and the moral quality of penitence. In the contradiction of individuality and collectivity, discussions on guilt and responsibility often go round in circles: How are group members supposed to get to grips with the guilt of their collectivity, if it is the collectivity itself that is about to be designated and needs to redefine itself? To what extent should moral sentiments like love, kindness, charity or conscience become part of political action?

The material aspect of restitution plays a major part here. Money is something external and measurable, guilt is not. Also, money fulfils another function, it makes something impossible possible: an exceptional political situation is transformed into mundane banality. At the end of the day, one pays reparations the way one pays the premium for an insurance, an insurance against evil. Certainly, this may not transform the fervour of ethnic and national struggles into cosmopolitan peace, but it is a small step in that direction.

This is precisely what restitution may achieve. It need not inevitably lead to a common narrative of erstwhile victims and perpetrators. It need not lead to a common 'we', but it does realize and acknowledge that politics may accept irreconcilable plurality as a given. This is another lesson to be learnt from the history of German-Jewish *Wiedergutmachung*.

'Restitution' as a cultural concept does not just comprise refunding stolen property and reparations for personal losses, but also apologizes for historical crimes. Often, the answer to the question about the essence of a historical crime is already a part of the negotiations between the victims and the perpetrators: With some historical crimes, the actions of the perpetrators already appeared as criminal to their contemporaries. This was not necessarily so with other cases, such as slavery or forced displacements (which were considered as a 'population transfer' legitimized by the state during the negotiations following World Wars I and II and are today called 'ethnic cleansing').

The principle of restitution resolved this ambiguity. It primarily involves negotiated history, in which various groups, linked across national boundaries and cleavages, seek to overcome the conflict in quest of a common narrative. In doing so, they are also changing their own identity to a certain extent and creating new opportunities for political action, as Hannah Arendt argues. But here, too, a word of caution is advised: A common narrative is not common in the sense that both sides would tell the same story. Instead, the recognition of the different narratives is the crux of the matter. As is commonly known, the reparations that Germany, e.g., paid to the victims, have not led to a common narrative.

Restitution creates compensation for historical injustice and it might become an instrument for compromise between multiethnic society and the nation-state, or a model of conflict resolution in cases where the traumatizing effects of historical crimes strain the relations between peoples or different groups. At the same time, our case studies demonstrate that the increasing pervasion and the privatization of restitution politics broadens and changes the national perspective.

'Perspective': Guilt and Forgiveness

As collective patterns of memory are becoming less centred on the state and the nation, they create new moral interdependencies which, in turn, rest on cosmopolitan memories. This opens up spaces in which new 'communities of fate' emerge that go beyond national territories and identities. Thus, the increasing propagation of restitution politics can provide a normative alternative to the disintegration of traditional communities and networks of solidarity. All they need in common is to have suffered and to identify as victims.

Therefore, a 'history' freed from the national container can no longer be one of glory. A skeptical narrative of history begins to emphasize the past injustice committed by its own nation. People realize their guilt. Cosmopolitan memory then means to acknowledge the history (and the memories) of the Other and to incorporate them into one's own, overriding the narrative of the self-righteous nation. This calls for 'boundary politics within a boundary-less modernity', which involves continuously recalling the boundaries of the definitions of the Holocaust, genocide, human-rights violations and restitution. Therefore, our analysis reveals a paradox: The nation is being remembered in order to overcome it. At least in Europe, it is the memory of national chauvinisms that is laying the foundations for fundamental transnational institutions and a human-rights regime that is politically consequential and is co-determining national politics in many areas (e.g., the European Court of Justice and the European Convention on Human Rights).

In the modernity of the nation-states, the distinction between the memories of perpetrators and victims was an important element of mutual non-understanding and served as a means to distinguish oneself from others. In cosmopolitan modernity, a compromise is achieved which, however fragile it may be, is sustained by the mutual recognition of the Other's history. This connection of perspectives makes this act of reconciliation a key experience of memory. Thus, in many ways, it is not so much the original crimes that are on the agenda – many victims and perpetrators having died in the meantime; rather, it is the question of how their descendants deal with these histories and memories. In other words, the inclusion of the Other alleviates the distinction between the memories of perpetrators and victims. What remains is the memory of a common history which cannot be divided. The cosmopolitan memory of the past emerges from the conscious and intended inclusion of the Other's suffering – not from the idea of some community of fate, inspired by mythical delusions and serving to construct some false historical continuity. Thus, new moral and political fields of action and responsibility emerge from communication and interdependencies.

Transnational and cosmopolitan memories, however, must permanently define themselves via national experiences. Boundaries may become fluid, but they do not disappear; they even get redrawn, however temporarily this may be. Different conclusions from memory cultures of the Holocaust are evident in transatlantic relations (Levy, Pensky and Torpey 2005).

Especially in West Germany, a growing majority feels morally committed to multilateralism, which is explained as a consequence both of the defeat of 1945 and the ensuing re-education by the Americans. For them, radical distancing from the Nazi past is the most important priority in politics and remembrance. For Germany, remembering the Holocaust has been instrumental for making the switch from 'Germanizing Europe' toward 'Europeanizing Germany'. Yet they are perceiving reality only from their own national perspective of 'Never again fascism'. However, this does have its downside – after all, it means closing one's eyes to the ongoing universalization of the Holocaust. This threatens to downplay the potential opposition between territorially based national sovereignty and the human rights regime. In American memory, on the other hand, the horror of terror has taken centre stage to the point of relegating the horror of war in Germany and other parts of Europe to the sidelines.

The way the Nazis did away with international law has been one of the major subjects of interest, not only with students of the Holocaust. Parallel to that, individuality was replaced with the idea of ethnic community (*Volksgemeinschaft*). The Nazis considered international law as a mixture of British imperialism and rootless Jewish spirit (the latter was emphasized, above all, by Carl Schmitt). Not having fully recovered from this experience yet, even today many Germans still identify the renunciation of international law as the beginning of a new process of destruction. The only difference is that, turning things completely upside down, those who once liberated Germany from the Nazis are now being declared the new war criminals. It is one of the empirical objectives to point out the dissolution of boundaries in Holocaust remembrance; at the same time, however, we seek to shed light on the limitations of this dissolution of boundaries. Germany's much-cited 'special responsibility' and the political conclusions that were drawn from it in recent years all fit neatly into a 'deterritorialized' cosmopolitan memory. The slogan 'never again war' is transforming into 'never again Auschwitz', for example in Joschka Fischer's (the former German Foreign Minister) parlance. All this begs the question if the integration with the West, which used to be West Germany's *raison d'être par excellence*, is now seeking to finally complete itself on the field of politics of remembrance. In the face of the current transatlantic tensions, this question will have to remain open for the time being.

References

Arendt, H. (1986), *Eichmann in Jerusalem* (München: Piper Verlag).
Barkan, E. (2000), *The Guilt of Nations: Restitution and Negotiating Historical Injustices* (New York: Houghton Mifflin).
— and Karn, A. (eds), *Taking Wrongs Seriously: Apologies and Reconciliation* (Stanford: Stanford University Press).
Beck, U. (2000), 'The Cosmopolitan Perspective: Sociology of the Second Age of Modernity', *British Journal of Sociology* 51, 79–105.

— (2002), *Macht und Gegenmacht im Globalen Zeitalter. Neue Weltpolitische Ökonomie* (Frankfurt am Main: Suhrkamp).

— and Bonß, W. (eds) (2001), *Die Modernisierung der Moderne* (Frankfurt am Main: Suhrkamp).

Diner, D. (2003), *Gedächtniszeiten. Über Jüdische und Andere Geschichten* (München: C.H. Beck).

Gross, J.T. (2001), *Nachbarn. Der Mord an den Juden von Jedwabne* (München: C.H. Beck).

Hilberg, R. (1961), *The Destruction of the European Jews* (Chicago: Quadrangle Books).

Levy, D., Pensky, M. and Torpey, J. (eds) (2005), *Old Europe, New Europe, Core Europe: Transatlantic Relations after the Iraq War* (London: Verso).

Levy, D. and Sznaider, N. (2001), *Erinnerung im Globalen Zeitalter: Der Holocaust* (Frankfurt am Main: Suhrkamp).

— (2005), *The Holocaust and Memory in the Global Age* (Philadelphia: Temple University Press).

— (2005), 'Forgive and not Forget: Reconciliation between Forgiveness and Resentment', in Barkan and Karn (eds).

Mauss, M. (1990), *The Gift: The Form and Reason for Exchange in Archaic Societies* (New York: W.D. Halls).

Spengler, O. (1991), *Der Untergang des Abendlandes* (München: PUB MISS).

Zweig, S. (1988), *Die Welt von Gestern. Erinnerungen eines Europäers* (Frankfurt am Main: Suhrkamp).

PART III
Tensions

Chapter 7

An Accented Radio:
Fostering Cosmopolitanism through
Media in Berlin

Steven Vertovec

Since the early decades of the twentieth century, Berlin has been associated with broad characterizations of cosmopolitanism. In the 1920s, the city was world-renowned as a site of cultural creativity spawned by an influx of foreign artists and intellectuals. During the Nazi reign, Hitler and other leaders despised Berlin's cosmopolitanism (which, for them, was associated with leftists and Jews). By the 1970s and 1980s, Berlin was again largely associated with free-thinkers and immigrants – this time represented by an alternative sub-culture of radical Germans alongside a large population of Turks and other identified *Ausländer* (foreigners). Indeed throughout the rest of Germany today, Berlin is often viewed as a 'city of foreigners' (Richie 1998, 791).

The proliferation of a public discourse of multiculturalism, coupled with local government's and business's self-conscious drive to be recognized as a *Weltstadt* (global city), has meant that Berlin's cosmopolitanism – or capacity to flourish by way of cultural diversity – is currently celebrated in a variety of ways. The following article examines one initiative to both display and foster a sense of cosmopolitanism in Berlin.

The Return of Cosmopolitanism

Throughout a number of academic disciplines there has rather recently been a kind of revitalization surrounding the notion of 'cosmopolitanism'. The term has been invoked to describe complex cultural repertoires, to modify understandings of hybridity, to portray the agendas of new social movements, and to suggest political alternatives to both ethnocentric nationalism and particularistic multiculturalism (see Brennan 1997; Cheah and Robbins 1998; Breckenridge et al. 2000; Dharwadker 2001; Vertovec and Cohen 2002).

As a corrective to the common stereotype of cosmopolitans as privileged, bourgeois, politically uncommitted elites, there is currently an increasing interest in recognizing that 'cosmopolitan' philosophies, institutions, dispositions and practices – 'actually existing cosmopolitanism' (Robbins 1998) – exist among a wide variety of non-elites, not least migrants and refugees. In this approach to cosmopolitanism there is emphasis on more positive, socio-culturally and politically transformative meanings of the term (see for instance Schein 1998a; 1998b). And it is in this sense that James Clifford describes how the term cosmopolitanism undermines the 'naturalness' of ethnic absolutisms (1998, 365), points to 'worldly, productive sites of crossing; complex, unfinished paths between local and global attachments' (Clifford 1998, 362), and 'presupposes encounters between worldly historical actors willing to link up aspects of their complex, different experiences' (Clifford 1998, 365).

While the trend towards positively re-appropriating notions of cosmopolitanism is to be welcomed for its socially and politically transformative potential, practically all the recent writings on the topic remain in the realm of rhetoric. There is little description or analysis of how contemporary cosmopolitan philosophies, political projects, outlooks or practices can be formed, instilled or bolstered. In short, there are few recipes for fostering cosmopolitanisms.

One important exception has been Martha Nussbaum's (1994) call for 'cosmopolitan education'. Such an educational agenda, forming the basis for the construction of attitudes as well as institutions, would have among its goals: to appreciate how common ends are variously instantiated in many cultures, to vividly imagine the different based on a mastery of facts, and to stimulate in every person an overall 'process of world thinking' (Nussbaum 1994, 4).

In addition to the educational system, the fostering of cosmopolitanism is a process that would need to be located among a number of intermediary institutions in public space, including journals, meetings and political discussions. The media, in its variety, also represent an obvious site for stimulating cosmopolitan awareness and highlighting cosmopolitan practices. To date, this has mostly been addressed through media structures and programmes surrounding the presentation of cultural diversity or multiculturalism.

Multiculturalism and the Media

Given the increased recognition of cultural diversity in Western societies over the past two or three decades, there has arisen a need for giving expression to difference in the public sphere, for 'creating a public in which all the groups can and must communicate' (Sandercock 1998, 199). Indeed, to guarantee media systems that adequately articulate the ethnic diversity of the citizenry has come to be considered an essential part of democracy itself (Husband 1994).

Since the 1980s the Council of Europe, for instance, has been actively engaging issues surrounding cultural diversity and the media through a series of conferences and policy documents (such as Council of Europe 1987; 1994). Most of its discourse and resultant recommendations address the highlighting of difference through notions of cultural rights and the preservation of immigrant cultures. Deniz Göktürk points out, however, 'The focus on cultural difference which claims to be liberating, in practice, often covers up existing crosscultural traffic and makes dialogue and interaction more difficult' (1999, 7). And 'Let's be honest', says BBC producer Anil Gupta, 'there has been an awful lot of crap put out in the name of right-on, PC, quota-fulfilling, multi-culturalism' (1998, 6). In this sense, then, the multicultural strategies in many forms of media, although providing a much-needed presence for ethnic minorities in public space, have not necessarily generated or sharpened cosmopolitan sensitivities in minority or majority populations.

More recently, the Council has broadened its discourse to recognize the desirability of media creating 'transverse links, i.e. ones that transcend the boundaries between identities' (Perotti 1997, 25). This seems to echo the advice of Ella Shohat and Robert Stam (1994, 346) who call for the media to encourage ethnic/cultural interlocution and an interweaving of voices.

> Dialog can be painful and polyphony can become cacaphony. But cultural polyphony would orchestrate a multifaceted polylog among all those interested in restructuring power in more egalitarian ways. It would promote a mutually enriching proliferation of emancipatory discourses, transcending a mere coexistence of voices to foster a mutual adoption of other voices and accents.

Such a call seems to have found its way, too, into the media policy recommendations that emerged from the 1997 United Nations World Television Forum. These include proposals for the transformation of broadcasting organizations to create structures in which different voices participate in collective dialogue. This would be intended to make media services more responsive and open to culturally alternative sources of programming and, ideally, stimulate new, hybrid forms of programming (Robins et al. 1997).

Complex, cross-over dialogues and representations in public space via diverse media programmes, it is suggested, can be one way of fostering cosmopolitanism. Public space cosmopolitanism would draw attention to, and increase awareness of, everyday forms of cultural multiplicity. This represents a rather different agenda than much current media multiculturalism, which can often be read as a patronizing form of ethnic exceptionalism. In other words, 'the media can normalize as well as exoticize other cultures' (Shohat and Stam 1994, 347).

Such a strategy has been adopted by the radio station SFB4 in Berlin, a context that, in a number of ways, lends itself to concepts of cosmopolitanism.

Context Berlin

The historical view of cosmopolitanism in Berlin was mentioned at the outset of this article. Today it has become practically *de rigueur*, when publicly addressing the city, to invoke approvingly Berlin's legacy of worldliness and cultural admixture. Since 1991, for instance, Berlin's Commissioner for Foreign Affairs

(*Ausländerbeauftragte*), Barbara John, has conducted a series of public discussions, led by invited German and foreign politicians, writers, scientists and publishers, on the theme '*Berlin – tolerant und weltoffen*', that is, Berlin – tolerant and liberal/cosmopolitan, or literally 'world-open' (its derivative noun *Weltoffenheit*, 'world-openness', is the word usually used synonymously with cosmopolitanism; see Vertovec 1996). In a recent joint policy statement naturalization issued to the Berlin Senate, representatives of the Social Democrats, Democratic Socialists and Greens commenced by invoking 'Berlin as a tolerant, *weltoffen* Federal Capital' (in Junge 1999). In his inaugural address, Chancellor Gerhard Schröder described how the renewed capital Berlin opens itself to Germany and the world in a 'cosmopolitan' fashion. 'Berlin is for a *weltoffen* climate', Schröder said (in Bundesregierung 1998, 35–6).

Barbara John observes how *weltoffen* used to mean something like 'Berlin is welcoming to the world'; 'now the world is here', she says, and various agencies must help Berlin's population to realize this reality (personal communication). Berlin is home to 440,247 registered 'non-Germans' (*Nichtdeutsche*) whose origins lay in 184 other countries – practically every country in the world (Ausländerbeauftragte 1998). They comprise no less than 13 per cent of Berlin's total population of 3,387,901 in 1997. The category includes some 137,000 Turks, 28,000 Poles, 22,000 'former Soviet Union', 18,000 Bosnians, 13,000 Italians, 13,000 Croats, 11,000 Greeks and over 37,000 listed simply as 'former Yugoslavia' (Ausländerbeauftragte 1998).

Ethnic and cultural diversity is one of Berlin's hallmarks. Heidrun Suhr (1990, 234–5) remarks:

> Most contemporary West Berlin authors now incorporate *Fremde* [Others, foreigners] into their narratives as part of the Berlin setting. As an integral part of the city's local color, they are present as a backdrop, in all forms of fiction. *Szeneliteratur* [a genre depicting the Berlin 'scene'] in particular always includes some reference to foreigners as proof of its authenticity, its direct link to Berlin reality.

Due to the fact of its diversity and its popular image suggesting some kind of *Weltoffenheit* (alongside its renewed position as capital city), policy makers in Berlin believe it is this city's role to provide a model of positively functioning cultural diversity for the rest of Germany. In other words, they wish Berlin to be the 'integration workshop of the nation' (John 1997). For a while Frankfurt am Main could contest Berlin's model role. In the late 1980s and early 1990s Frankfurt's local government office for multicultural affairs promoted many high profile projects communicating information and encouraging discussion in the city's public sphere in order to facilitate the 'growing together' (*Zusammenwachsen*) of all resident ethnic groups (Welz 1992; Friedmann and Lehrer 1998). Yet overall since 1981, when Berlin was the first German *Land* to establish an office of Commissioner for Foreigners' Affairs, Berlin's policies and initiatives – some reinforcing communalism, other encouraging cosmopolitanism – have indeed been exemplary for the rest of Germany (see Schwartz 1992; Vertovec 1996).

Broadcast media in Berlin have recently been the focus of considerable public attention concerning potential trajectories for the future of the city's ethnic diversity. On the one hand, from outside the city, new forms of transnational media, especially satellite and cable television, have significantly transformed patterns of listening and viewing (Robins 1998; Çağlar 2001). This is particularly the case with Turkish television programmes broadcast from Istanbul and watched in real time in Berlin. Much public debate has ensued following claims that Berlin Turks' consumption of media from Turkey has led to communalist viewing patterns, an 'ethnicization' of the media landscape and, therefore, increased cultural isolation and social ghettoization (Becker 1997).

On the other hand, a new self-conceived 'media experiment' called Radio Multikulti has been established in order to promote a rather different pattern.

SFB4 Radio Multikulti

The fourth station of public radio Sender *Freies Berlin* (SFB), nicknamed Radio Multikulti, first went on the air in September 1994. The station was initially financed (with a very low budget of 6.5 million DM) for the trial period 1994–97 by the media institute of Berlin-Brandenburg, the Federal Ministry of Labor, and licence-funded SFB. After the trial, SFB4 Radio Multikulti has subsequently been awarded permanent funding due to its recognized success over its initial three years.

For media service promoting 'life in cultural diversity and awareness of others', in 1995 the radio station was awarded the CIVIS prize from the Federal Commissioner for Foreigners' Affairs, the Freudenberg Foundation and the national broadcasting systems WDR (*Westdeutsche Rundfunk* (West-German Broadcast)) and ARD (*der Arbeitsgemeinschaft der öffentlich- rechtlichen Rundfunkanstalten der Bundesrepublik Deutschland* (Working Committee of Public Broadcasting Corporations of the Federal Republic of Germany)). Also in 1995 UNESCO recognized the station as German partner for the World Decade for Cultural Development. In 1997 Radio Multikulti was proclaimed radio station of the year by the media organization *Internationale Medienhilfe* (International Media Support).

Radio Multikulti was established as an experiment based on certain innovations in the media treatment of multiculturalism. 'Multi-cultural radio should not be like "normal" radio', insists Radio Multikulti station director Friedrich Voß. 'It should offer the cultural diversity of everyday Berlin' (Voß 1995). The station's goals focus on the keywords: 'Integration' and '*Weltoffenheit*' (see SFB4 Multikulti 1998). Like many other public institutions in Berlin, SFB4's strategy is formulated with reference to highlighting the importance of the city – especially as renewed capital – as an example for other parts of Germany.

A city, which in the future will attract more and more businessmen, diplomats, artists and other foreign guests, must show that it is also able to demonstrate peaceful and constructive living-together (*Zusammenleben*). The goal is integration, not assimilation. A prerequisite for effective integration is information. Prejudice and discrimination result from ignorance, from lack of knowledge of others. Here lies an essential task of the media. (SFB4 Multikulti 1998)

Providing 'information' has two meanings with regard to the radio station's strategy. One is the sense of conveying basic information about the various groups and cultural backgrounds now existing in the city in order to fashion a general climate of acceptance and integration. Another sense is supplying practical assistance to the public – often specifically immigrants and ethnic minorities – by way of information on developments concerning legal conditions and social programmes. Alongside news and public information, the station produces diverse forms of entertainment. The total effect is to foster different understandings of cosmopolitanism, directed at both German and 'non-German' people, in everyday settings of Berlin.

Highlighting the fact that 440,000 migrants from 184 nations live in Berlin, Radio Multikulti's promotional material (brochures and pamphlets, posters, postcards, Internet site) claims that the station provides around-the-clock 'borderless' radio 'for them and all *weltoffenen* Berliners'. It proclaims 'Multikulti is the radio of cultural diversity with information about cultural living-together (*das Zusammenleben der Kulturen*) among ourselves (in Berlin) and elsewhere'. The station sees itself as 'a bridge of sound' (*eine Brücke, die klingt*) both between different cultural groups living in the city, and between each group and its homeland.

'We speak with an accent', boasts the station through its promotional material. Many if not most of the people presenting programmes on Radio Multikulti speak German with a foreign accent (Turkish, Italian, Polish, Croatian and so forth). The strategy here is to normalize difference by recognizing that Berliners come from many origins. The radio station's journalists, technicians and other employees are themselves comprised of Germans and a wide variety of 'foreigners': most Radio Multikulti personnel see their own successful cooperative activity as a kind of model too (Bergling 1998).

The daily structure of programming reflects other important aspects of Radio Multikulti's strategy. Following five minutes of news (each hour on the hour), from 6:05 to 9:00 each morning the day begins with the Breakfast programme. This includes reports on developments in world politics, European news, and events in Berlin and elsewhere in Germany. 'World music' is played intermittently throughout this and all daily programmes: the station specifically excludes 'Anglo-American rockpop'. The latter is avoided as it is implicitly regarded as part of a globalizing, hegemonic uniformity represented in most popular media.

Examples of the two- to four-minute reports during the Breakfast programme are: a year's overview of developments among Bosnian refugees in Berlin; a series on the meaning and implications of European monetary union, including an account of Britain's reluctance to join; an excerpt from an Iranian literary satire; an interview with the Green party politician Cem Özdemir about dual citizenship; a report on the election of Minnesota's ex-wrestler Governor Ventura; during Ramadan, daily readings from the Qur'an; a discussion with Berlin Muslims about breaking the fast during Ramadan; a description of Russian Christmas celebrations in Berlin; information about indoor-skiing in Berlin; and a report from Cuba about celebrations for the anniversary of the Revolution contrasted to scenes of daily life.

From 9:05 to 12:00 a variety of light entertainment segments are linked under the programme title Meridian. This includes a fifteen-minute 'Travel Fever' show (descriptions of reporters' travel experiences plus a contest, based on knowledge about other countries and people) and a music magazine show including interviews with touring musicians (such as a South African choir, an Australian didgeridoo player and Berlin street musicians). News in English from the BBC World Service is broadcast at 10:00, and in French from RFI at 11:00. Examples of musical presentations in Meridian include songs from a world music CD of the week and live performances by a local Kurdish band, a mixed ethnicity all woman band, and a Jewish Klezmer band.

Metro, 'the Berlin magazine', is broadcast from 12:05 to 14:00. During this part of the day a variety of segments probe specific issues relevant to the social and political scene in Berlin and elsewhere in Germany. Examples include: accounts of the Christian Democrat (CDU) campaign against dual citizenship, a report by a journalist accompanying Berlin's mayor as he meets foreign ambassadors new to Berlin; a review of a new theatre production of Gogol's *Dead Souls*, an historical overview of Russian exile writers in Berlin, a visit to a German-Arab association in the Berlin district of Moabit, and an interview with a local (Turkish) psychologist about possible psychological implications of dual citizenship.

For a 'siesta' between 14:05 and 15:00 the station presents Diwan, a mixture of music, poetry and story around varying themes. A studio discussion program called Viaduct – 'a forum of understanding in diversity' – is conducted each day from 15:05 to 16:00. Here, invited guests from a range of backgrounds discuss and criticize new activities and initiatives surrounding 'everyday culture and the multicultural day' (*die alltägliche Kultur und den multikulturellen Alltag*). Recent themes have covered the meanings of European monetary union for 'foreigners' in Berlin, the functions of the regional employment office for women and youth, the implications of the Russian economic crisis, and the successes and problems of Radio Multikulti's own Turkish-language programmes (see below).

From 16:05 to 16:45, *Heimspiel* (home-play) provides a space for various foreign-origin people to present aspects of their homelands such as kinds of music, food and drink, festivals, linguistic expressions. This is followed, 16:45–17:00 by a report on some world or local event (such as the visit of a foreign dignitary to

Berlin) which developed during the day, usually having been briefly announced during the Breakfast programme.

From 17:00 to 22:30 Radio Multikulti switches from German language programmes to a succession of programmes in 'the languages of the world-city'. The duration of the programmes, as well as their broadcasting daily or weekly, vary (from an hour in Turkish daily to fifteen minutes in Roma twice per month). Other languages of programmes in this time slot are Albanian, Arabic, Kurdish, Persian, Polish, Russian, Vietnamese, Italian, Spanish and Greek. Radio Multikulti inherited the SFB's programme established in the 1960s for Yugoslav 'guestworkers' that was originally broadcast in Serbo-Croatian; now, reflecting the breakup of Yugoslavia, Radio Multikulti produces separate programmes for Serbs, Croats, Slovenians, Bosnians and Macedonians.

Each non-German language programme has its own editor and reporters who are usually well known to the respective language communities in Berlin. Editors and reporters canvass such communities for the kinds of information and material that members would like publicly presented or interrogated. Interspersed with popular and traditional music, the programmes usually include news reports and analysis from respective 'homelands', local and international news, interviews and reports concerning law, health and social services in Berlin, and local cultural events. The issues are not always confined to the language-group, however; often a report, interview or discussion from one of the German-language programmes or from a non-German language programme (e.g. Turkish) is translated and broadcast during another non-German language show (e.g. Polish).

Some examples of miscellaneous material in the non-German language programmes are: (in Russian) a report on amnesty for deserters of the Russian army and a piece on the opening of a Russian film festival in Saarbrücken; (in Polish) an account about ethnic Poles from Kazakhstan migrating to Poland, a review of a new play opening in Berlin, and interviews with Moroccan students in Berlin on the difficulties they find in maintaining the Ramadan fast; (in Arabic) news from Baghdad about secret cooperation between Unscom and the United States, a discussion of the work of Goethe, and a review of a new art exhibition in Potsdam; (in Turkish) a survey of newly privatized telephone services in Germany and a discussion with Berlin Turks who translate Yiddish texts; (in Serbian) an interview with the editor of an independent Serbian newspaper and on-the-street interviews with Serbs in Berlin concerning the CDU's campaign against dual citizenship; and (in Croatian) handball and tennis results, a description of difficulties regarding the transference of foreign driving licences to German ones, and a report on unemployment in Croatia. Practically every non-German language programme also conducts discussions with invited guests and radio phone-in shows concerning issues like dealing with everyday racism and addressing questions surrounding naturalization and dual citizenship.

The non-German language editors, together with other senior editors of Radio Multikulti, claim to maintain close contacts with key associations and other members of the various ethnic-linguistic communities resident in Berlin. For the station managers such contacts are the 'best audience research studies' conveying up-to-the-minute needs and interests within these communities (Wolfgang Holler, personal communication). The managers, editors and journalists are ever conscious of conflicting political sensitivities existing within various communities in Berlin. The editors seek to ensure that they do not propagate the views of any one group or movement.

The shift of programming between languages – one of the most experimental aspects of Radio Multikulti – was originally viewed by station managers as a potential mistake. Now, some years after the station's establishment, this is regarded as wholly unproblematic. The shifts in programme language have apparently not lost the station listeners: according to Wolfgang Holler, many people throughout the city have acquired the opinion 'that's my channel' and will either simply tune out during another language programme and tune-in again later, or listen through some (albeit non-understood) non-German language programme simply to hear the intermittent music (personal communication).

Following the non-German programmes, each night from 22:30 to 22:45 the station provides a course on German as a foreign language, prepared by the Goethe Institute. A 'musical trip' or fictional fantasy is presented between 22:45 and 23:00. Then, from 23:00 to 6:00 the station is devoted entirely to world music. Throughout the week this includes alternating, hour-long world music programmes broadcast from radio stations in Lausanne, Paris, Helsinki, Istanbul, Vienna, Madrid, Basel, Halle, Toronto and London.

On weekends there are special programmes for rap and hip-hop (especially oriented towards young listeners), drum-and-tribe, bhangra, jazz and 'global dance', along with a weekly live concert. Weekend broadcasting also includes a literary programme called Papyrus (in which literature from around the world is critiqued and discussed) and a world religions programme called From Abraham to Zarathustra (largely comprised of basic teachings of different religions, descriptions of major festivals, and interviews with Berlin-based believers).

SFB4 Radio Multikulti is generally thought to appeal to Berlin's 'globetrotters and cosmopolitans' (Messmer 1998, 33). One survey shows that SFB4 Radio Multikulti held only about 0.7 per cent audience share for Berlin (1 per cent in the former West Berlin). While low, this figure actually represents more than many others in Berlin – especially in public radio, and not least SFB1, the classic 'culture' radio station – in a city with no less than 36 radio stations. Perhaps more importantly, one needs to bear in mind that this official survey of listeners only questions 'Germans'. 'Foreigners' are overlooked. Therefore it is estimated that perhaps three-fifths of Radio Multikulti's listeners are not counted because they don't have German citizenship (Braun 1998). The station's own informal inquiry, according to SFB4's Senior Editor Wolfgang Holler, suggests that Multikulti has an enormous share of the audience among ethnic minority communities: from perhaps 40 per cent of the city's 28,000 Poles up to 90 per cent of the 8,000 Vietnamese in Berlin (personal communication). Radio Multikulti now also reaches much further than Berlin, and than Germany, by way of the internet (see http://www.multikulti.de).

While the listening audience may not be massive, the members of SFB4 Radio Multikulti believe they are making a difference and that their experiment is already a success. The station has indeed become a kind of media role model. The national ARD network of radio and television stations now transmits Radio Multikulti-produced programmes to numerous other parts of Germany. KISS FM, a commercial Berlin radio station built around popular music, has recently followed Multikulti by creating a programme in Turkish, largely devoted to German-Turkish hip-hop, for young German-born Turks in the city. But for Wolfgang Holler, Radio Multikulti's impact has been more subtle: 'The idea behind this all, we are realizing now. Just to be there, we are changing minds. Just to be on air, just that German listeners are listening to people with an accent and are getting used to it. And they're seeing: hey, it's normal' (personal communication).

Conclusion

While arguably having broken new ground in the public representation of cultural diversity, SFB4 Radio Multikulti also exhibits occasional evidence of 'non-cosmopolitan' thinking. Sometimes the treatment of specific groups sounds rather bounded and essentialist, particularly when addressing needs of cultural retention among migrants. This is reminiscent of what David Hollinger (1995) has called pluralism, in describing a multiculturalist approach he considers to be the opposite of cosmopolitanism. For Hollinger, cosmopolitanism represents an emphasis on individual, multiple affiliations, while pluralism emphasizes inherited boundaries and the importance of protecting and preserving ethnic identities. In this respect, Radio Multikulti's presentation often slips back and forth between cosmopolitan and pluralist multiculturalisms.

Radio Multikulti does succeed in communicating a variety of meanings of cosmopolitanism. That is, concerning cosmopolitanism as a socio-cultural condition, the station's programmes are filled with descriptions of Berlin as a culturally complex environment reflecting globalization and other large-scale processes. As ideology or philosophy, Radio Multikulti's general approach to a range of issues reflects deep concerns with conceived universal values such as human rights and anti-racism, and its programming strategies are arguably based on a humanistic view of peoples of the world who can be united not only around such universal values, but around diverse expressions of art and music as well. Cosmopolitanism as a political project of transnational institutions is supported by Radio Multikulti's abundant reporting of (and obvious support for) political frameworks such as dual citizenship and institutions such as the European Union. The cosmopolitan political project of representing multiple identities is seen to be supported by Radio Multikulti's mode of addressing the complexity of Berliners themselves – as networked in multi-origin communities yet still as Berliners, and as women, youths of the first, second and third generation, as deeply concerned with district and neighbourhood politics as well as with city and Germany-wide politics. The facilitation of cosmopolitan dispositions – open to gaining familiarity and ease with that which is different – is underscored in practically every programme SFB4 produces since their *raison d'être* is exactly to expose the public to difference. And finally, cosmopolitanism as practice is represented on the air in numerous ways, from the presenters 'with accents' through the playing of hybrid forms of music to interviews and debates involving 'non-German'-origin Berliners.

The slogan 'We speak with an accent' is resonant with Hamid Naficy's (2001) recent description of exilic and diasporic filmmaking as 'accented'. By this Naficy suggests the marker 'accented' refers not just to speech, but also to cultural fragmentation, multilingualism, socio-political displacement and critical juxtaposition. 'Accented' modes of cultural production, says Naficy, are 'situated in the interstices of cultures' (Naficy 2001, 4). In this way we can describe Radio Multikulti as 'accented radio,' since it consciously seeks to create, highlight and develop such interstices as positive and stimulating facets of Berlin.

As James Clifford (1998, 362) has remarked, cosmopolitanism is especially to be found in people's lived encounters in 'worldly, productive sites of crossing'. But 'The process of cultural meeting and mixing', Deniz Göktürk points out, 'cannot be ordered through cultural politics and definitely not steered from above' (1994, 33). Radio Multikulti attempts to foster modes of cosmopolitanism by conveying or offering the space, the interstices, for everyday realities of cultural crossing, rather than by moralistically prescribing good ethnic relations. Staff at the station importantly believe that the best way to foster change is to provide (alongside a variety of music and stories of popular interest) basic information and good journalistic description about a range of cosmopolitanism attitudes, practices and sites of cultural production throughout Berlin.

Acknowledgements

I wish to express my sincere thanks and appreciation to numerous people who graciously provided information, advice and feedback surrounding this piece, especially Thérèse Bergling, Ayşe Çağlar, Tom Cheesman, Robin Cohen, Dorota Danielewicz-Kerski, Jürgen Maintz, Deniz Göktürk, Wolfgang Holler, Barbara John, Kevin Robins, Alisdair Rogers, Robin Schneider and Friedrich Voß.

References

Ammann, R. and von Neumann, B. (eds) (1997), *Berlin: Eine Stadt im Zeichen der Migration* (Darmstadt: Verlag für Wissenschaftliche Publikationen).
Ausländerbeauftragte des Senats (1998), *Bericht zur Integrations- und Ausländerpolitik* (Berlin: Verwaltungsdruckerei).

Becker, J. (1997), 'Taking Turkishness Seriously: The Rise of Turkish Media Culture in Germany', in Robins (ed.).

Bergling, T. (1998), *Intercultural Communication: A Case Study of SFB4 Multikulti, a German Radio Station. Sociology Diploma Thesis* (Uppsala: Uppsala University).

Braun, R. (1998), 'Beispielloses Integrationsprojekt', *Mainzer Allgemeine Zeitung*, October 2, 4.

Breckenridge, C., Pollock, P., Bhabha, H. and Chakrabarty, D. (eds) (2000), *Cosmopolitanism*. Special issue of *Public Culture* 12(3).

Brennan, T. (1997), *At Home in the World: Cosmopolitanism Now* (Cambridge, MA: Harvard University Press).

Bundesregierung Deutschlands, (1998), *Die Regierungserklärung von Bundeskanzler Gerhard Schröder* (Bonn: Presse und Informationsamt der Bundesregierung).

Çağlar, A. (2001), 'Constraining Metaphors and the Transnationalisation of Spaces in Berlin', *Journal of Ethnic and Minority Studies* 27: 4, 601–13.

Cheah, P. and Robbins, B. (eds) (1998), *Cosmopolitics: Thinking and Feeling Beyond the Nation* (Minneapolis: University of Minnesota Press).

Clifford, J. (1998), 'Mixed Feelings', in Cheah and Robbins (eds).

Council of Europe (1987), *Migrants and the Media – From 'Guest Workers' to Linguistic and Cultural Minorities* (Strasbourg: Council for Cultural Co-operation of the Council of Europe).

— (1994), *Meeting Report: The Role of the Media in Promoting Integration and Equal Opportunities for Immigrants* (Strasbourg: Council of Europe).

Dharwadker, V. (ed.) (2001), *Cosmopolitan Geographies: New Locations in Literature and Culture* (London: Routledge).

Douglas, M. and Friedmann, J. (eds) (1998), *Cities for Citizens. Planning and the Rise of Civil Society in a Global Age* (Chichester: John Wiley & Sons).

Friedmann, J. and Lehrer, U. (1998), 'Urban Policy Responses to Foreign In-Migration: The Case of Frankfurt am Main', in Douglas and Friedmann (eds).

Göktürk, D. (1994), 'Muselmanisch Depressiv', *Die Tageszeitung*, 3 September, 33.

— (1999), *Turkish Delight – German Fright: Migrant Identities in Transnational Cinema*. ESRC Transnational Communities Programme Working Paper No. 16. <http://www.transcomm.ox.ac.uk> accessed 2 July 2006.

Gupta, A. (1998), 'We Were Seen as a "Minority Show" Even Though We Were All Full-Time Writers and Actors', *The Guardian*, November 2, 6–7.

Haxthausen, C.W. and Suhr, H. (eds) (1990), *Berlin: Culture and Metropolis* (Minneapolis: University of Minnesota Press).

Hollinger, D.A. (1995), *Postethnic America: Beyond Multiculturalism* (New York: Basic Books).

Husband, C. (1994), *The Multi-Ethnic Public Sphere: A Necessary Project*, paper presented at the European Film and Television Studies Conference, 19 July 1994, London.

John, B. (1997), 'Berlin – Integrationswerkstatt der Nation', in Amann and von Neumann (eds).

Junge, B. (1999), 'Hauptstadt für Doppelpaß', *Die Tageszeitung*, January 15, 17.

Messmer, S. (1998), 'Klänge aus aller Welt', *Die Tageszeitung*, September 26, 33.

Naficy, H. (2001), *An Accented Cinema: Exilic and Diasporic Filmmaking* (Princeton: Princeton University Press).

Nussbaum, M. (1994), 'Patriotism and Cosmopolitanism', *Boston Review* 19:5: 3–34.

Perotti, A. (1997), *Practicing Cultural Diversity in Culture and the Media* (Strasbourg: Council for Cultural Co-operation of the Council of Europe).

Richie, A. (1998), *Faust's Metropolis: A History of Berlin* (London: Harper Collins).

Robbins, B. (1998), 'Introduction Part I: Actually Existing Cosmopolitanism', in Cheah and Robbins (eds).

Robins, K. (1998), *Spaces of Global Media*. ESRC Transnational Communities Programme Working Paper No. 6.<http://www.transcomm.ox.ac.uk> accessed 15 March 2006.

— (ed.) (1997), *Programming for People: From Cultural Rights to Cultural Responsibilities* (New York: United Nations World Television Forum).

—, Cornford, J. and Aksoy, A. (1997), 'Overview: From Cultural Rights to Cultural Responsibilities', in Robins (ed.)

Sandercock, L. (1998), *Towards Cosmopolis: Planning for Multicultural Cities* (Chichester: John Wiley & Sons).

Schein, L. (1998a), 'Forged Transnationality and Oppositional Cosmopolitanism', in Smith and Guarnizo (eds).

— (1998b), 'Importing Miao Brethren to Hmong America: A Not-So Stateless Transnationalism', in Cheah and Robbins (eds).

Schwartz, T. (1992), *Zuwanderer im Netz des Wohlfahrtsstaats: Türkische Jugendliche und die Berliner Kummunalpolitik* (Berlin: Parabolis).

SFB4 Multikulti (1998), *Ziele: Integration und Weltoffenheit*. <http://www.multikulti.de/ziele.htm> accessed 2 September 1998.

Shohat, E. and Stam, R. (1995), *Unthinking Eurocentrism: Multiculturalism and the Media* (London: Routledge).

Smith, M.P. and Guarnizo, L.E. (eds) (1998), *Transnationalism from Below* (New Brunswick: Transaction).

Suhr, H. (1990), '*Fremde* in Berlin: The Outsiders' View from the Inside', in Haxthausen and Suhr (eds).

Vertovec, S. (1996), 'Berlin Multikulti: Germany, "Foreigners" and "World-Openness"', *New Community* 22, 381–99.

— and Cohen, R. (eds) (2002), *Conceiving Cosmopolitanism: Theory, Context and Practice* (Oxford: Oxford University Press).

Voß, F. (1995), *Radio Multikulti: Babylon auf dem Äther*. FU:N (Freie Universität Nachrichten) 8–9, <http://www.fu-berlin.de/fun/8-95 > accessed 21 October 1996.

Welz, G. (1992), 'Multikulterelle Stadtpolitik: das Frankfurter Modell', *Multikultur Journal 1992* (Tübingen: Tübinger Vereinigung für Volkskunde e.v.).

Chapter 8
Cosmopolitanism and Feminism in the Age of the 'War on Terror': A Twenty-first Century Reading of Virginia Woolf's *Three Guineas*

Gillian Youngs

Cosmopolitanism, the Individual and Gender

Cosmopolitanism is fundamentally about the individual's relationship to the world, his or her orientation to senses of connection with it, and mobilization of such connections in and through her or his identity. Cosmopolitanism essentially concerns questions of transcendence and, in common sense terms, what might be thought of as worldliness. As such, it is perhaps a controversial concept to revisit in times of the unilateral military hegemony of the United States, the so-called 'war on terror' and Iraq war at the beginning of the new century. However, these conditions remind us that cosmopolitanism, often regarded as a Western or Eurocentric notion, should be considered not only in abstract philosophical terms, key as these are, but also in relation to power and the practices of power.

The normative dimensions of 'moral cosmopolitanism' as discussed in the introduction indicate that it is as much about ideal aspiration as reality. War, conflict and many forms of violence, seem to counter its very possibility in practice. So as these are so characteristic of twentieth and twenty-first century history so far, it seems we live, at the very least, in compromised cosmopolitan times. 'Political cosmopolitanism', as the introduction goes on to explain, is located more firmly in the realm of practice, and so operates in more basic terms relating to equal and shared principles governing the behaviours of states to one another and their citizens, along the lines of international legal principles.

However, 'the might is right' principle frequently comes into play to disrupt this picture, as in the current Iraq war for example. This reminds us that power relations do not necessarily sit comfortably alongside universally oriented frameworks such as cosmopolitanism. 'Cultural cosmopolitanism' is the softer side of such universalism, focusing on inter-cultural linkages and respect for cultural differences and their richness, as the introduction explains. This is the kind of cosmopolitanism that is most prevalent in everyday approaches to the world, particularly in the contemporary era of global travel, global brands and mass media advertising. There is an emphasis here on the mobility and consumption of cultures, both our own and others. The shared experience is often one defined by market activities as much as any other, and these developments have done much to democratize ideas associated with cosmopolitanism, which still carry a heavily elitist baggage.

Critical social science has been helping us to unpack that baggage so that when we think about the individual and cosmopolitanism we realize that working with a traditional abstract notion of the individual is severely limited. It is more revealing and precise to go beyond such abstractions and recognize that, especially when we are talking about an individual's relationship to the world, all aspects of her or his social positioning will be relevant to considerations of what it means to be cosmopolitan. These aspects include socio-economic or class status, gender, ethnicity, cultural or multicultural identifications.

The 'intersectional' (Crenshaw Williams 1994) perspective recognizes how different forms of inequality across these are woven together to produce complex and differentiated individual and collective circumstances. In some cases deep inequality may exist across all these areas, in others it may exist across some with emphasis on one or two areas in particular, and in others it may just exist in one such as gender. Gender is the area I will focus on in this discussion. Whether we are thinking of moral, political or cultural forms of cosmopolitanism, the abstract notion of the individual is usually assumed in masculine terms, as is common across mainstream social science. In other words the dominant notion of the social actor, while articulated as gender neutral, is in fact assumed to be male.

This follows the powerful gender dualism of modernity positioning men as subjects and women as objects in the world. From this cosmopolitan worldview it is men who are predominantly conceived of as having made the world (as acting subjects), and women who have inhabited it, predominantly as passive objects of the processes and effects of masculine agency. Public/private configurations come into play here. The public sphere has historically, and continues to a significant extent, to be dominated by men, gendered patterns of paid work, and institutional influence largely associated with masculine identities. The private sphere of domesticity, unpaid social reproductive work and care, has historically been the residual realm associated largely with women and feminine identities. Systems of patriarchy have asserted male power across public and private, not least through gendered access to resources, and gender identities reflecting the public (male) over private (female) hierarchy (Youngs 2000).

Cosmopolitan imaginaries as primarily locked into the public sphere have traditionally been shaped by masculine characteristics. A familiar historical cosmopolitan archetype might be a lone male figure standing on the prow of a ship looking out across the waters and destinations to come, with a sense of being in command of all he surveys, with freedom of movement and thought, excited about all he is yet to discover and how he will relate that to what he has discovered so far.

Comparable contemporary archetypes might be the hyper-masculine types who bestride the realms of the global investment arena, or corporate types whose mobile lifestyles reflect the reach of their transnational businesses (see, for example, Hooper 2000). These are images steeped in the dynamics of physical and intellectual mobility, power through footloose freedom and senses of control. In gendered terms they are masculinist framings, although increasing numbers of women are joining their arenas (Kofman 2000). But they are in stark gendered contrast to the harshest types of substantially feminized global mobility such as migrant domestic labour and trafficked and enslaved sex workers (Chang and Ling 2000; Pettman 1996).

Feminist perspectives interrogate the gender assumptions of dominant masculinist archetypes and their implications. They investigate how their construction is linked to social structures of gendered power and the ways in which they work to identify man/woman as subject/object, and the diverse forms of empowerment and disempowerment that follow from these, including contrasting freeing and constraining of mind and body. Thus cosmopolitanism can be looked at as part of understanding gendered (as well as other) power dynamics and social and international positionings. Such dynamics and positionings relate to 'self-transformation' as the introduction explains, but such 'self-transformation' may be experienced as subject or object, and therefore be of quite different qualities.

Put quite simply, the global business magnate and the trafficked sex worker are both experiencing some kind of cosmopolitan mobility that impact on mind and body. But in the subject/object positioning, mobility is more likely to be transformatively empowering for the former and transformatively disempowering (oppressive or worse) for the latter. Agency exists in both cases, and is expressed in complex ways, but the constraints on it are likely to be far more negative for those crossing borders as objects rather than subjects.

Such understandings lead us away from an abstract notion of the cosmopolitan individual (or an assumed masculinist interpretration of that individual) and towards the potential for more nuanced and gender sensitive approaches to cosmopolitanism. This has purchase not just for now but for how we view the past.

Cosmopolitanism and Virginia Woolf's *Three Guineas*

This is one of the reasons I have chosen in this chapter to undertake a reading of Virginia Woolf's *Three Guineas* (hereafter referred to as *TG*). It was published in 1938 in the build up to World War II and a prolonged period of history where major conflict or the threat of it, and thus arms build ups and expenditures, were prominent issues in international relations. *TG* is a controversial tract and part of this as always with Woolf's work is the privileged social position from which she critiques gender inequalities. This is explicit in *TG* (118) in her concern with 'the daughters of educated men'.

TG may not seem the most obvious text to focus on in relation to cosmopolitanism. I have chosen it deliberately because it deals with some of the human forces (war, violent human conflict and the threat of it) that are most in tension with ideal aspirations of cosmopolitanism. The competing ideological and violent struggles of the 'war on terror' as well as recent arguments about 'clash of civilizations' (Huntington 1998) are among the proofs that we continue to live in anti-cosmopolitan as much as cosmopolitan times. The gender analysis offered by *TG* identifies male domination of society as blameworthy for militarism and war. It is a detailed critique of funding priorities, the masculinist nature of education, and its relationship with patriotic warrior-like tendencies. As Michele Barrett (1993, xxxvii) has argued from a contemporary standpoint 'Woolf's argument linking masculinism and war is both prescient and uncontentious'. *TG*'s central concern with education as a means by which the world may (or may not) be transformed from a warlike to a peaceful one is pertinent to the cosmopolitan debate. It helpfully associates the transformative role of education at the individual level to social change at the large scale.

I also see its form as part of its relevance to the cosmopolitan debate. It is a self-reflective debate on a range of associated social (universal) questions. This is very much an individual's (interior) engagement with the world in the interests of its potential transformation. Its mode is feminist in positioning the author as thinking, critical woman. She is subject rather than object, an active agent rather than an object of social processes. The approach disrupts the male over female (subject over object) traditional positioning of men and women, the masculine and the feminine, while the content represents a deep critical engagement with the consequences of such positioning in relation to war and peace, and an envisioning of how transformation from war to peace might take place. It links self-transformation (of gendered identities and roles) with social transformation.

The content also has much relevance for the contemporary concerns of feminism. Much has changed for many women in terms of socio-economic circumstances and access to all levels of education over the twentieth century. But the global picture remains an uneven and gendered one with women most represented among those who are illiterate and lacking access to even primary education in the poorest parts of the world (Youngs 2007, 91, 99–100). And while women are increasingly active in politics, with some even holding some of the highest positions in some countries, it is still the case that international relations is a predominantly masculine sphere dominated by men and shaped by masculinist values.

Feminist international relations scholars have written extensively about the problem of women's missing voices and influences in relation to the 'war on terror', in ways that echo directly and indirectly the kinds of concerns raised in Woolf's essay (see, for example, Youngs 2006 and *International Feminist Journal of Politics* 2006). Woolf's critique focuses on social processes that lead to masculinist cultures disposed more to war than peace. As leading feminist international relations scholar Cynthia Enloe (2004, 218) has recently commented: 'Whether the process of militarization is stalled, reversed or propelled forward in any society is determined by the political processes that bolster certain notions of masculinity and certain presumptions about femininity over their gendered alternatives.'

Feminists continue to be engaged in the kind of consciousness-raising about the gendered nature of war that Woolf undertakes in *TG*. She highlights the partial and gendered nature of education, dominated as it is by men, their influence and masculinist values. At heart, Woolf's analysis is sociological, in the sense that it recognizes societies and their values are not just accidental or haphazard but produced by gendered structures of power and the particular and partial worldview they perpetuate as universally relevant. For Woolf education is a fundamental aspect of producing a gendered world, as it was for her well-known predecessor of two centuries earlier Mary Wollstonecraft (1985). *TG* reminds us how central education is to an individual's outlook on the world and his or her sense of possibility within it, also her or his associational proclivities within it as citizens, national patriotic or cosmopolitan, or combinations of both. Woolf's statement that 'a woman has no country' remains the most famous catchphrase from *TG* but, of course, it is frequently cited without the full context of the text. I consider that context and its relevance for debates about cosmopolitanism.

Reflectivity and the Politics of Individual Agency

The form of Woolf's text positions the female author/commentator in reflective mode, thinking about the past and its relationship to the present and future, making clear connections between individual (interior) thought and analysis and social (exterior) reality. If we can think of Woolf presenting a picture of the cosmopolitan woman, for reasons I will continue to elaborate below, it is as someone who can think about the big social issues, war and peace, education and economic independence/dependence. This is a socially grounded and connected individual with a confident and fluent voice, grasping historical continuities and problems, and relating them to the potential for social change and the difficulties standing in the way. 'Three years is a long time to leave a letter unanswered, and your letter has been lying without an answer even longer than that' (*TG*, 117). This starting point is subtle in taking you into the interior world of the author within a lengthy timeframe, indicating the time and capacity for prolonged consideration.

The question that has been posed, 'How in your opinion are we to prevent war?' (117), could not be grander and more challenging. When we think about what Woolf does not say about this question as well as what she does say, we note that there is no indication that the question is too big, merely that it is of such substance as to require a great deal of thought. It is quickly implied that we are dealing with an individual consciousness quite capable of addressing weighty social matters and confident in so doing. She immediately signals why this is important when she remarks on how 'remarkable ... perhaps unique' such an inquiry is of a woman by an 'educated man' (117). But while admitting that they both come from the 'educated class' she wants to highlight the 'gulf' that stalks communication between them in a world where a man's education is at the expense of his sisters (118–19).

Woolf emphasizes here the gendered differences in the intellectual resources which men and women can draw on to address large questions such as the goal of peace. Furthermore, she is explicitly making this point in a relational (feminist) fashion. She stresses that gendered priorities within families allocate resources for male education and professional development at the direct expense of females such that: 'the noble courts and quadrangles of Oxford and Cambridge often appear to educated men's daughters like petticoats with holes in them, cold legs of mutton, and the boat train starting for abroad while the guard slams the door in their faces' (119). While women may not be able to draw on the learning from disciplines concerned with war like politics, international relations and economics, they have to rely on 'unpaid-for education' of experience and understanding of human nature (psychology). But the major gender line is soon drawn: 'to fight has always been the man's habit, not the woman's' (120). So while women lack first hand understanding, they will need to consider the biographies of others, of men.

It is interesting to think that more than half a century later although gender changes have occurred with women's involvement in the military and combat in some countries' armed forces, and women's participation in terrorist acts including suicide bombing, the domain of warfare remains largely a male affair, and certainly the masculinist culture of warfare prevails. This reminds us that women's expanding engagement in even the most masculine of arenas such as the military does not necessarily rapidly transform the nature of those spheres. Were that to happen, and of course it is not inevitable, it could be expected to be a long historical process. And this would be likely to be dependent on women's relatively equal or greater influence at all levels including the most senior over a substantial length of time. Such structural shifts may be happening incrementally with small changes one by one, but any resulting major transformations may be long in gestation and dependent on certain tipping points being reached.

In looking at male perspectives Woolf notes that while there are different positive and negative views of war there is a majority in favour, and 'overpowering unanimity' that 'it is better to kill than be killed' (123). But this 'patriotism' and defence of England may well have a different meaning for 'the educated man's sister' who is differently positioned in 'the home of freedom' than her brother (123). Here Woolf focuses on the lack of women's roles and influence across the public sphere. She notes the absence of women not only from the military but also the Stock Exchange. 'Thus we can use neither the pressure of force nor the pressure of money' (126–7). Even while they were now being admitted to the Bar and the Civil Service, their influence was limited, as in politics too (127–8).

Again, while gender change has impacted on all these areas giving women more influence now than in Woolf's days it is worth noting that women's representation in national parliaments across the world is still low enough to cause comment, and their minimal representation on the boards of companies even more so. A recent report from the Equal Opportunities Commission (2006, 1) in the UK explained that women 'are still not reaching the top of their professions in significant numbers. They represent 10 per cent of directors at FTSE 100 companies, and barely 20 per cent of Members of Parliament. Among those few women who do make it to the top, ethnic minority women make up just 0.3 per cent of MPs and 0.4 per cent of FTSE 100 directors, despite the fact that they comprise 5.2 per cent of the population and 3.9 per cent of the labour market'.

The gender picture of public and working life is different now compared to Woolf's times, but the struggle she was articulating to bring women's influence fully into the operation, cultures and values of those spheres, is still far from over. This is of course clearly the case in such deeply entrenched realms as the military, war and all forms of violent conflict. Woolf places useful emphasis on 'memory and tradition' (*TG* 133) and their impact on gendered identities involving 'mind and body'. She indicates in such ways the importance of history and its impact on contemporary conditions. 'Though we see the same world, we see it through different eyes' (133), she says of educated men and women. What I want to touch on here are the historical roots of present day gendered positionings, and their relevance to the possibilities for change. Her perspective reminds us that such conditions cannot necessarily be easily or quickly transcended: being established over long periods of time, it is unlikely that they will be simply and quickly disrupted or overturned.

Pertinent to our media rich times is Woolf's use of imagery to support her points. She ridicules through detailed description, and the inclusion of photos, the elaborate and formal costumes of 'public attire' (134). 'It not only covers nakedness, gratifies vanity, and creates pleasure for the eye, but it serves to advertise the social, professional, or intellectual standing of the wearer' (137). Woolf certainly does not mince her words when she likens this to tickets in a grocer's shop and even worse compares it to 'a barbarity which deserves the ridicule which we bestow upon the rites of savages' (137). In a turn of phrase that deftly equates motherhood with male professional achievement, Woolf dismisses the practice even further by a sharply drawn piece of comparative imagery. 'A woman who advertised her motherhood by a tuft of horsehair on the left shoulder would scarcely, you will agree, be a venerable object' (137).

Through these discursive strategies Woolf manages to invert the symbolic power of the pomp and circumstance, the dressing up, that accompanies the public parading of the social significance of masculinist institutions. She reduces it to a rather pathetic and superficial form of claims to status depicting, for example, 'a clever man' and 'a very clever man' (137). The tickets in the grocer's comparison, has multiple meanings including the reference to inanimate objects (vegetables or other foodstuffs) rather than human subjects, and of course, in a wider sense to the female domestic domain. We are left with the impression of the silliness of the male world of ceremony, as if the fussiness of the whole endeavour is an attempt to make much more of what is being claimed than should actually be the case.

This is a penetrating critique saying much about the symbolic social representation of male power and its roles in affirming and validating that power. Such a critique is if anything more potent in the context of contemporary media saturation than it was in Woolf's times. All our media are swamped with images of men of action and influence, whether in politics, business, the military, the world of the professions or increasingly these days of sport and entertainment. The symbolic public arena of masculinist power may be very different from the mid-twentieth century but it is if anything more prevalent, more prosaic and less escapable. Senses of masculinist cosmopolitanism are represented and influenced as much by images as words in these media-saturated times, whether we are thinking about diverse media from print to television, film and the Internet, factual photojournalism, corporate prospectuses, or glossy adverts for goods and services associated with cosmopolitan lifestyles.

Woolf emphasizes that the various uniforms of the male world are significations of masculine power, so rejection of such uniforms would be a meaningful way of working against rather than for war (138). She continues on to discuss how education, as part of the overall system of power seeking and competitive 'possessiveness', can be considered part of the problem of war: 'if we help an educated man's daughter to go to Cambridge are we not forcing her to think not about education but about war? – not how she can learn, but how she can fight in order that she may win the same advantages as her brothers?' (152). An alternative education contrary to passing on 'the arts of dominating other people ... of ruling, of killing, of acquiring land and capital' should 'teach the arts of human intercourse; the art of understanding other people's lives and minds' (155).

Such an alternative education could be regarded as cosmopolitan in its orientation towards individual engagement with other people and the world, and enhanced understanding of the lives that others live and the kinds of perspectives they generate. It could be argued as potentially more horizontal than vertical, more concerned with connection than conflict, harmony than domination. But even in the absence of such an orientation in education the imperative to support education for women remains for Woolf. It offers the opportunity for independent living and the possibility for women to exert social influence as a result, including as independent voices against war (158–62). This is a feminist challenge that still applies today: the challenge of harnessing current masculinist conditions of existence and routes to power, as part of a process of working towards transcending and transforming them.

This touches on a whole range of tensions related to feminist practices, many of which are not easily resolvable, not least because pursuing masculinist routes to power means engaging with the masculinist values associated with them. Is it possible then to influence and ultimately transcend them? It may depend on how much those values come to reshape the subjectivities of those involved and their sense of agency. There is not space to explore this complex area at length here, but it is worth stressing that it continues to be relevant to feminist theory and practice today. It can be argued that gender change towards greater equality where it has been achieved is definitely an indication that influence is possible, and that the potential for transformation may remain in the future. So education is key and the first guinea goes towards rebuilding a college.

Women's Missing Voices in Shaping a Cosmopolitan World

Woolf emphasizes the political point that continues to hold sway these days, that even when women get an independent income it does not automatically give them equal public voice, or as importantly, equal weight of influence. This relates to what has now become the familiar problem of the glass ceiling where the limited number of women at the top of public institutions and businesses contributes directly to perpetuating masculinist systems and values as dominant. Woolf's satirical discourse continues to be powerful on this point. She comments on how women are concentrated at the lower ends of the salary brackets in government and public bodies. 'The sex distinction seems ... possessed of a curious leaden quality, liable to keep any name to which it is fastened circling in the lower spheres' (170).

Woolf states that women lose out money-wise in both their public and private contributions to society, through their (comparatively lower) paid work and their unpaid work through marriage and in the home. This issue remains as current as ever, with widespread feminist critiques of the unpaid nature of social reproduction, caring and nurturing duties predominantly undertaken by women, and the accompanying undervaluing and lack of recognition and status for these contributions. While such functions are fundamental to the health and well being of any society, women continue to lose out because such work is unpaid. It also inhibits them engaging in paid work, or progressing to higher paid work, and often forces them into the lowest forms of flexible, home or contract jobs in order to fit in with their commitments to children and family.

Woolf points out that there are three routes through which women's influence is limited:

> The first is that the daughters of educated men are paid very little from the public funds for their public services; the second is that they are paid nothing at all from the public funds for their private services; and the third is that their share of the husband's income is not a flesh-and-blood share but a spiritual or nominal share, which means that when both are clothed and fed the surplus fund that can be devoted to causes, pleasures or philanthropies gravitates mysteriously but indisputably towards those causes, pleasures and philanthropies which the husband enjoys, and of which the husband approves. *It seems that the person to whom the salary is actually paid is the person who has the actual right to decide how that salary shall be spent.* (179–80, my emphasis)

This picture has changed over time, with for instance welfare state cultures recognizing the importance of some public funding support for families, especially poorer ones, and the more recent introduction of maternity and paternity leave systems.

But some of the core principles of Woolf's arguments still hold sway, especially the last point that I have highlighted. It makes clear that how much money does reach women independently counts, because it is only via that means that women's influence can be guaranteed. If less money reaches them, which continues often to be the case even in paid employment spheres, then they are likely to have less independent influence. And if money comes to them via men, as it still often does, then this may allow them influence, but it may also continue to allow them limited or no influence.

Substantial wealth or status not only brings with it the possibilities of influencing whatever sphere those monies are made in, but also extends influence including into the non-profit spheres where surplus funds can be directed. So this unequal wealth and status amounts to all-encompassing kinds of influence in the world across profit and non-profit realms. The gendering of wealth and the power attached to it does not just touch on influence in and the shaping of business and public institutions but also that of the charitable sector, where visions of social improvements and transformations, including of a cosmopolitan kind, can be supported and pursued.

Not surprisingly even in these unequal circumstances Woolf presses home the political significance of critical thought. In what seems like a clarion call to women to use the power of thought towards the transformation of such conditions Woolf argues:

> Let us never cease from thinking – what is this 'civilization' in which we find
> ourselves? What are these ceremonies and why should we take part in them?
> What are these professions and why should we make money out of them? Where
> in short is it leading us, the procession of the sons of educated men? (187)

As Woolf draws a fairly detailed picture of women participating in the structures and rituals of a male-dominated world, she deftly sketches women as thinking reflecting subjects rather than merely objects in this world, women who through such critical orientation can generate their own authentic perspectives on the meanings of this world and where it is leading.

Woolf's positioning of women in this discourse looks towards the future and associates the individual reflections of women with the universal in cosmopolitan mode through the reference to the notion of 'civilization'. The implication is that as things stand such a 'civilization' is predominantly man made but it could be different. However women will need to be critically engaged with what is happening all around them for this to be a prospect. This is a public sphere orientation. The resulting agency of women is viewed as holistic: important as much for (re)shaping the non-profit and profit sector.

If a guinea is to be given to help women enter the professions then the desire would be for this to be on a different basis from the past, so that the 'possessive' and 'combative' qualities that lead to war can be overturned (191). This includes freeing women from their position as 'victims of the patriarchal system' to become 'champions of the capitalist system' with substantial incomes, and the philanthropic power that would result to support, for instance, women's colleges, politics and other women's causes (192–3). But Woolf is brutal in her description of the narrowing effects of the professional world: the constraints such lifelong focus produces on participating in activities beyond work, including relationships with children or 'friendships, travel or art', and the tendency for making money to become a consuming force (194–7).

This is a potent rhetorical shift from the earlier discussions about male wealth, power, status and influence. While Woolf has spent some time exploring the grounds and manifestations of these, she is now undermining them dramatically by depicting their by-product as a diminished humanity. This again is a fascinating element of *TG* in relation to cosmopolitan debates. While, as I have stressed, cosmopolitanism focuses on the relation of the individual to the wider world, Woolf depicts the professional path as one that can inevitably shrink that relation, cut off the individual from seeing, listening and talking to the extent that: 'Humanity goes' and the result is 'a cripple in a cave' (197). Woolf emphasizes that the professional path can be a distorting one where a 'sense of proportion – the relations between one thing and another' (197) is lost.

She presents us with an individual cut off from the world in many ways, rather than actively engaged with it, or impacting on it and being affected by it in human, relational, aesthetic and cultural terms. This feminist perspective is overtly transformative and especially relevant to cosmopolitanism, which is oriented towards exposure to and interaction with diverse cultural influences. Woolf is arguing for a wider sense of the professional than has been familiar in the historically established masculinist model, perceiving this as narrowing rather than expanding in terms of human, social and cultural interactions.

Not surprisingly therefore Woolf depicts the choice between such a narrowing destiny and the one which the daughters of educated men have generally been condemned to as a choice between two bad options rather than one good and one bad. 'The one shuts us up like slaves in a harem; the other forces us to circle, like caterpillars head to tail, round and round the mulberry tree, the sacred tree, of property. It is a choice of evils. Each is bad' (199) And in a comment prophetic of her own suicide by drowning in 1941: 'Had we not better plunge off the bridge into the river; give up the game; declare that the whole of human life is a mistake and so end it?' (199).

In a more positive vein looking at the lives of women it could be seen that there was evidence of them doing work for its own sake rather than for recognition (201). This path of greater humility and means just sufficient to 'the full development of body and mind', turning away from 'pride' most notably of nationality but also beyond that of, for example, religion, family, sex, could be a way forward (205). Here we have more transformative suggestions related to alternative ways of thinking about identity and work and social relations. These may be regarded as rather idealized in the extent to which they emphasize limits: for example sufficient means only; resistance to 'fame and praise'; and 'freedom from unreal loyalties' in denying the forms of 'pride' referred to above (205). In some ways they make interesting if not straightforward links to some of the newer forms of cosmopolitan thinking related to social movements for sustainability and global justice (see, for example, Shiva 2005; Hutchings 2007; see also Hutchings 1999). Such movements raise issues of the need for limits to production and consumption in universal interests, and the importance of identifications beyond the narrow confines of state and immediate social networks in the interests of wider humanitarian ones. So on this complex and challenging basis a guinea goes towards helping the daughters of educated men enter the professions.

Feminist Cosmopolitanism: a Woman has No Country

The last section of *TG* is where Woolf makes probably what is her most well known and often quoted claim that a woman has no country. I had first heard it like many others I am sure without actually knowing about *TG* and its full content in any great detail. As a feminist I had some idea of what Woolf was referring to but at that time I had more a sense of *TG* as some kind of pacifist tract, and less as a general piece of feminist analysis of gender inequalities. It is equally both of these, and each aspect of the analysis informs and supports the other. So there is a crucial mutual reinforcement across the pacifist and feminist interpretations Woolf is offering.

I would argue that Woolf's comment about a woman having no country is best understood in relation to the fullness of *TG* and its intertwined pacifist and feminist positions. It is a penetrating and frequently bitingly satirical discussion of two interrelated areas: masculinist cultures and values as they are embedded in the major male-dominated institutions and their rituals (politics, the Church, the military, the professions, business, education and so on); and the exclusions or limited presence of women from and in them. This logically positions women's identities and affiliations differently from men's in society. Women's exclusions from core institutions and the masculinist values linked to them inevitably works to detach women from the core of society, or at least leaves them with much looser or weaker senses of attachment to or investment in it.

Woolf's points in the first two parts of *TG* which have been discussed above in outline terms (there is much more detail to be found in the text than I have touched on here) are very much the basis for the final points she goes on to make in the last part. She attacks vigorously the rejection of the value of women's opinion indicated by all the exclusions and inequalities discussed in the first two parts of *TG* (212) and warns against committing 'adultery of the brain' – writing for money something you do not want to write (218–19). Again here, Woolf's rhetoric is powerful in feminist regards. It inverts the conventional moral hierarchy as applied to women between selling one's body and one's mind, arguing that the latter ('brain prostitution') is far more damaging than the former (219). The truthful written word, 'intellectual liberty', is a way forward to work for the prevention of war, so freedom of thought and expression are paramount (222).

Woolf's correlation of feminists' fight against 'the tyranny of the patriarchal state' with the fight in that period against 'the tyranny of the Fascist state' (227–8) is well ahead of its times in aligning different struggles for equality, of sexes, races, religions (see Barrett 1993, xxxviii). In working to prevent war a woman is an 'outsider' opposing masculinist 'patriotic demonstrations', 'national self-praise' and 'military displays', proclaiming a universal rather than nationalistic affiliation, saying 'as a woman, I have no country. As a woman I want no country. As a woman my country is the whole world' (234). What meaning patriotism for a woman whose 'sex and class has very little to thank England for in the past; not much to thank England for in the present' (233).

The remainder of this last section of TG includes a discussion of different aspects of women's rights and the benefits for all. For example a call for the state to pay a wage to 'those whose profession is marriage and motherhood' that could lighten the 'slavery' of work for men (236–7). In the end the guinea is 'given freely' to the society aiming to maintain peace but the outsider status is preserved, the argument being that women can help best by not joining the society but cooperating in the shared aim of rights for all (272). The emphasis on 'difference' (229) as a basis of women's social contribution continues as an aspect of feminist debates. Woolf argues that this approach promises 'new words' and 'new methods' (272). Feminist theory and practice echoes such sentiments today and the struggle for recognition of feminist arguments as valid and socially meaningful in a male-dominated world also goes on.

Some Closing Thoughts on Feminism, Cosmopolitanism and War

The times in which I am writing this piece do not engender much optimism about a more peaceful world, with terrorism a major problem, and the Iraq war enduring for years rather than months, with horrendous civilian death and injury tolls. The achievement of peace in the world remains the greatest challenge in international relations. As in Woolf's time, masculinist military cultures and values continue to dominate, and women's and feminist voices and influence are too little heard or acted on. War continues to be predominantly decided on and engaged in by men, with women too often powerless victims. Women and feminists along with others, individually and collectively through NGOs and political processes and protests, continue to campaign against war and all its destructiveness. War remains perhaps the most fundamental obstacle to moves towards a universal cosmopolitan utopia. State-based and other forms of violence, such as terrorism, pitting different groups of people and ideologies, cultures and religions against each other, continue to contribute to dividing peoples of the world rather than connecting and uniting them.

Do women, feminists and feminist perspectives have particular contributions to make to transformations towards a more peaceful cosmopolitan world? The discussion in this chapter and in much other feminist analysis would suggest they do. As Woolf elaborates in *TG*, there are plenty of reasons why they should at least be part of the process. But this will never be wholly the case while women's influence remains highly restricted at the top of core institutions in society including governments.

TG envisages feminist transformations in education, attitudes to professional, familial and national identities in the interests of a less competitive, acquisitive and narrow society, one that looks beyond as well as within its national boundaries. Her statement that a woman has no country and the diverse meanings it carries along with it is bound to be a catchphrase of *TG* that is far more well known than the text as a whole. The catchphrase alone makes *TG* worthy of inclusion in critical reflections on cosmopolitanism, but the deeper transformations *TG* proposes, and the bases for them it outlines, adds much more to the debate.

If the past is anything to go by we do need 'new words' and 'new methods' to lead us towards peace. Cosmopolitan engagement would favour listening to different and contrasting views, including from women and feminists. *TG* is a sound illustration of the broad nature of such contributions, well beyond their relevance to deeper understandings of gender dynamics. The ways it highlights education as a transformative realm are especially noteworthy. They help us to understand new kinds of learning as central to cosmopolitan possibilities: a point as useful now as when *TG* was first written. This is also one of the many areas of *TG*'s assessment that powerfully binds individual and social transformations from the smallest to the largest scale.

Acknowledgement

This research was developed out of the ESRC Research Seminar Series (RES-451-25-4188) 'Ethics and the War on Terror: Politics, Multiculturalism and Media' (2006–2008) which I led in collaboration with Simon Caney (University of Oxford) and Heather Widdows (University of Birmingham).

References

Barrett, M. (1993), 'Introduction. A Room of One's Own/Three Guineas', in Woolf.

Chang, K.A. and. Ling, L.H.M. (2000), 'Globalization and its Intimate Other: Filipina Domestic Workers in Hong Kong', in Marchand and Runyan (eds).

Crenshaw W.K. (1994), 'Mapping the Margins: Intersectionality, Identity, and Violence against Women of Color', in Fineman and Mykitiuk (eds).

Enloe, C. (2004), *The Curious Feminist: Searching for Women in a New Age of Empire* (Berkeley, CA.: California University Press).

Equal Opportunities Commission (2006), *Sex and Power: Who Runs Britain? 2007* (Manchester: Equal Opportunities Commission).

Fineman, M. and Mykitiuk, R. (eds) (1994), *The Public Nature of Private Violence* (London: Routledge).

Hooper, C. (2000), *Manly States: Masculinites, International Relations, and Gender Politics* (New York: Columbia University Press).

Huntington, S.P. (1998), *Clash of Civilizations and the Remaking of World Order* (New York: Simon & Schuster).

Hutchings, K. (1999), *International Political Theory: Rethinking Ethics in a Global Era* (London: Sage).

— (2007), 'Feminist Perspectives on a Planetary Ethic', in Sullivan and Kymlicka (eds).

International Feminist Journal of Politics (2006) 8(1). Theme issue: 'Feminist International Relations in the Age of the War on Terror: Ideologies, Religions and Conflict'.

Kofman, E. (2000), 'Beyond a Reductionist Analysis of Female Migrants in Global European Cities: the Unskilled, Deskilled, and Professional', in Marchand and Runyan (eds).

Marchand, M.H. and Runyan, A.S. (eds) (2000), *Gender and Global Restructuring: Sightings, Sites and Resistances* (London: Routledge).

Pettman, J.J. (1996), *Worlding Women: A Feminist International Politics* (London: Routledge).

Shiva, V. (2005), *Earth Democracy: Justice, Sustainability and Peace* (Cambridge MA: South End Press).

Sullivan, W. and Kymlicka, W. (eds) (2007), *The Globalization of Ethics* (Cambridge: Cambridge University Press).

Tehranian, M. and Clements, K.P. (eds) (2005), *America and the World: The Double Bind* (London: Transaction).

Wollstonecraft, M. (1985), *Vindication of the Rights of Woman* (London: Penguin. First published 1792).

Woolf, V. (1993), *Three Guineas* (London: Penguin. First published in 1938).

Youngs, G. (2000), *Political Economy, Power and the Body: Global Perspectives* (London: Macmillan).

— (2005), 'Feminism and Peace: Towards a New World?', in Tehranian and Clements (eds).

— (2006), 'Feminist International Relations in the Age of the War on Terror: Ideologies, Religions and Conflict', *International Feminist Journal of Politics* 8:1, 3–18.

— (2007), *Global Political Economy in the Information Age: Power and Inequality* (London: Routledge).

Chapter 9

Cosmopolitan Capital or Multicultural Community? Reflections on the Production and Management of Differential Mobilities in Germany's Capital City

Kira Kosnick

Undesirable Elements

It is the summer of 2003, and Berlin is basking in a heatwave. On a hot and sunny Saturday afternoon, scores of residents have come to Berlin's centrally located park, the *Tiergarten*, and set up barbecue fires. Families are roasting pieces of lamb and chicken on portable grills, seated around blankets, with children playing nearby. Most of them are of immigrant background, part of Berlin's sizable labour migrant and refugee population.

A steady stream of visitors trickles through the gates of a nearby building, the House of World Cultures. It is the only place that offers toilet facilities in this area of the park, though many have come for a different reason: one of Berlin's most prominent cultural institutions, the House is hosting the In Transit Festival, a series of performances, talks, exhibitions and installations that deal with issues of migration and mobility. Today's performance is 'Undesirable Elements', a theatre project staged by American-Chinese director Ching Pong that deals with individual experiences of migration and exclusion. The House takes pride in featuring cutting-edge cosmopolitan artwork that embodies the artistic and cultural consequences of globalization and intercultural cooperation.

It is not just on the main stage of the House that exclusion is at issue, though. Two heavy-set bouncers flank the main gates of the building, trying to separate those who have come for the festival from those who want to use the building's toilet facilities. The latter are sent to the back entrance of the building. Women with features deemed Middle Eastern, headscarves and children by their side are turned away immediately. Young boys with empty water bottles in their hands are chased away with even less courtesy. Visitors who fit the stereotypical embodiments of non-immigrant Germans are let through. There is some hesitation with male adults of apparently Middle Eastern origin. If they are determined enough, not hesitating on their way inside, the guards watch closely, but let them through without a word. Others are turned away. No-one seems to protest.

The scene above encapsulates the tensions that arise from an urban cultural agenda of cosmopolitanism, central to Berlin's attempts to position itself as a world city, and its inescapable rootedness in a particular geographical location that is marked by unequal diversity – tensions that are dealt with through different forms of managing and reterritorializing[1] space and culture(s). The Tiergarten park is part of the most desirable inner city area, bordering on the residence of the German Chancellor, the Reichstag parliament building, ministerial offices and Berlin's most notorious mega-project for real estate development, the Potsdamer Platz. In the midst of an urban restructuring process that increasingly restricts access to this area on the basis of political privileges and consumer power, the park is still open to city residents that are lacking both. Large parts of Berlin's migrant population are far removed from the centres of political decision-making, and at the same time disproportionately affected by poverty and the city's dramatic unemployment crisis.

This chapter explores the contradictions between restructuring efforts that seek to capitalize on Berlin's image as a cosmopolitan city and the management of its 'really existing' ethno-cultural diversity. Culture and mobility is a key to the production and regulation of urban space along both of these lines, with different consequences for various groups of urban dwellers. Cosmopolitanism and multiculturalism function as practical ideologies in efforts to market the city to affluent and economically successful groups that appreciate diversity, and to contain the consequences of an increasing socio-economic polarization that is heavily ethnicized. While the creative cosmopolitan urbanite is widely expected to be both geographically mobile and have the ability to draw upon vocabularies and discourses from a variety of cultural repertoires (Hannerz 1990; Škrbiš, Kendall and Woodward 2004), the alleged cultural differences of economically weak migrants are often identified as culprits in urban conflicts and as central targets for integration measures. The mobility exhibited by migrants who do not muster the necessary economic, social and cultural capital to qualify as cosmopolitan in this sense is similarly seen as problematic. While Berlin vies with other metropolitan aspirants for the attention of global business elites and culturally eclectic world citizens, the city's strategies for managing and containing poor migrants have a very different localizing intention and impact. Importantly, it is not just in the field of urban restructuring and transformation of public space that such differential management can be observed: urban cultural institutions such as the House of World Cultures (*Haus der Kulturen der Welt*) and the wider field of cultural policy in Berlin perform strikingly similar tasks with regard to conceptualizing and localizing cultural diversity. In their practices and discourses, the 'cosmopolitan' city is one that offers its cultural riches to the sampling connoisseur of global

---

1   Neil Brenner (1999) has highlighted the importance of considering relatively immobile forms of territorial organizations such as cities in the context of globalization, pointing out that the latter is linked to a reterritorialization of socioeconomic and political-institutional spaces rather than to deterritorialization.

trends, not to be confused with the ethnic minority bearers of a cultural diversity that are mostly dealt with in terms of 'multicultural' policies and agendas.

This chapter presents empirical material that was gathered by the author in Berlin as part of a three-year European Union Fifth Framework project on cultural policy and immigrant inclusion in different European cities (www.citynexus. com). The results of comparative qualitative research that included interviews with cultural policy makers, representatives of cultural institutions and immigrant artists, as well as participant observation at cultural events, have been published in more detail elsewhere (Kosnick 2007; Meinhof and Triandafyllidou 2006). This chapter focuses on selected material that can demonstrate how cultural policy and interlinked institutional practices in Berlin mirror the management of urban 'diversity' in other policy domains. It compares the self-understanding and mission statements of two cultural institutions that exemplify complementary strategies of producing Berlin as a city both cosmopolitan and multicultural, and draws upon additional interview material with policy makers and artists to show how managing diversity involves both the commodification and reification of cultural differences.

Cosmopolitanism and Multiculturalism

As with many key concepts that promise to open up new interdisciplinary perspectives as well as fields of academic and political engagement, debates on cosmopolitanism almost inevitably involve questions of definition. Noting the dangers of a cosmopolitan universalism that proclaims loyalty only to a rather abstract category of humanity as such, controversies range around the deployment of the term as a moral and philosophical concept, as a foundation for a globally thinking political theory, as a distinctive methodological approach or as emergent mundane practice (Beck 2004; Featherstone 2002; Held 2003; Roudometof 2005). 'Cosmopolitanism, indeed, is another word for disputing about cosmopolitanisms' (Beck 2002, 35). The uses of cosmopolitanism are manifold, and its meanings highly contested.

Controversies regarding an authoritative definition of cosmopolitanism easily run the danger of fetishizing the concept as if there was some definite meaning to be extracted and revealed, instead of focusing on its possible heuristic value in concrete projects of inquiry. A turn towards cosmopolitanism in practice offers the chance to address both the *Erkenntnisinteressen* (knowledge or cognitive interests) that inform scholarly projects of inquiry into matters deemed cosmopolitan, and the multiple situated meanings of the term that are produced in different socio-historical settings. These settings involve not just the outlooks and practices of 'ordinary' individuals, but also those of institutions, interest groups and policy makers who mobilize cosmopolitanism for a variety of political projects. Thus, what is the purchase that cultural institutions, commercial interest coalitions and city representatives hope to gain from promoting Berlin as a cosmopolitan city?

And what is its relationship to other concepts that have guided and fuelled different forms of urban diversity management and its cultural representation, most notably that of multiculturalism?

Like cosmopolitanism, multiculturalism in its various appearances as intellectual discourse, normative ideal and political project has been centrally concerned with respect for cultural diversity and tolerance towards cultural (usually meaning ethnic or 'racial') others (Taylor 1992; Kymlicka 1995). Both cosmopolitanism and multiculturalism exhibit in terms of ethics, interests and orientations a certain openness, eagerness and ability to engage with different cultural traditions and orientations that are 'strange' in their origin. Cosmopolitanism shares with multiculturalism the rejection of exclusively parochial or national cultural attachments, as well as the political aim to reconcile the principle of equality with the recognition of positively valued difference. Contemporary interest in both concepts is related to the perception of a 'shrinking world' in which human beings are confronted with 'others' and cultural 'otherness' in unprecedented ways. Yet, while cosmopolitanism considers the world to be its appropriate referent and scale of interest, multiculturalism tends to be more 'inward looking' and concerned with territorially limited spaces such as nation-states, cities or even local neighbourhoods. Various critiques of multiculturalism have criticized its culturally essentialist underpinnings (Beck 2002; Bhabha 1996; Reckwitz 2001; Werbner and Modood 1997). In contemporary discussions across the social and cultural sciences, multiculturalism appears as not only theoretically and politically problematic in its treatment of difference, but also seems somehow outdated, as talk of transnational connections and 'the global' has increasingly taken centre stage (Tsing 2000).

In line with its 'inward looking' orientation, multiculturalist urban policies and discourses treat the city as a local space and communally defined territory that needs to integrate its residential ethnic minority populations, seemingly regardless of their transnational affiliations and mobilities. Dominant invocations of urban cosmopolitanism, however, regard the city not as a local space that contains diversity but as a node in a global cultural network, open to a diversity of cultural flows. This is different from the multicultural city that focuses on the coexistence of cultures related to immigration, without the added sense of navigating different cultural repertoires and connectedness to the world. Multiculturalism seeks to ensure equal rights and recognition for 'minority cultures' that cohabit as a result of migration, whereas cosmopolitanism looks outward towards the world, acknowledging otherness as a universal condition and challenge. The multicultural city is conceptualized as the end point of migratory movements that produce cultural mosaics, while the cosmopolitan city appears as a node in global cultural flows, ideally structuring their intermingling harmoniously and benefiting from them as sources of innovation.

Despite these differences, cosmopolitanism and multiculturalism can easily coexist and complement each other as different strategies and emblems of managing cultural diversities in concrete fields of urban policy making and cultural production. If cities have historically been the 'privileged, if not necessarily exclusive, sites for the emergence of the form of life that we call the cosmopolitan' (Abbas 2000, 772), they have also been a privileged site for developing and implementing multiculturalist policies that have in turn influenced national debates.[2] In Berlin, both cosmopolitanism and multiculturalism figure prominently in efforts to transform, to govern and to successfully market the city. The division of labour that exists between them allows for existing contradictions and potential conflicts to remain submerged and subdued, operating along a 'fuzzy logic' of ideology that is decidedly pragmatist in its orientation.

'Weltoffenes' Berlin

Once a year, the acting mayor of the city and the *Berlin Partner GmbH*, a public-private partnership organization that markets the city as an attractive investment and business location, organize an illustrious party at the city hall. The *Hoffest* party is designed to bring together prominent 'movers and shakers' from politics, the business world, sports, culture and academic institutions, while presenting Berlin as a world open city, as the invitational brochure states:

> Berlin – creative, innovative and world open city. Berlin is a city of contrasts, a city in motion: here you find old next to new, experience next to innovation, metropolitan life and lots of culture next to peace and relaxation in parks and countryside. This mixture and the openness of Berliners towards the new attract young people and creatives from all over the world. They bring new life to the city and are themselves providing the impulse for the creative climate … Half a million people from 180 nations live in Berlin. Together with embassies, cultural institutes, institutions and organizations acting worldwide, they create a world open atmosphere. They are joined each year by 6,5 million visitors from all over the world.

Whenever the term 'weltoffen', the German translation for cosmopolitan, appears in conjunction with the city of Berlin, it is almost always its value as an economic location factor that is at issue. In a global climate where major cities increasingly feel themselves to be in transnational competition with each other, public-private partnerships seek to restructure and market urban space in order to attract foreign investment and tourism (Redak 1998). The city's cosmopolitan qualities are thus an essential selling point – to attract not the world as such, to

---

2 Examples include the anti-racist campaigns and educational programmes of the Greater London Council (Back 1996); the Agency for Multicultural Affairs in Frankfurt/ Main and the Office for Foreigner Affairs in Berlin, both of which inspired similar initiatives at the national level; the Intercultural Affairs Bureau in Montreal and the Hastings Institute in Vancouver (Sandercock 2004).

which it is allegedly open, but those who are currently the developers' main hope for economic success and global reputation. Openness is key to the cosmopolitan city. This openness means more than simply tolerance of difference: it signals an active embrace of particular influences that come from the city's outside. Valuing the new implies movement and progress, the continuous transformation of city life as captured in the term 'innovation'. Linking change to improvement, the term is firmly embedded in the language of business and marketing strategies: Berlin is presented as an attractive location for evolving business sectors that regard innovation as an essential factor of economic survival and success.

This is anything but extraordinary. In the wake of what might be called 'a dramatic explosion of global place-marketing' and inter-urban competition (Cochrane and Jonas 1999, 145), Berlin is simply emulating strategies that are employed by cities and urban growth coalitions all over the world in order not to be sidelined by the emerging networked geographies of globalization (Sassen 2000; 2002). Its position, however, is anything but promising. A city that has officially declared bankruptcy after a spate of financial scandals, has lost national subsidies after unification and has seen its manufacturing industries collapse, post-unification Berlin has the slowest economic growth of all new federal states in the Eastern part of Germany. The move of the capital to Berlin has not had the invigorating impact on the labour market that was hoped for. The city's unemployment rate is at a staggering 18 per cent, and little has remained of the reunification boom that saw an unprecedented building industry and redevelopment frenzy in the early 1990s.

Far from fulfilling the criteria necessary to qualify as a world city in Saskia Sassen's sense of the term, Berlin can only try to capitalize on its cultural-industrial potential. Thus, even though the terms in which the city's advocates attempt to present it as a dynamic and desirable location are far from original, the emphasis on the creative cultural potential, ethno-cultural diversity and youthful world-openness of Berlin carries extra weight precisely because the city cannot capitalize on most of the other factors seen as essential for metropolitan development (Bilger 2003; Krätke 2001). Instead, marketing strategists promote Berlin increasingly as a 'city of talents', pointing to the actually emerging clusters of '"knowledge intensive" industries which rely on creative knowledge and innovative capacity' (Krätke 2004, 516). Berlin's culture and media industries in particular have seen surprising growth in a period of overall economic decline, including film and television production, design, music and publishing, performing arts and multimedia. The city is hailed as Germany's 'music capital', and in 2005, UNESCO appointed Berlin to its worldwide 'Creative Cities Network', awarding it the title of 'City of Design'.

Berlin's socio-cultural qualities take on special importance in this context. Its city planners and developers have fully taken on board the lessons taught by Richard Florida concerning urban attractiveness for the so-called 'creative class' that is essential to economic growth in contemporary metropolitan centres (Florida 2002). Only cities that provide a vibrant climate of talent, technology and tolerance will succeed in becoming powerhouses of economic development,

Florida has argued. In his more recent *Flight of the Creative Class* (Florida 2005), he claims a key advantage for tolerant cities with a high percentage of immigrants and liberal policies regarding different lifestyles, sexual orientations and beliefs. Such cities are able to attract 'creative' people who want to live not just where the jobs are, but where living conditions seem particularly attractive. As Krätke (2004, 518) argues in his analysis of Berlin:

> Cities of this kind are perceived as a living space with a socio-cultural milieu that is marked by great openness and an atmosphere of tolerance. This in turn enhances their attractiveness for creative talents and makes them a source of inspiration for cultural producers, etc. A marked social and cultural variety and openness, therefore, represents a specific 'cultural capital' of a city, which is highly attractive for the actors of the creative economy.

Berlin's policy makers and marketing strategists have learnt their lesson. Despite its bankruptcy, the city continues to spend a substantive amount of its yearly budget on funding cultural institutions and activities. The city is clearly living beyond its means, supporting a cultural life that is second to none in Germany despite crippling debts (Burns and Van der Will 2003). The national government lends additional support to institutions that are deemed to boost Berlin's positive image as a capital city both nationally and internationally. The House of World Cultures mentioned at the beginning of this chapter has received federal funds since 2001, in order to help turn Berlin into a 'global city of cultures'.[3] Its online mission statement presents an agenda that aims to remain at the cutting edge of contemporary cultural and globalization theories.

> Migration, international networks, encounters with other traditions and other modernities have transformed cultural conditions throughout the world and created new conditions for art. National cultures, even where they are still experienced as homogeneous by many people, no longer ensure binding cultural affiliation. … All over the world, artists, authors and scientists are relating to these changes in their works. In co-operation with them, the House of World Cultures seeks to develop a programme presenting responses and artistic models that reflect these international conditions in terms of what they mean for the individual and for human beings living together in a global world. (<http://www. hkw.de/en/hkw/selbstdarstellung/2.php> accessed 2 February 2007)

---

3   As it was envisioned in a speech by the then Senator for Science, Research and Culture, Christoph Stölzl, given on December 7, 2000: '*Auch wer in die* Kultur *investiert, baut an einem Zukunftsbild unserer Stadt: einer* global city *der Kulturen.*' (Those investing in *culture* also contribute to the future image of our city: a *global city* of cultures.) <http:// www.berlinews.de/senwfk/archiv/95.shtml> accessed 10 January 2007.

Its artistic cosmopolitanism links up with art institutes all over the world, aided by an advisory board of artists and scholars of 'international standing', as the director of the House put it in an interview.[4] Arjun Appadurai and Homi Bhabha were among those who crucially influenced his vision, he stated, helping him realize that there was something wrong with the concept of culture still dominant in Germany:

> I know one thing for sure, there is still a very rigid concept of culture predominant here in Germany. Cultures are understood as islands that ought to be within calling range. But what we need is a virtual, flexible, completely open concept of culture.

It is such an 'open' understanding of culture that informs thematic orientations at the House, with activities such as the yearly *In Transit* festival emphasizing mobility and change, shifting cultural boundaries and emerging aesthetic processes. A 2007 focus on New York takes the city as paradigmatic for contemporary megacities, modelling 'the interrelationships of cultures as they have developed in the age of globalization'. New York can set examples for major European cities like Berlin, it is argued, since the metropolis 'is a catalyst of artistic-cultural and aesthetic processes which are received in the city on the Hudson from around the world, transform themselves in the urban context, and radiate back with new – and also commercial – meaning'.[5] The House can certainly not be accused of exclusively foregrounding the commercial potential of the cultural developments it is trying to highlight. However, there are obvious parallels between the 'virtual, flexible, completely open' concept of culture that the House wants to promote and the 'creative, innovative and worldopen' image of Berlin that is marketed in order to compete for the attention of global 'creative classes'.

'Multicultural' Berlin

The numbers of members of the 'creative class' flocking to Berlin are small, however, when compared to a different kind of immigration that makes up a substantial part of the city's population. Of the 13 per cent of Berlin residents who carry a foreign passport, most have come as labour migrants or refugees with low educational status and few job qualifications. The invitation the city once extended towards 'guestworkers' has long expired, and they are the primary victims of the socio-economic polarization that has taken place in Berlin over the past 15 years. Their descendents are disproportionately failed by the school system and face

---

4   Author's interview with Hans-Georg Knopp, 21 August 2003.
5   Quotes stem from the online preview of the New York event, to be found at <http://www.hkw.de/en/programm2007/new_york/projekt-detail_3.php> accessed 6 February 2007.

extremely high rates of unemployment. In terms of spatial segregation, the urban poor of which they form a part are concentrated in a number of inner-city districts and neighbourhoods that are defined as urban 'problem zones', targeted by special management and policing measures.

Ever since the political admission that Germany's labour migrant population was 'there to stay', culture and cultural differences have figured large in national debates on migrant integration and the place of ethnic minorities in German society. They have been heavily influenced by debates and policies that were developed in urban contexts, where the large majority of labour migrants had settled. Cities such as Frankfurt am Main and Berlin set up departments for 'multicultural affairs' and appointed commissioners for 'foreigners', proceeding from the assumption that (a) each ethno-national group of immigrants had its own 'culture', and that (b) cultural traditions and differences were a major factor to be reckoned with when it came to social integration. Such basic tenets of multiculturalist thinking tied into a field of cultural policy making and institution building that had developed in Germany in the 1970s, namely the field of socio-culture. Distinct from the 'high cultural' arena of artistic excellence, socio-culture has been concerned with cultural production as a form of self-realization and social participation, geared towards the social integration of participants (Deutscher Städtetag 1992). The concept of *Soziokultur* emphasized the importance of creative activities for personal growth and social cohesion, particularly at the grass-roots level of neighbourhoods and city districts. Multiculturalist paradigms have been integrated into socio-culture with the claim that 'maintaining one's own culture' would promote the social integration of migrants and put them on an equal and harmonious footing with their non-migrant neighbours. Berlin's city districts with high levels of immigrant residents all feature their own 'day of cultures' (*Tag der Kulturen*) to promote 'peaceful cohabitation' among different ethnic groups. These events feature music, dance, theatre and 'ethnic' foods, usually supported by different migrant organizations and funds from different sources ranging from the 'social city programme' to European Union funds and federal funds.

At the city level, resident immigrants can apply to obtain money for cultural projects from a fund called 'project support in the area of cultural activities of foreign-descent citizens', which is part of the meagerly funded socio-culture category within the overall culture budget of Berlin. Its aims are to fund artistic and socio-cultural projects of immigrants '(...) that focus on the protection and development of cultural identity and/or on the promotion of intercultural dialogue'.[6] A similar agenda is pursued by a cultural institution that receives funding from the city's Commissioner for Integration and Migration, the Workshop of Cultures (*Werkstatt der Kulturen*). Whereas the House of World Cultures has its home within a stone's throw of the German Chancellor's office in the centre of the city, the Workshop is located in one of Berlin's poorest neighbourhoods with a high

---

6 This text can be found in the 2003 leaflet published by the Berlin Senate Administration for Science, Research and Culture.

percentage of immigrant residents. Conceptualized as a 'workshop for integration in a new Berlin' in the early 1990s, the Workshop wants to play an active role in facilitating intercultural encounter, exchange and transformation among different ethnic, cultural and religious groups. As a 'forum for the multicultural civil society', it foregrounds not so much artistic as social criteria and goals, stating in its online profile that it understands itself 'as a place of active citizenship and self-determined engagement with the legal and political processes of the democratic society'. Its main high-profile activity is the yearly Carnival of Cultures, advertised as a demonstration of Berlin's cultural diversity by 'participants from more than eighty nations living in Berlin'.[7] In this context, the cultural diversity of urban life in Berlin is understood as a multiplicity of ethnic groups, mobilized to display their cultural distinctiveness in public. A form of 'picturesque multiculturalism' (Frei 2003) which reduces culture to a marker of ethnic or national group identity is central to the Carnival's choreography and reception.

The Carnival manages to draw around 1.5 million visitors a year and thus significantly contributes to Berlin's marketable cosmopolitan image. But the visibility of 'otherness' in such heavily aestheticized and commodified terms – picturesque diversity as a tourist event – does nothing to address the actual forms of marginalization and conflict that mark the lives of many immigrants in the city. Neither does it unsettle the division of labour between the Workshop of Cultures and the House of World Cultures that was introduced above: the Workshop of Cultures operates as a firmly socio-cultural institution, rather than an arts-oriented one. The House of World Cultures, on the other hand, strongly rejects sociocultural projects as part of its own agenda. It also rejects any particular responsibility for showing the work of immigrant or postmigrant artists, or targeting immigrants as part of its audience, deeming this the task of the Workshop of Cultures. Importantly, then, a correlation can be detected between immigrant and postmigrant cultural production and the domain of socio-culture, with institutional structures and public funding schemes favouring the recognition and evaluation of such production in integrationist terms (Kosnick 2004).

While the Workshop mobilizes and addresses mainly underprivileged migrants within a multiculturalist agenda that foregrounds social integrationist aims, the House addresses cultural globalization, migration and diversity as challenges to Eurocentric conceptions of high art that need to open up towards the non-Western world in order not to lose touch with creative progress worldwide. World openness at the House means to be tied into global developments in the arts, and to be part of a worldwide network of art institutions that link Berlin to cities like Singapore, Seoul, Sao Paulo, Beijing, Mumbai, New York and Los Angeles. Multiculturalism at the Workshop means to address social problems of immigrants via cultural means, in order to promote 'intercultural' harmony and integration.

---

7   2003 leaflet published by the Berlin Senate Administration for Science, Research and Culture.

Migrant Artists: Facing the Double Bind

For artists with migrant backgrounds living and working in Berlin, the divide between cosmopolitan and multicultural orientations in different areas of urban policy making leads to a curious dilemma: unless they have already made a name for themselves internationally, the city offers rather unfavourable conditions for developing one's reputation as an artist. The various funding opportunities available in the context of 'socio-culture' at the level of neighbourhoods, districts or the above-mentioned city-wide project support address migrant artists as representatives of ethnic minorities, whose work ought to preserve cultural identities or promote intercultural dialogue within a multiculturalist frame. Their work is valued with regard to social-integrationist aims, not as artistic contributions in their own right. It is thus rare to see the work of Berlin's migrant artists represented at the House of World Cultures, for example. Its director has been adamant that the House has no role to play in promoting the artistic careers of local migrant artists:

> Time and again people try to take such socio-cultural projects to the House of World Cultures, and we have to be very sharp in our opposition ... We don't support these makeshift socio-cultural exhibitions, projects, whatever, that meet no standards. I still think that an artist is either good or he (sic) isn't. No matter where he comes from, no matter in which milieu he is working, he is either good or not. And I don't give any credit because of someone's origin, not in an art project. Neither positive nor negative.[8]

While the concern with 'quality' is understandable given the House's lack of interest in socio-cultural integration goals, the director problematically equates an interest in Berlin's locally developing migrant artists with a socio-cultural agenda, deeming them implicitly unfit to meet the criteria for 'good' artwork. Local migrant artists find themselves in a double bind, because the very policy measures undertaken to promote migrants' art reveal themselves to function as barriers, tying them to the production of 'migrant art' that embodies only multicultural and never cosmopolitan visions. Even the very affirmative action tool intended to increase the participation of migrant artists, the city fund for 'citizens of foreign descent', has become something of a trap, keeping artists out of other funding circuits which offer considerably more money and opportunities for career development. A Senate Administration representative for the fund stated in 2003 that the jury that makes funding decisions in the area of non-institutionalized theatre projects regularly turns away migrant applicants, advising them to rather submit an application to the 'foreign descent' fund.[9] Instead of providing additional assistance for migrant artists, the fund thus actually poses a hindrance to migrant participation in

---

8 Author's interview with Hans-Georg Knopp, see above.

9 Author's interview with Manfred Fischer at the Berlin Senate Administration for Science, Research and Culture, 20 May 2003.

'mainstream' categories of cultural production, effectively limiting their artistic activities to the realm of socio-culture.

Another problem arises with regard to the actual 'openness' of Berlin's mainstream cultural establishment to non-Western art forms. Turkish and Ottoman music provides the most pertinent example. Despite more than four decades of Turkish migration to Berlin, it took until 1999 for a German university, the University of the Arts (*Universität der Künste, UdK*) to offer a first introductory class on 'The Music of Turkey', staffed by members of Berlin's privately-run Conservatory for Turkish Music. Its founder Nuri Karademirli has been fighting for years to get his Conservatory accredited by German state agencies – without success. German administrators decided that it lacked a broad enough range of subjects as well as sufficiently qualified staff (Greve 2002). Karademirli felt that the real problem was both the unwillingness of the Berlin administration to seriously consider his application and their lack of competence to evaluate his school's instruction.[10] Given the relative dearth of exceptional Turkish musicians qualified to teach at an institution of higher education in Berlin, his Conservatory was conceptualized as a transnational project from the start. Members of Istanbul's prestigious State Conservatory regularly come to Berlin to teach and to conduct exams. For students, the lack of accreditation means that they cannot apply for student loans and are not eligible for tax breaks and other reductions such as cheap public transport tickets. But what is more, the institutional and wider popular disregard for Turkish musical traditions and genres means that few of them can hope to enter professional musical careers in Germany.[11]

Instead, many of those studying at the Conservatory orient themselves towards a possible career in Turkey. Since the arrival of satellite television in many Turkish migrant households over the course of the 1990s, channels from Turkey are a familiar presence in daily life routines, even for young people. Karademirli proudly revealed that several of his students had performed well in Turkey's state television singing competition, broadcast on the widely available channel TRT-International. Nationwide amateur singing contests have been a regular feature of state broadcasting, but in 2000, a separate competition was started for Turkish migrants living in Western Europe. Its 2001 finale took place in Berlin, and one of Karademirli's students came in first place, securing immediate publicity and a possible recording career in Turkey.

A number of singers rising to fame in the country have a personal migration background, most prominently pop-idol Tarkan. While Karademirli shuddered to think that his students might join the ranks of Turkey's pop industry, his students

---

10 Author's interview with Nuri Karademirli, 11 September 2003.

11 Berlin's Music Council (*Landesmusikrat*) has added the *bağlama*, Turkey's most famous plucked string instrument, to its *Jugend Musiziert* youth competition in 2002 (Greve 2002). This marks an important first step in the acceptance of non-Western musical traditions and instruments, but young talents cannot move on and compete at the national level.

were much more open to the thought. Given the lack of recognition and interest in Germany, a career in Turkey seemed like the only at least vaguely realistic option. The relatively young genre of Turkish pop is widely perceived as 'westernized' music in Turkey, making it easier for migrants to play a role despite their alleged disconnection from Turkish musical traditions. Media liberalization, in conjunction with the movement of multinational companies into Turkey's music industry, has against most expectations not led to diversification but to a 'stifling conformity' (Stokes 1999, 127) that favours the new genre of Turkish pop. Paradoxically, the industrially manufactured pop star whose success relies upon heavy advertising investment and distribution systems of major industry players might just as well be a young migrant 'discovered' on television as someone emerging from Turkey's music academies. The contemporary forms of capitalist music commodification thus appear to offer an opening to young migrant artists who have little hope of being admitted to the high cultural establishment in Turkey or Germany.

In Germany, commercial recognition for musicians with a migration background from Turkey has been exclusively reserved for rap and hip hop artists. Well-known musicians Aziza A., Islamic Force, Cartel and Erci E. were among those who encountered rap and hip hop in the context of Berlin's youth centres, where rapping was offered as an appropriately urban cultural activity for young people, with heavy class and racialized inflections. Celebrated as an authentic and creative expression of marginalized youth, cultural forms such as rap, breakdance and graffiti were not simply 'discovered' by young migrants. Instead, they were mediated through specific institutions such as the Berlin Senate, agencies for social work, nonprofit organizations and youth centres, specifically in neighbourhoods with a large proportion of immigrants (Çağlar 1998). Here again it was a social policy agenda that promoted the spread of hip hop as a form of cultural creativity appropriate to disadvantaged migrant youths. While not 'culturalist' in the ethno-national sense of multiculturalist paradigms, a different kind of culturalism is implied in the celebration of rap: the celebration of ghetto culture as a cultural space at the periphery of the centre, as Ayşe Çağlar (1998) has put it.

Yet, does the engagement with an almost globally successful musical genre not provide 'a language and sound to a "peer group" of youths world-wide' (Soysal 1999, 138), connecting Turkish to a 'global ecumene' and helping them to articulate a cosmopolitan vision? Various arguments have been made that connect Turkish-German hip hop youths to different cosmopolitan visions of culture, by way of forming transnational networks (Burul 2003), developing 'cosmopolitan and transnational third cultures' as members of a diaspora (Kaya 2001, 211), or by connecting 'in tangible dreams to their counterparts in Sheffield, Rotterdam, Paris, and New York' (Soysal 1999, 169). Indeed, Aziza A. names close friends in Berlin, New York and Istanbul in her song *Outro* on her album *Kendi Dünyam*, and moves seemingly effortlessly between English, German and Turkish. In the song *Selaminaleyküm*, MC Boe-B of *Islamic Force* wants to connect with his Turkish roots in Kadiköy, a neighbourhood in Istanbul. And Soysal's hip hop informants refer to universal ideas of tolerance and unity-in-diversity in their fight against racism and gang warfare, true to the motto 'Think Globally – Act Locally' (Soysal 1999, 150).

However, in the work and statements of most rap artists, the 'ghetto' or 'the street' remains the central point of reference, and ties to a marginalized urban territorial space are mobilized to authenticate one's experience and claim to represent. It is to 'their counterparts' that migrant hip hop artists may legitimately connect in the world, even if their music can, once commodified and circulated, feed into the lifestyle and consumption practices of more privileged youth cultures. They know quite well that heavily aestheticized tales of ghetto life and strife resonate well with a global music industry that trademarks and markets cultural exoticisms in various guises. This is not to say that migrant youths cannot display agency and cultural creativity in rap music, and that their visions need to remain localized. But interpreting their activities as forms of resistance to marginalization and cultural essentialism risks to ignore their embeddedness into both state policies of urban integration and global culture industries that relentlessly turn cultural differences into consumer items and thus shape the experiences of 'banal cosmopolitanism' (Beck 2002; Nghi Ha 2005). Investing hope in the rebellious and liberating qualities of music as cultural politics is problematic, John Hutnyk has argued, because 'co-option into the assimilation project of the multiculture of capital is all too readily always on offer', and offers rewards only to a select few (Hutnyk 2000, 122).

Aziza A. herself was not particularly drawn to hip hop, but was told that this was the genre where she could accomplish her breakthrough. For her second album, released in 2001 and featuring very different sounds, integrating soul, jazz and only very few rap vocals, she had to move to Istanbul's worldmusic label Doublemoon Records. In Berlin, her career could not progress beyond occasional concerts in small venues, a weekly radio show on Berlin's public service radio station *Radio Multikulti*, and different cooperative projects within Berlin's Turkish-German music and film scene. While her work and life could be described cosmopolitan in the strong sense of a self-reflexive openness towards and creative engagement with different global cultural influences, Berlin's cultural policies and cultural industries emplaced and trapped her as firmly multicultural, forever concerned with German-Turkish identity issues and questions of ghettoized belonging. In 2006, she decided to move to Istanbul altogether. By then, the Turkish-German hip hop scene had by and large exhausted its promise of commercial potential for the music industries serving the German market. Its protagonists had begun to fade from the feature pages of music magazines and from the all-important German music channels, if not from the repertoire of youth centres and state-funded nonprofit organizations targeting young migrants in Berlin. Once producing the work of Aziza A. and other local talents, Berlin producer Ünal Yüksel has become pessimistic regarding Turkish-German musicians' chances to break into the German music market. Local producers, he said, have mostly folded operations or have entered into alliances with Turkey's music industry.[12] His company now promotes the German sales of Turkey's megastars such as Sezen Aksu, signed by Plak Records which is now a division of the multinational Warner Bros Records. Even Berlin's own commercial Turkish radio station *Metropol FM* shies away from showcasing the music of local talent, and relies on 'safe' music imports from Turkey that have the backing and support of large corporations.[13] Thus, as young Turkish-German artists look towards Turkey when planning their music careers, their 'everyday transnationalism' acquires a somewhat bitter taste, enforced by cultural politics and commercial pressures that leave them little hope for local success.

Culture and Mobility

The trials and tribulations of a Turkish-German hip hop artist, barbecues and back doors in the park, cultural policy provisions and urban marketing strategies – this assortment of seemingly disparate observations reveals more systematic qualities once we ask how culture and mobility figure in related projects of boundary management in the production and transformation of Berlin as a cosmopolitan and multicultural city.

Despite the long genealogy of the concept of cosmopolitanism, it has taken on new and much more urgent connotations as a political and social science concern in the context of contemporary globalization. Whereas early modern and enlightenment *kosmopolitês* ('citizens of the world') could imagine the world as a space of bounded places, contemporary cosmopolitanism relates to a 'world of flows'. The mantra of globalization evokes visions of unfettered mobility and unbounded space (Massey 2005), in which the ability to productively cope with strange encounters has become a necessity rather than a chosen vocation. The cosmopolitan city similarly needs to navigate global flows in order not to be left behind (time seems to annihilate space) or submerged (in wholly naturalized 'waves' of undesired migrants, for example). In a world that is perceived to be in constant flux, control over motility (people's mobility potential) and movement become central concerns for projects of management and governance – individual, state, commercial, and also urban. As strategies of managing and governing the city, cosmopolitanism and multiculturalism exercise control over mobility in different, yet complementary ways.

Berlin's urban cosmopolitanism presents the city as a node that intensifies and consolidates cultural flows for the ultimate purpose of relentless business innovation. Opening the city to investors, tourists and creative classes, its cultural diversity is presented as both consumer item and as evidence of a tolerant and world-open habitat in which creatives can thrive. Berlin's multiculturalism, on

---

12 Author's interview with Ünal Yüksel, 23 September 2003.
13 Author's interview with Werner Felten, acting director, 11 June 2003.

the other hand, conceives the city as a spatially fixed mosaic of bounded ethnic groups, in which both cultures and places are in need of protection and integration. Whereas the motility of those targeted by cosmopolitan marketing strategies is taken as a given, multiculturalist policies seek to control and limit the motility and movement of economically expendable migrants in cultural and spatial terms. The state-promoted hip hop culture that celebrates the ghetto as the only possible and authentic experience of the real feeds into the politics of spatial containment and segregation that are shored up by privatization of public space and new strategies of policing the poor (Eick 2003). In Berlin, such strategies involve the declaration of neighbourhoods, squares or districts as 'problem areas', 'disadvantaged areas' and 'dangerous places' (*gefährliche Orte*) where the police can suspend civil rights.[14] Fifteen areas have been targeted by special district management teams (*Quartiersmanagement*), trying to set up local coalitions of government, private sector and civil society organizations in order to build local capacities and start community programmes. Their measures are framed in the social capital discourse of urban restructuring that focuses on marginalized local residents as agents of their own survival (Mayer 2003). Self-help and grassroots participation are to empower and re-integrate marginalized populations, but not in the sense of tackling the causes of inequality. Rather, the goal is to transform urban disadvantaged groups into '"social capitalists", whose "belonging" is conditional on their mobilizing the only resources they have as a form of capital' (Mayer 2003, 125).

In Berlin's 'disadvantaged areas', 'security' has emerged as a central focus of urban restructuring, and poor local residents themselves are mobilized and drawn into order and control measures. Thus, welfare recipients are retrained and employed as low-wage security workers by local nonprofits in the interest of neighbourhood 'self-regulation', enforcing control practices that target particularly often young migrant men. Permanent patrolling of public space and expulsion of those deemed dangerous or disruptive, enclosure projects and 'clean-up' drives combine to limit movement in public space and produce new forms of social and spatial exclusion. Interestingly, as Eick describes, the 'order and control measures ... are called "integrative projects" by all the involved actors' (Eick 2003, 376). The language of community empowerment and grassroots activism hides the fact that poor are employed against poor, and that they are employed to control and discipline, rather than to enforce and promote common rights.

New forms of governance that practice exclusion through 'integration' measures stabilize a polarization of urban space that results from the competitive transformation of Berlin into a node of neo-liberal globalization flows. This transformation has no economic need for the large majority of poorly educated and qualified migrants who are disproportionately located in those quarters designated as 'disadvantaged areas'. More than half of young migrants in hot-spot districts such as Kreuzberg were effectively unemployed by the turn of the millennium,

---

14 Leading to identity checks without credible suspicion, body searches, evictions (see Eick 2003).

a situation that is expected only to worsen in the future. The unsurprising consequences of rising poverty, unemployment and steadily shrinking welfare state provisions are making headlines in culturalist terms: violent behaviour and delinquency are discussed as signs of a failed cultural integration, calling for more 'integrationist' measures that feed both the growing security industry and multiculturalist agendas aiming for harmony and tolerance between ethnic groups. Instead of targeting the causes of poverty and unemployment, 'security' measures and 'multicultural integration' work towards the local containment and self-regulation of groups that have no stake in Berlin's cosmopolitan world city dreams. Yet, as ideologies that enable and guide complementary practices of urban restructuring in the city, cosmopolitanism and multiculturalism stand revealed as being intimately related. In Berlin, there is indeed 'no cosmopolitanism without localism' (Beck 2002, 19), albeit with a twist that does not mirror the optimism of the prominent advocats of cosmopolitan transformations.

This chapter has tried to argue that ideologies of cosmopolitanism and multiculturalism can figure prominently in contemporary urban policies that seek to both manage and capitalize on cultural 'diversity'. Far from being incompatible, in Berlin they fuel complementary practices of selling the city as a cosmopolitan node in global networks of creative and profitable innovation, while at the same time advancing policies whose culturally essentialist underpinnings are key to managing and policing increasingly segregated urban spaces without tackling the root causes of social and economic inequality.

References

Abbas, A. (2000), 'Cosmopolitan De-scriptions: Shanghai and Hong Kong', *Public Culture* 12:3, 769–86.

Back, L. (1996), *New Ethnicities and Urban Culture: Racism and Multiculture in Young Lives* (London: Routledge).

Beck, U. (2002), 'The Cosmopolitan Society and its Enemies', *Theory, Culture & Society* 19:1–2, 17–44.

— (2004), 'Cosmopolitical Realism: On the Distinction between Cosmopolitanism in Philosophy and the Social Sciences', *Global Networks* 4:2, 131–56.

Bhabha, H. (1996), 'Culture's In-Between', in Hall and Gay (eds).

Bilger, A. (2003), 'Metropole der Kultur(en): Berlin als Standort der neuen Inhaltsindustrien', in Raiser and Volkmann (eds).

Brenner, N. (1999), 'Globalisation as Reterritorialisation: The Re-scaling of Urban Governance in the European Union', *Urban Studies* 36:3, 431–51.

Burns, R. and Van der Will, W. (2003), 'German Cultural Policy: An Overview', *International Journal of Cultural Policy* 9:2, 133–52.

Burul, Y. (2003), 'The World of Aziza A.: Third Spaces in Identities', *New Perspectives on Turkey* 28–9, 209–28.

Çağlar, A. (1998), 'Verordnete Rebellion. Deutsch-türkischer Rap und türkischer Pop in Berlin', in Mayer and Terkessidis (eds).

Cochrane, A. and Jonas, A. (1999), 'Reimagining Berlin: World City, National Capital or Ordinary Place?', *European Urban and Regional Studies* 6:2, 145–64.

Deutscher Städtetag (1992) (ed.), *DST-Beiträge zur Bildungs- und Kulturpolitik: Fünf Jahrzehnte kommunale Kulturpolitik. Vol. C.* (Köln: Deutscher Städtetag).

Eick, V. (2003), 'New Strategies of Policing the Poor: Berlin's Neo-Liberal Security System', *Policing and Society* 13:4, 365–79.

Featherstone, M. (2002), 'Cosmopolis: An Introduction', *Theory, Culture & Society* 19:1–2, 1–16.

— (ed.) (1990), *Global Culture: Nationalism, Globalization and Modernity* (London and Newbury Park: Sage).

Florida, R. (2002), *The Rise of the Creative Class: And How It's Transforming Work, Leisure, Community and Everyday Life* (New York: Basic Books).

— (2005), *The Flight of the Creative Class: The New Global Competition for Talent* (New York: Harper Collins).

Frei, K. (2003), *Wer sich Maskiert, Wird Integriert. Der Karneval der Kulturen in Berlin* (Berlin: Hans Schiler).

Greve, M. (2002), 'Der Marsch in die Institutionen: Auf der Suche nach Deutsch-türkischer Musikausbildung', *Üben & Musizieren* 1, 16–22.

Hall, S. and Gay, P.D. (eds), *Questions of Cultural Identity* (London: Sage).

Hannerz, U. (1990), 'Cosmopolitans and Locals in World Culture', in Featherstone (ed.).

Held, D. (2003), 'Cosmopolitanism: Globalisation Tamed?', *Review of International Studies* 29, 465–80.

Hutnyk, J. (2000), *Critique of Exotica: Music, Politics and the Culture Industry* (London: Pluto Press).

Kaya, A. (2001), *'Sicher in Kreuzberg': Constructing Diasporas: Turkish Hip-Hop Youth in Berlin* (Bielefeld: transcript Verlag).

Keyder, Ç. (ed.) (1999), *Istanbul: Between the Global and the Local* (Lanham, Maryland: Rowman & Littlefield Publishers).

Kosnick, K. (2004), 'The Gap between Culture and Cultures: Cultural Policy in Berlin and its Implications for Immigrant Cultural Production', *European University Institute Working Papers*, RSCAS No.41.

— (2007), *Migrant Media: Turkish Broadcasting and Multicultural Politics in Berlin* (Bloomington: Indiana University Press).

Krätke, S. (2001), 'Berlin: Towards a Global City?', *Urban Studies* 38:10, 1777–99.

— (2004), 'City of Talents? Berlin's Regional Economy, Socio-Spatial Fabric and "Worst Practice" Urban Governance', *International Journal of Urban and Regional Research* 28:3, 511–29.

Kymlicka, W. (1995), *Multicultural Citizenship. A Liberal Theory of Minority Rights* (Oxford: Oxford University Press).

Massey, D. (2005), *For Space* (London: Sage).

Mayer, M. (2004), 'The Onward Sweep of Social Capital: Causes and Consequences for Understanding Cities, Communities and Urban Movements', *International Journal of Urban and Regional Research* 27:1, 110–32.

Mayer, R. and Terkessidis, M. (eds) (1998), *Globalkolorit: Multikulturalismus und Populärkultur* (St. Andrä/Wördern: Hannibal Verlag).

Meinhof, U. and Triandafyllidou, A. (eds) (2006), *Transcultural Europe: Cultural Policy in the Changing European Space* (Basingstoke: Palgrave).

Nghi Ha, K. (2005), *Hype um Hybridität. Kultureller Differenzkonsum und postmoderne Verwertungstechniken im Spätkapitalismus* (Bielefeld: transcript Verlag).

Raiser, S. and Volkmann, K. (eds) (2003), *Die neue Welt der Städte: Metropolen in Zeiten der Globalisierung* (Berlin: Osteuropa-Institut der Freien Universität Berlin).

Reckwitz, A. (2001), 'Multikulturalismustheorien und der Kulturbegriff: Vom Homogenitätsmodell zum Modell kultureller Interferenzen', *Berliner Journal für Soziologie* 11:2, 179–200.

Redak, V. (1998), 'Demokratie in der Metropolenkonkurrenz', *Kurswechsel* 1, <http://www.beigewum.at/TCgi_Images/beigewum/20050215150759_1-98(6)redak.pdf> accessed 02 February 2007.

Roudometof, V. (2005), 'Transnationalism, Cosmopolitanism and Glocalization', *Current Sociology* 53:1, 113–35.

Sandercock, L. (2004), 'Sustaining Canada's Multicultural Cities: Learning from the Local'. Breakfast on the Hill Seminar Series, <http://www.fedcan.ca/english/pdf/fromold/breakfast-sandercock0204.pdf> accessed 23 January 2007.

Sassen, S. (2000), 'Ausgrabungen in der "Global City"', in Scharenberg (ed.).

— (ed.) (2002), *Global Networks, Linked Cities* (London and New York: Routledge).

Scharenberg, A. (ed.) (2000), *Berlin: Globale City oder Konkursmasse? Eine Zwischenbilanz zehn Jahre nach dem Mauerfall* (Berlin: Karl Dietz Verlag).

Škrbiš, Z., Kendall, G. and Woodward, I. (2004), 'Locating Cosmopolitanism: Between Humanist Ideal and Grounded Social Category', *Theory, Culture & Society* 21:6, 115–36.

Soysal, L. (1999), *Projects of Culture: An Ethnographic Episode in the Life of Migrant Youth in Berlin* (Doctoral Dissertation submitted to the Department of Anthropology, Harvard University, Cambridge), May 1999.

Stokes, M. (1999), 'Sounding Out: The Culture Industries and the Globalization of Istanbul', in Keyder (ed.).

Taylor, C. (1992), *Multiculturalism and 'The Politics of Recognition'* (Princeton: Princeton University Press).

Tsing, A. (2000), 'The Global Situation', *Cultural Anthropology* 15:3, 327–60.

Werbner, P. and Modood, T. (eds) (1997), *Debating Cultural Hybridity: Multi-Cultural Identities and the Politics of Anti-Racism* (London and New Jersey: Zed Books).

Chapter 10

Religion and the Challenges of Cosmopolitanism: Young Portuguese Volunteers in Africa

Maria Rovisco

Introduction

Volunteering has many different meanings and definitions which are rooted in particular cultural and political traditions across different nation-states. In the Western world, volunteering is conventionally understood as an activity that is generally 'unpaid, formal and part-time' (Anheier and Salamon 1999, 51). But defining volunteering as free time that is freely given to the benefit of others does not preclude that the volunteer benefits from his or her work in terms of both material (e.g., paid work) and subjective (e.g., life satisfaction, self-esteem, educational and occupational achievement) rewards (see Wilson 2000).

Volunteer work involves, traditionally, a strong religious dimension. Research has shown that people who are actively involved in the activities of churches and religious organizations are more likely to undertake volunteer work than nonreligious people (Wilson and Janoski 1995; Wuthnow 1994). Churches have indeed encouraged the culture of beneficence that characterizes volunteering (Wuthnow 1990, 30). Moreover, religious orders, organized missionary societies and religious organizations of several types and faiths have been at the forefront of the internationalization of volunteering through the grass-roots base of organized religion, creating alternative geographies of knowledge which shape particular worldviews (see Harvey 2005, 227–8). There is evidence that the meanings and patterns of volunteering are changing; individualization and secularization are redefining volunteering and, today, volunteering is less linked to religion or to notions like 'service to the nation' (Anheier and Salaman 1999, 46). This is particularly apparent in the ways in which formal volunteering is being increasingly tied to understandings of civic participation, and internationalized in the work of NGOs and social movements active in civil society at both the national and supranational levels. Organizations such as the UN and the European Union foster greater recognition and support of volunteering in initiatives such as the 'International Year of the Volunteer 2001' or the 'European Voluntary Service for Young People'. These are informed by cosmopolitan ideas such as a commitment to the protection of human rights, the tolerance towards otherness, solidarity, and the fight against poverty and inequality on a worldwide scale. It is in this vein that an official publication issued by the United Nations Development Programme (UNDP) suggests that 'when networks of voluntary organizations are created which link different interest groups, the increased interaction leads to improved understanding and increased tolerance of diversity' (UNDP 2003, 1) Cosmopolitan ideas are discursively embedded in the mission statements, manifestos and other public documentation channelled by international organizations (e.g., European Union, UN), even though a notion of cosmopolitanism is rarely part of the self-definition of such institutional structures (see also Rumford 2005).

There is ground to argue that volunteering is more and more institutionally defined in terms of cosmopolitan values and ideas. Yet, there is so far little empirical evidence to suggest that cosmopolitan ideas and values actually play a significant role in helping volunteers to make sense of what they do. Drawing on Wilson's (2000, 218–19), theorization of volunteer work, my contention is that cosmopolitan ideas and values do not necessarily explain the reasons why people volunteer on an *ad hoc* basis (i.e., people do not necessarily volunteer because they have cosmopolitan predispositions), but play rather a significant role as cultural resources that individuals use to meaningfully interpret their experiences as volunteers.

By using a cultural-sociology approach, this chapter probes some of the ways in which young Portuguese volunteers active in development, cooperation and relief efforts in the PALOP (*Países Africanos de Língua Oficial Portuguesa*) (Community of Portuguese Speaking African Countries) use cosmopolitan ideas and values (e.g. openness, selflessness, solidarity, defence of an essential humanity) as cultural resources to negotiate patterns of cultural proximity and distance with people and cultures they experience as different from 'them'. Cosmopolitanism is here understood in the sense of an actually-existing cosmopolitanism that involves a reality of multiple attachments (Robbins 1998) and, thereby, implies some degree of reflexivity and self-transformation (see Nowicka and Rovisco, this volume).

Ultimately, this chapter aims to explore some of the linkages and tensions between religion and cosmopolitanism which remain largely unelaborated in the literature. Religion is rarely seen as an instance of cosmopolitanism, a notion that is more easily equated to worldliness and secularism, while religious allegiances are usually understood to condemn the believer to parochialism, absolutism and lack of tolerance (Van der Veer 2004, 14). This chapter raises the question of whether young volunteers invoking particular religious orientations as reasons for volunteering actually develop cosmopolitan ways of imagining the world and engaging the otherness of other people and cultures. It further asks how their cosmopolitan outlook compares to the cosmopolitan mindset displayed by volunteers who are motivated by nonreligious orientations. We will see that, in the Portuguese context, international volunteering appeals to the young and is primarily institutionalized in church-based organizations and informal groups of the Catholic Church.

Methodologically, this research draws on secondary sociological literature on volunteering, publications and public communication issued in the print and electronic media by organizations that promote or implement volunteer work, as well as on 14 in-depth interviews[1] with associational leaders and young programme volunteers. These are individuals who have undertaken international volunteer work in the area of Cooperation for Development in Africa, for at least two months, within the framework of two different types of organizations: a youth association with a secular orientation – ISU – *Instituto de Solidariedade e Cooperação Universitária* (Institute for Solidarity and University Cooperation) and organizations and informal groups connected to the Catholic Church. The focus on international volunteering is justified by the fact that international volunteers are more likely to adopt a cosmopolitan outlook because they are more overtly exposed to cultures, values and places that they experience as alien *vis-à-vis* their own cultural frames of reference. Arguably, they are also more prone to easily gain a sense of the oneness of the world as they actively engage with 'others' in distant world sites, than those people who volunteer solely at the local community level.

International Volunteering of Young People in Portugal

Portugal is a country with a low tradition of formal volunteering. A study looking at the volunteering rates in associations of the nonprofit sector in several European countries shows that in 1999 only 16 per cent of the Portuguese population is involved in volunteer work. This rate contrasts with high volunteering rates in Northern European countries such as Sweden (68 per cent), Denmark (56 per cent) or the United Kingdom (34 per cent) (see Vala and Cabral 1999). According to Delicado (2002, 34–5), such low rate of participation in volunteer work can be explained,

---

1   Fourteen college-educated programme volunteers, six males and eight females, aged between 20 and 35 years old were interviewed. Only one interviewee carried out volunteer work for cooperation and development in the condition of a married volunteer with a young family. Half of the interviewees had been involved in more than one volunteering programme in particular African locations. The interviews were conducted in public settings (mostly public gardens and cafes) at a location of the interviewee's choice, and ranged from 40 minutes to two hours in length. Two participants with responsibilities on project management, volunteering training, and recruitment, were also interviewed in the condition of privileged informants with valuable experience and knowledge about international volunteering of young people in the Portuguese context. They also worked as key contacts to gain entry in the organizations and to facilitate speedy access to the programme volunteers who comprise the sample. This intentional sample covers people displaying a diversified range of volunteering experiences in considering the following criteria: gender; the duration of the volunteering programme (short or long-term); the recurrence of participation in volunteering programmes; and the type of organization where the volunteer work is carried on (i.e., religious or nonreligious organizations; and formal or informal organizations).

in part, by the socio-historical circumstances that shaped the late transition to democracy in 1974 after 40 years of dictatorship. These historical circumstances are at the root of low levels of civic participation and a weak civil society through the democratic years. But low literacy rates in Portugal[2] and the absence of a tradition of sponsoring or encouraging volunteer work in both the private and public sectors also account for low levels of involvement in formal volunteering. Hence, it is not surprising, as I was told by one my privileged informants, that financial support to volunteer programmes is highly dependent on informal personal networks and connections sustained by the organizations that implement volunteer work (e.g., religious congregations, NGOs, youth associations). Notably, volunteering in the Portuguese nonprofit sector is dominated by the Catholic Church through its networks of congregations, informal parish groups and charities. In the Portuguese context, it is interesting to note that the volunteering rate in religious organizations is significantly lower when compared with other European countries such as Britain or Sweden (see Delicado 2002, 33–6).

International volunteering programmes targeting the young and directed to areas such as grassroots aid and development for cooperation and education in the PALOP had a timid start in the late 1980s under the umbrella of movements and associations linked to the Catholic Church. Founded by a group of university graduates linked to the Jesuits, the NGDO *Leigos para o Desenvolvimento* (Lays for Development) was the first association to send in 1988 a group of young volunteers to an African country in order to implement a project of development aid. This startup enterprise was followed by further initiatives put forward by the *Jovens Sem Fronteiras* (Youth without Borders), an international missionary movement of young people organized through local parishes, also in 1988, and *GAS África*, a youth association of the Portuguese Catholic University in Lisbon in 1990 (see Fundação Evangelização e Culturas 2004, 5). From 1998 onwards, there is a considerable expansion in the number of organizations and informal groups that under the spirit and sponsorship of the Catholic Church promote and deliver volunteer work within the scope of the so-called missions *ad gentes* (missions with other peoples). According to statistical data provided by the *Fundação Evangelização e Culturas* (Evangelization and Cultures Foundation) (FEC), between 1988 and 2006, a total of 2,519 people had been involved in missionary volunteering programmes developed in the scope of Church-based organizations. Thirty-one per cent of all volunteering programmes carried out took place in Mozambique; eighteen per cent in Cape Verde; and 17 per cent in Angola. Seventy-five per cent of all programme volunteers were involved in short-term programmes with two months duration, while projects requiring a commitment for more than 11 months in the field account for only 18 per cent of all programme volunteers. Furthermore, it is noteworthy that such projects appear to appeal more

2   This is interesting, especially when considering that the level of education is the most consistent predictor of volunteering (see McPherson and Rotolo, 1996 cited in Wilson 2002, 219).

to young females as 66 per cent of all programme volunteers are female. The recruitment, training, planning and delivery of this particular type of volunteering – missionary volunteering – has a strong institutional framing in organizations, informal parish groups and congregations of the Catholic Church, and is typically carried out on a full-time basis for a period of time ranging from two months to two years.

Importantly, an understanding of missionary volunteering falls outside the scope of the legal definition of volunteering in the Portuguese context. According to the law 71/98 of 3 November 1998, volunteering is 'the activity of public or community interest, unpaid, continuous, and carried out within the scope of a sponsoring organization, following a project or program, in the areas of civic work, social services, health, education, science and culture ...'[3] (cited in Delicado 2002, 37–8). This legal definition is one that values formal volunteering that is typically carried out in the context of organizations while dismissing more informal forms of volunteering – such as helping friends, neighbours and kin living outside the household – which are usually more private and occasional (see Wilson and Musick 1997, 700). Yet, it does not recognize the specificity of missionary volunteering, which is strongly informed by religious orientations and other forms of international volunteering, which are, typically, secular, partially paid, and occasional.[4] But a definition of missionary volunteering is intrinsically linked to the self-understanding of those Catholic associations and organizations that target, in particular (but not exclusively), young people between 18 and 34 years old for participation in the missions *ad gentes*. This is why for the purposes of this research, we consider important to distinguish between 'missionary volunteering' (a type of volunteering informed by religious orientations) and 'international volunteering for cooperation' which is developed by people without particular religious affiliations.

Missionary Volunteering and the New Evangelization: the Mission ad Gentes

The *Fundação Evangelização e Culturas* (FEC), an NGDO created in 1990 by the Portuguese Catholic Church to act as a religious platform connecting a set of 40 Catholic entities that implement volunteer work in developing countries (mostly in the PALOP), has played an important role in the institutionalization of missionary volunteering in Portugal. As stated in FEC's web site, 'missionary volunteers are all those lay people who, in connection with one of the entities associated with this (Catholic) movement, are willing to work in projects of cooperation or evangelization with the Catholic Church'. This kind of volunteering

---

3 Quotes from works, web sites, and interview transcripts in Portuguese are the present author's translations. All page references are to the Portuguese editions.

4 In order to overcome this inconsistency, specific legislation is currently under preparation to regulate the so-called international volunteering for cooperation. See Delicado (2002, 38).

work focuses in the areas of pastoral work, catechesis, education and health. The aims of missionary volunteering are closely linked to the goals of the discourse of the New Evangelization which comprehends 'new ways of bringing the Gospel to all' in a world faced with 'a progressive process of de-Christianization and the loss of the essential human values' (Ratzinger 2000). But the mission *ad gentes* is seen, above all, as a pathway to bring closer lay Christians and their Church and to identify potential leaders: 'the announcement of Christ, through the testimony of faith and service, that the lay missionary experiences in the mission, leads one to be more available upon one's return to integrate and help to mobilize a group, parish or diocese, namely in a missionary dimension' (Fundação Evangelização e Culturas 2004, 20).

As a religious discourse, the New Evangelization emphasizes ecumenical understanding, religious pluralism and the protection of an essential humanity (see e.g. John Paul II 1990). This rhetoric has swiftly appropriated and disseminated cosmopolitan ideas such as self-reflexivity about one's place and role in the world, the idea of an essential humanity, and openness to the reality of other people and cultures. As former cardinal Ratzinger, and current Pope Benedict XVI, puts it in a keynote address to Catechists and Religious teachers:

> The Greek word for converting means: to rethink—to question one's own and common way of living; to allow God to enter into the criteria of one's life; to not merely judge according to the current opinions. ... Not aiming at the judgment of the majority, of men, but on the justice of God—in other words: to look for a new style of life, a new life. (Ratzinger 2000)

This institutional discourse resonates with the old Christian cosmopolitanism that, in the sixteenth century, reveals a preoccupation about the 'inclusion of the Other' in the intellectual debates led by Vitoria and de Las Casas about the rights of the Amerindians, and the rights of the Spanish of declaring war in foreign land. Christianity was then a cosmopolitan project with a planetary consciousness which sought to incorporate the Americas in the global vision of an *orbis christianus* with the Occident as the frame of reference (Mignolo 2000). Significantly, this Christian cosmopolitanism was informed by a strong ethical acumen; 'to be a Christian meant to be self-conscious and to act consciously on behalf of the common good' (Mignolo 2000, 729). But this intellectual narrative of cosmopolitan orientation, although championing a series of fundamental rights for all peoples or *gentes*, contrasted with the *de facto* generalized assumption that the Amerindians and non-Christian people were not equal but inferior. The reflections of the missionary Las Casas and the theologian Vitoria emerged in a historical moment marked by the extreme violence and abuse of Indian populations, the expulsion of the Jews from the Iberian Peninsula, and the rise of slavery. But while the rhetoric of this 'classical evangelization' was ultimately shaped by a civilizing mission and a cosmopolitan project which had European values as a framework of reference, the contemporary discourse of the New Evangelization equates Christian values with essential human values, which are secular and are believed to be of universal applicability (see Fundação Evangelização e Culturas 2002, 1). It is in this sense that a booklet issued by FEC goes on to identity as motivations for missionary volunteering 'a sense of co-responsibility and justice towards the state of the world, a strong sense of solidarity, an enormous will to dislodge oneself to fight against passivity, and even a deep divine call' (Fundação Evangelização e Culturas 2002, 1).

Youth Associations and International Volunteering: the Case of the Institute for Solidarity and University Cooperation (ISU)

International volunteering of young people developed outside the scope of religious organizations and without particular religious orientations is much less prominent in the Portuguese context.[5] International Volunteering for Cooperation is primarily carried out by ISU – *Instituto de Solidariedade e Cooperação Universitária* (Institute for Solidarity and University Cooperation) a youth association and NGDO, which was founded in 1989 by a group of university students in Lisbon. As a youth association, ISU started its activities of volunteering at local community level by providing some help and assistance to university students of African origin and by developing activities of social work in a disadvantaged neighbourhood in Lisbon. ISU has a clear secular orientation and places great emphasis on goals such as civic participation, the empowerment of local populations, and sustained development in the volunteer programmes it promotes both internationally (namely, through its participation in the European Voluntary Service for Young People Programme) and at local community level.

The volunteering programmes implemented by ISU focus on the civic participation of concrete young people in the world understood as a whole. It is implicit here a rejection of ethnocentrism and the affirmation of an ethics of solidarity which emphasizes self-reflexivity and altruism. As Margarida,[6] an associational volunteer at ISU with responsibilities in planning and training, tells me:

> In volunteering the idea is that looking at the world in which we live today, from a global perspective, we propose volunteering as a proposal to intervene there. That is, in the world it is not enough to have a great awareness that there are a lot of deprived people everywhere, and go out to see the World Press Photo and say 'poor things, they suffer so much', but to have an obligation to do something.

---

5 Due to the lack of organized statistical data about the number of youth associations, NGOS, and volunteers involved in volunteering programmes outside the networks of the Catholic Church, it is not possible to provide an adequate picture of the scope of this type of international volunteering in the Portuguese context. However, ISU emerges, in both the literature and the expert interviews I conducted, as a key reference as a NGO that has consistently carried out international volunteering without a religious orientation.

6 All names are pseudonyms.

And my option could be to do sustained consumption, which is to consume organic products in fair trade shops, but it could also be to do volunteering. And this is the proposal that is put forward in the general training course.

Within the scope of the volunteering programme *Nô Djunta Mon*,[7] one of the goals stated in the programme's handbook has strong cosmopolitan underpinnings: 'to promote volunteering as a way of gaining awareness and actively participate in a global society through a strong path shaped by personal growth and self-discovery' (see Dias e Azevedo 2005). And although a notion of cosmopolitanism is not explicitly mentioned in ISU's public communication, its institutional discourse clearly mobilizes cosmopolitan ideas and values as it tries to challenge perceived inequalities and challenges facing the world, and to promote the tolerance of difference and the respect for the value of a common humanity. As mentioned in the association's web site, ISU's vision is 'to promote the dignity of the human person and its recognition on all levels'. And among ISU's stated aims and goals for the areas of cooperation and development one finds the need 'to promote the closeness and sharing of values and cultures', 'to sensitize for issues of development and interculturality', and to 'provide future volunteers with a space of reflection about the state of the world, and the inequalities and asymmetries which are devastating the world today'. This institutional discourse is consistent with the current rhetoric and culture of development which is predicated on the idea that 'in a partnership, development co-operation does not try to do things for developing countries and their people, but with them. It must be seen as a collaborative effort to help them increase their capacities and do things for themselves' (Crewe and Harrison 1991 cited in Baaz, 2005, 3).

Social Networks and the 'Volunteering Calling'

The recruitment and training of young volunteers is strongly anchored on a range of social networks and organizational memberships that supply information, make contacts, foster trust, and create obligations (cf. Wilson and Musick 1997, 695). In the concrete case of missionary volunteering, membership of Catholic congregations and informal parish groups plays a key role in motivating and supplying information about volunteering opportunities to young Catholics through the institutional networks of the Catholic Church. Active participation in local parish groups for the young or youth movements aggregated to religious congregations constitute important settings for the recruitment of the young. In fact, most of the missionary volunteers I spoke to started by doing volunteer work at community level prior to making the decision of doing a mission *ad gentes*.

---

7   This volunteering programme involves projects in the area of Development for Cooperation in Cape Verde, Angola and Guinea Bissau, and is carried on in collaboration with a local partner, usually for a two month period.

Young people who participated in ISU's volunteering programmes for cooperation invoke, more commonly, personal networks (e.g., family and friends), and previous volunteer experience at community level and in ONGs, as means for obtaining the information and encouragement they required to make a decision to get involved in international volunteering. This research finding is consistent with research indicating that extensive social networks, multiple organizational memberships, and prior volunteer experience, all increase the chances of volunteering. Few people learn about opportunities through the mass media while face-to-face invitations are more effective than public appeals (Wilson 2000, 223).

The young volunteers I interviewed all have university qualifications in subjects such as international relations, education, engineering, economics, mathematics and geography. These data support evidence that highly educated people are more likely to volunteer. People with high education levels are, indeed, more likely to have the social and technical skills that gives them more confidence to engage with other cultures and people, and this makes them more desirable as volunteers (cf. Wilson and Musick 1997, 710).

In the Catholic organizations and associations the need to reduce uncertainty about the profile of the missionary volunteer led to the set up of more formal training schemes with a strong spiritual dimension. As Sara, an associational volunteer at FEC, explains:

> we understood that there are more and more people willing to depart and also that there was not capacity to know the type of people that we were sending. At the beginning, it was people that were close and already knew each other, the friend of a friend, and if we knew the person already, and we knew that she had maturity, then, perhaps the risk was not so high. I think that at a certain point this became a little bit more mass-oriented … and we had to devise something more structured. Through training programs it is possible to filter people because, either they give up by themselves (because they understand that this is not for them), or, if there is a lot of people, one has even to create criteria to select them.

As I talked to Sara, it became clear that along with university level education credentials, religious training is a key factor to reduce the risks of selecting people without the 'right' motivations, i.e., people displaying instrumental motives – such as the desire to improve one's curriculum vitae, to overcome a personal crisis or an unemployment situation.[8] In the end, social ties to organizations and informal associations linked to the Catholic Church help to define the volunteer role and, thereby, make it easier to perform (cf. Wuthnow 1991, 201). As the demand for volunteering opportunities in the missions *ad gentes* rises, the recruitment of missionary volunteers becomes increasingly dependent on a rigorous spiritual training which emphasizes an ethics of selflessness bind to religious duty.

---

8   See Barker (1993, 28) who draws a typology of the three motivational factors why people volunteer: altruistic, instrumental and obligatory.

At ISU, the recruitment of young people (usually university students and graduates) with the 'right' academic qualifications is not much of a problem. ISU places great efforts in targeting people with skills and competences that are not exclusively gained from educational qualifications. What is required beyond educational credentials is that the trainees become increasingly aware and reflexive about what makes them want to be volunteers. As Margarida stresses:

> ... what I think is that there are not motivations which are right or wrong, but a path of consistency that one follows. When people go abroad with us, beyond the general training course I talked about, they have to participate on a more specific training that regards the principles of cooperation, the reality of the countries where ISU acts, project management skills, interculturality, and so forth. And during this process people refine their own motivations.

The emphasis is therefore placed on an individual ethics of selflessness that is informed by altruistic motives, rather than by religious duty, as is more commonly the case in the context of the recruitment of missionary volunteers. International volunteering for cooperation is institutionally defined – in the case of ISU – as a way of promoting awareness about values of peace, interculturality, respect for difference, and tolerance, beyond one's own personal motivations. In this context, pursuing personal rewards, such as improving one's self-esteem, the desire for self-discovery, or occupational achievement, is seen as compatible with an ethics of beneficence that includes traditional altruistic notions such as a sense of solidarity towards the poor and promoting the dignity of the disadvantaged (cf. Barker, 1993 cited in Anheier and Saloman 1999, 56). This contrasts with the rhetoric of the Catholic organizations where religious orientations are seen as easily conflicting with the fulfilment of self-interest.

We have seen that the organizational settings in which international volunteering is carried on play a very significant role in raising awareness of a range of secular and religious values which are underpinned by a cosmopolitan orientation. These values are enforced through various institutional channels, ranging from public communications and social networks to formal training schemes, which help people make sense of why they volunteer. Some research has suggested that while traditional religious values and selfless motivations appear to be losing ground in view of greater trends of individualization and secularization in the developed world, instrumental orientations have increased since the 1980s, particularly, among the younger cohorts (Anheier and Salamon 1999, 55–6). However, the question we want to ask here is not whether in today's world traditional religious values still do much to encourage the volunteering of young people, but rather to which extent the young who actually volunteer can uphold a mix of both secular and religious orientations, and do so by drawing on institutionally-embedded cosmopolitan outlooks and narratives.

Christian Cosmopolitanism and the Ethics of 'Caring for Others'

The rhetoric of the New Evangelization deploys a cosmopolitan outlook not only at the level of institutional discourse, but also, subjectively, in the personal narratives of the missionary volunteers as they attempt to explain what they do. To evangelize *ad gentes* (other people), means, in the first instance, to protect the dignity of every human being. This is predicated on the respect for particular religious traditions and cultural attachments. The classical view that evangelization is about the promotion of the Christian faith, or a matter of taking the word of the Gospel to other peoples, loses ground in arguments that posit the protection of the essential humanity of the 'other' as the primary goal of missionary evangelization *ad gentes*.

As Rui, a married voluntary who spent six years living and working in a mission in Mozambique, explains:

> [to evangelize] is a process that goes hand in hand with, on the one side, the knowledge of the life of Christ, and on the other, the knowledge that arises from one's chance of getting education, or a professional qualification ... Our ideal is, first, to make men and women that can think for themselves and then, secondly, that these men and women get to know Christ. If they get to know Christ or, for instance, Mahomet or another church, this is an issue that is up to oneself to make a choice. But we [the missionary volunteers] offer an alternative.

In a similar vein, Francisco, who spent one year working with a congregation in Guinea Bissau, argues that the evangelization *ad gentes* is tied to process of humanization and emancipation of the recipients in the local communities where the volunteer work is carried out:

> Pope John Paul VI said that 'before evangelization one needs to humanize' and I believe in this. So if the work of the Church in this case implies humanization, in the concrete case of the mission, that humanization is carried on through development that is gained through education. Because education facilitates the human advancement of children and this helps them in their future ... And what is important is to help people to understand what is good and evil in their own culture. In the end, we are dealing with emancipation in the sense of helping a person to become more human and, thus, little by little, Christianity becomes visible.

Furthermore, there is evidence in the volunteers' personal accounts that missionary evangelization is less about saving heathen souls or the desire to establish pure Christian communities, as was the case with past evangelization projects, but more about one's life testimony – the way one lives with others, cares for others and acts towards others. Hence, to live humbly, to share with locals basic public infrastructures and the reality of existing living conditions, to learn a local dialect or native language, or, simply, to spend time socializing with the locals and the recipients of the volunteer work, are seen by the interviewees as key aspects of missionary evangelization. In the words of Ines, a medical student who participated on a short volunteering programme in Cape Verde:

> People have a bit this idea that 'we go there and we change that'. I think we have to go there with our own experiences, to share our experiences, but also to understand why they are like they are. This is what I attempted to do with the children from the orphanage. The orphanage had children between four and 22 years old. With the little ones we played and organized fun activities. With the eldest we offered informal training courses.

Arguably, in such circumstances, the missionary volunteer goes on to display a cosmopolitan outlook that is primarily informed and shaped by a strictly defined religious obligation. As the late Pope John Paul II (1990) puts it 'missionary evangelization is ... the primary service which the Church can render to every individual and to all humanity in the modern world'. There is evidence of a truly Christian cosmopolitanism in the ways in which the missionary volunteers become highly reflexive and sensitive about the workings of the cultural boundaries that make 'them' feel different from the recipients of their volunteer work. They feel compelled to engage with the worldviews, idiosyncrasies and value-systems of the African regions where Christianity and modernization have had so far little impact. Yet, it is less clear whether they embrace them in their own western lifestyles or identity outlooks when they return (cf. Philips and Aarons 2007).

Francisco points out, for instance, that:

> I used to be horrified of seeing the men sat and playing checkers, while the women had to go and fetch water, carry wood and the children on their back as men did nothing! I mean this question of basic and simple human rights ... We are talking about a culture that is matriarchal and where there is polygamy, which is quite common in Guinea. But, there, these things are as natural as a normal relationship between a woman and a man here, that doesn't exist there. There, a cow has more rights than a woman because it works less!

There is also evidence that the missionary volunteers learn how to de-emphasize perceived differences and tensions between 'us' and 'them' in conditions of intense cultural interaction. Cultural exchange is an important rationale in development organizations (Baaz 2005, 50). In the case of missionary evangelization *ad gentes*, the importance of cultural exchange is institutionally channelled and implemented in selective training programmes where the prospective volunteers are schooled in topics such as solidarity and enculturation. Telma, a volunteer who spent two years in Mozambique working with a Catholic congregation, tells me that one thing she learnt on her volunteering training is that the missionary should be cautious about becoming part of the culture of the recipients:

We have to learn a little about the customs, traditions and ways of living of the place, of the people we are going to work with, so that we do not feel apart. We should be aware that if we want to do something, we have to show that we are there for them and not to stress the differences. But yet we can't transform ourselves into them. We have to be who we are but with caution in their culture.

Although many volunteers claim they adopt a self-reflexive stance regarding their own ways of relating and interpreting alien cultures, there is little sense in their personal accounts that the symbolic boundaries between 'us' and 'them' are being challenged, or called into question. The Catholic volunteers appear, in fact, more comfortable in listing objective differences between different cultures, than the volunteers involved in ISU's volunteering programmes for cooperation. This is to say that forms of collective self-understating – as Portuguese, Catholics, Christians or Europeans – are not significantly affected by situations of wide exposure to otherness because the 'other' is not expected to cross the boundaries of his or her culture into the volunteer's own recognizable and familiar world. Thus by demarcating and controlling the parameters in which their collective identities are conceived and reshaped (see Newman 2003, 15), the missionary volunteers also create otherness.

Significantly, the abstract commitment to the protection of human dignity or a deeply felt moral responsibility regarding the state of the world, which are often presented as reasons why Catholics volunteer in the institutional networks of the Catholic Church, are sometimes dismissed in the very concrete ways in which the volunteers talk about the differences between 'us' and 'them'. Although they are generally critical of the materialistic and individualistic orientations that blight Western and European societies, some of the missionary volunteers I interviewed explain their volunteer work via paternalistic arguments which are bound to an ethnocentric bias that morally elevates the culture of the helper. For example, a few volunteers speak of the naivety and 'poverty of spirit' of the Africans, and of their lack of ambition and entrepreneurship, as obstacles to development. They go on to frame their role as volunteers in terms of the valuable help and guidance – namely, through their own example as successful and educated western young people – they can offer Africans so they are able to overcome such cultural limitations. This paternalistic outlook brings to mind one of the predicaments of the cosmopolitan imagination: a sense of mastery of the reality of the other that goes hand in hand with a narcissistic streak of the worldly and sophisticated position of the cosmopolitan (Hannerz 1996, 103–4).

All in all, although volunteering in the scope of the missions *ad gentes* paves the way for an actually-existing Christian cosmopolitanism, this is not necessarily the result of the 'opening up' of the boundaries (see also, Jansen, this volume) of one's religious identity. In fact, the missionary volunteers rarely question their religious orientations or the theological precepts of Catholicism, even though a few of them are critical of the practical ways in which the Catholic Church carries out its business in a missionary context. In other words, they do not become less Catholic, or more African, or yet adept of more diffuse and syncretic religious beliefs and ways of living together, as a result of greater self-reflexivity and openness. On the contrary, the experience of missionary volunteering appears to foster the intensity of one's religious identity because one feels close to the roots of one's Catholic faith and the Church in the mission *ad gentes*. This can be explained, in part, by the fact that the volunteers are moved by an ethics of selflessness which entails self-sacrifice, the personal growth of the Christian and, above all, a moral obligation to 'care for others' in distant world sites that is institutionally enforced. This is consistent with the fact that missionary volunteering is highly institutionalized and dependent on volunteering training schemes, which provide moral and practical apprenticeship, and, as such, help filtering and schooling the appropriate candidates (cf. Wuthnow 1991 cited in Wilson 2000, 697).

Cosmopolitanism, Cultural Relativism, and the Individual Ethics of Selflessness

Unlike the missionary volunteers, college-educated volunteers who embark on ISU's volunteering programmes for cooperation find it harder to translate the distinctiveness of different cultures into a matter of essential differences between different human groups (for example, between North and South, between Europeans and Africans, or between Portuguese and Angolans or Mozambicans). In their personal narratives, they display a drive to deconstruct the symbolic boundaries between 'us' – as, say, Portuguese, European or Western – and 'them' – the recipients of their work, say, the locals, the Africans – by using the discourse of cultural relativism which helps them to overcome ethnocentric and essentialist readings of the 'other'. Basically, in adopting a highly reflexive and subjectivist stance, they attempt to explain how and why one cannot easily compare and evaluate different cultures; and how one's interpretations of how different one is *vis-à-vis* the 'other' are context-bound. They do so by critically engaging established and collectively shared cultural understandings about the 'other', which they believe to be anchored in western-centred cultural frames of reference.

Paula, a programme volunteer who spent two years in Guinea Bissau working with a local NGO, stresses that what is important when one comes upon a foreign culture is to:

> ... respect, I think this is what one learns in intercultural experiences, which is very good. In respecting [others] we do not judge them, and then we find ourselves in the stance of observers at the beginning. Just because we don't know [them], we should not take hurried conclusions. And to be tolerant it helps a lot, as well as to be able to dislodge ourselves a little bit from our own self, and our own references, in order to open ourselves to that difference.

In a similar vein, Mariana, an associational volunteer with extensive volunteer experience in Africa, concords that:

> This type of thinking 'I have my own truth and this is worth what is worth' is something that ISU stresses a lot. And this is the same here and there. But, there, it assumes different features, because it is more demanding as a challenge. Because, there, everything is different. The way people see life, and what matters for people. When suddenly I realize that, here, there is a certain consensus about being on time, or the importance of investing in education ... there, I have to be able to understand that farming and the goat are more important than any knowledge they might acquire ... If I understand that one lives in a survival scheme and that tomorrow is a very distant day, it is a lot easier to relativize the lack of timeliness, the fact that they fall asleep in training courses, the fact that they have huge difficulty in projecting their lives into the future.

This highly intellectualized discourse resonates with the stance of many academics, intellectuals, and activists who use cultural relativism and multiculturalism to rebut racism (see Lamont and Aksartova 2002, 10). Yet, it is important to bear in mind that one of the challenges these volunteers face is precisely the difficulty to conciliate the abstract rhetoric of development aid, which is predicated on a strong cosmopolitan ethico-political outlook that is institutionally channelled – and includes notions such as awareness of North-South inequalities, human rights, and co-responsibility towards underprivileged groups – with the practicalities of carrying on volunteer work in a terrain fraught with uncertainties; in a terrain where it is not always easy to 'manoeuvre between different systems of meaning' (Vertovec and Cohen 2002, 13). While on the one hand, they explain their volunteer role by invoking their commitment to the abstract notion of humanity and to global causes, saying, for instance, that 'beyond cultural differences we all share a common humanity', or 'it is part of the work carried out within ISU to have an altruistic mission'; on the other, they are baffled by how their exposure to 'other' worldviews and mindsets in concrete local sites also makes them more aware of the limits of their own cultural versatility. In other words, in contact with alien cultures the volunteers become more reflexive about their ability to discern the mix and the entanglement of cultures as they move between cultures.

As Mariana goes on to explain reflecting upon her own volunteering trajectory:

> One of the things I felt is that the more you stay [abroad], the more you learn, and the more you feel that there is a lot more to know. I start in Morocco, then go through Algeria, Guinea Bissau, Cape Verde, and think, this is a world! Because what I felt in each of these places, and the people I got to know, have nothing to do with each other. I can't find proximity. And suddenly Africa seems to me a very small concept to describe all these differences that I saw ... To speak about

Africa, or Europe, or about the continents, is very reductive, isn't it? What I feel
is that the more people learn, the more this reductive feeling arises.

In a similar vein, Luisa, a programme volunteer who participated in two
short-term volunteering programmes in Cape Verde, speaks of the fragilities and
difficulties the volunteer faces when one finds oneself away from familiar cultural
frames of reference:

> Over there, there is not any type of social mask one can use. Because one is
> twenty-four hours over twenty-four hours with people that are different and,
> then, because one is often in a context that is a liminal context, a context of risk,
> one is outside his own references: it is not with one's group of friends; it is not
> within one's own comfort zone; and all this provokes a series of things. I had to
> deal myself with several inner confrontations that arose during that first month:
> the fact that I was not enjoying being there [Cape Verde]; the fact that I was not
> in the Africa pure and virgin I was searching, because my initial aim was rather
> to be sent to Guinea, and also a great confrontation with what I thought I was.

Drawing on Ossewaarde (2007, 384), it could be argued that young programme
volunteers display cosmopolitan outlooks as they go on 'to develop the intellectual
ability to establish distance from their cultural pattern of group life, and detach
themselves from ... their old cultural patterns'. However, this does not mean
that they are to be seen as human beings in themselves without knowledge of
acquaintance in the borderless society of strangers, as Ossewaarde suggests.
In the concrete everyday life contexts in which they carry on their work, one's
commitment to the universal idea of a common humanity makes sense as a matter
of meaningfully engaging the problem of how to live with difference, not as a
matter of transcending group loyalties or exclusive local bonds.

In contrast to the missionary volunteers who rarely contest the identity of
the 'we' as they engage the 'otherness of the other' (cf. Benhabib 2002, 184),
nonreligious volunteers are more prompt to see the boundaries of cultures as
fluid, open and contested. However, they do not easily fit the canonic image of
the enlightened and worldly cosmopolitan (Thompson and Tambyah 1999, 221)
as someone who takes pleasure from the presence of the other (Appiah 1998, 91),
or one who moves blithely and swiftly between different cultures without fully
belonging, or even someone who is ultimately 'betwixt and between without being
liminal' (see Friedman, 1995 cited in Thompson and Tambyah 1999, 220). This
is even more pressing if we consider that only a few interviewees talk about their
volunteering experience in terms of a mundane or aesthetic consumption of cultural
difference. Instead, they all go on to deploy an individual ethics of selflessness that
is underpinned by a belief on the moral equality of all cultures and a deeply felt
concern with worldly affairs – apparent, for example, in their commitment to fight
global inequalities and non-democratic power structures. This individual ethics of
selflessness, no matter how abstractly conceived, helps them to account for why

they volunteer in more secular terms. But, equally important, is how such altruistic orientations are ultimately tied to a narrative of self-development which is framed by notions of mutual help, social learning and self-discovery (see also Nowicka and Kaweh, this volume). This is in contrast with the ethics of 'care for others' displayed by the missionary volunteers that rejects any expression of self-interest and is, ultimately, underpinned by a strong sense of religious duty and the self-enhancement of the Christian.

The narrative of self-development displayed by nonreligious volunteers is, for instance, apparent in the way Jorge, a software consultant who spent two months in Cape Verde after graduating, tells me that: 'I also feel I have a lot to learn from them, and that I came back enriched, in this respect. I think that these projects have an altruistic mission, but also a little bit of selfishness. We go there to give, but we end up receiving a lot more.'

Conclusion

This chapter has addressed the question of how young people who carry on work on volunteering programmes of cooperation and development in Africa make use of cosmopolitan ideas and values as cultural resources to account for their volunteer experiences. I have shown that these ideas are, to a great degree, appropriated by institutional rhetoric and channelled in selective training programmes. By comparing the arguments used by young people who volunteer in Catholic organizations and young people who volunteer in a nonreligious organization – I have demonstrated that the fact that the missionary volunteers uphold strong religious orientations as reasons for volunteering does not prevent them acquiring a cosmopolitan mindset. They are not to be seen as less cosmopolitan (or more parochial) than those nonreligious interviewees – who more overtly invoke an ethico-political cosmopolitan outlook to explain what they do – just because in their self-definition as volunteers their engagements with others and their commitment to the protection of a common humanity are bound to a religious particularism.

But whether one upholds religious orientations does make a difference in terms of the cosmopolitan narratives, worldviews and ideas that the volunteers mobilize in personal accounts of the volunteer role. Arguably, then, different instances of an actually-existing cosmopolitanism are tied to very distinct ways of engaging otherness and the struggle for a better world. We have seen that the missionary volunteers rarely question the boundaries of the 'we' as they engage the reality of an alien culture, and that they do so by drawing on cosmopolitan values which are embedded in the Catholic discourse of the New Evangelization. This is a religious discourse that posits the defence of the essential humanity of all cultures and human beings in the context of the mission *ad gentes*, which is seen as a pathway for the making of better Christians. This Christian cosmopolitanism contrasts with the cosmopolitanism of the young who develop their work in the scope of ISU, an organization with nonreligious orientations. Moved by an individual ethics of selflessness, these volunteers actively deconstruct the symbolic boundaries between 'us' and 'them'. We have seen that they do so as they juggle the cultural relativism inherent to their experience of the irreconcilable diversity of cultures in concrete everyday life settings and their commitment to the abstract rhetoric of development aid. The latter is informed by a strong cosmopolitan ethos; one that is predicated on the moral imperative to protect humankind taken as a whole.

References

Anheier, H. and Salamon, L. (1999), 'Volunteering in Cross-National Perspective: Initial Comparisons', *Law and Contemporary Problems* 62: 4, 43–65.
Appiah, K. (1998), 'Cosmopolitan Patriots', in Cheah and Robbins (eds).
Baaz, M. (2005), *The Paternalism of Partnership – A Postcolonial Reading of Identity in Development Aid* (London and New York: Zed Books).
Barker, D. (1993), 'Values and Volunteering', in Smith (ed.).
Benhabib, S. (2002), *The Claims of Culture – Equality and Diversity in the Global Era* (Princeton and Oxford: Princeton University Press).
Cheah, P. and Robbins, B. (eds) (1998), *Cosmopolitics – Thinking and Feeling Beyond the Nation* (Minneapolis: University of Minnesota Press).
Delicado, A., Nunes de Almeida, A. and Ferrão, J. (2002) (eds), *Caracterização do Voluntariado Social em Portugal* (Lisboa: Comissão Nacional para o Ano Internacional do Voluntariado).
Dias, P. and Azevedo, M. (2005), *Como Fazer o Nô Djunta Mon em 8 Lições* (Lisboa: Instituto de Solidariedade e Cooperação Universitária).
Fundação Evangelização e Culturas (2002), *Voluntariado Missionário – Guião Informativo* (Lisboa: Fundação Evangelização e Culturas).
— (2004), *Voluntariado Missionário em Portugal – 18 de Anos de Acção* (Lisboa: Fundação Evangelização e Culturas).
Hannerz, U. (1996), *Transnational Connections: Culture, People, Places* (London: Routledge).
Harvey, D. (2005), 'The Sociological and Geographical Imaginations', *International Journal of Politics, Culture, and Society* 18:3–4, 211–55.
John Paul II (1990), *Redemptoris Missio – On the Permanent Validity of the Church's Missionary Mandate*, <http://www.vatican.va/holy_father/john_paul_ii/encyclicals/documents/hf_jp-ii_enc_
07121990_redemptoris-missio_en.html>, accessed 15 October 2007.
Lamont, M. and Aksartova, S. (2002), 'Ordinary Cosmopolitanisms: Strategies for Bridging Racial Boundaries among Working-Class Men', *Theory, Culture & Society* 19:4, 1–25.
Mignolo, W. (2000), 'The Many Faces of Cosmo-polis: Border Thinking and Critical Cosmopolitanism', *Public Culture* 12:3, 721–48.
Newman, D. (2003), 'On Borders and Power: A Theoretical Framework', *Journal of Borderlands Studies* 18:1, 13–25.

Ossewaarde, M. (2007), 'Cosmopolitanism and the Society of Strangers', *Contemporary Sociology* 55: 367–88.

Phillips, T. and Aarons, H. (2007) 'Looking "East": an Exploratory Study of Western Disenchantment', *International Sociology* 22:3, 325–41.

Ratzinger, J. (2000), *The New Evangelization – Building the Civilization of Love*, Address to Catechists and Religion Teachers, Jubilee of Catechists. <http://www.ewtn.com/new_evangelization/Ratzinger.htm, accessed 15 October 2007.

Rumford, C. (2005), 'Cosmopolitanism and Europe – Towards a new EU Studies Agenda?', *Innovation*, 18:1, 1–9.

Smith, J. (ed.) (1993), *Volunteering in Europe 2* (Berkhamsted: The Volunteer Centre).

Robbins, B. (1998), 'Actually Existing Cosmopolitanism', in Cheah and Robbins (eds).

Thompson, C. and Tambyah, S. (1999), 'Trying to Be Cosmopolitan', *Journal of Consumer Research* 26:3, 214–41.

United Nations Development Programme (2003), 'Volunteerism and Development', in *UNPD Essentials* (ed.).

UNPD Evaluation Office 12. <http://www.worldvolunteerweb.org/resources/policy-documents/united-nations/doc/undp-essentials-on-volunteerism.html>, accessed 15 October 2007.

Vala, J. and Cabral, M.V. (eds) (1999), *Estudo Europeu dos Valores* (Lisboa: Instituto de Ciências Sociais).

Van der Veer, P. (2004), 'Transnational Religion: Hindu and Muslim Movements', *Journal for the Study of Religions and Ideologies* 7, 4–18.

Vertovec, S. and Cohen, R. (2002), 'Introduction: Conceiving Cosmopolitanism', in Vertovec and Cohen (eds).

— (eds) (2002), *Conceiving Cosmopolitanism – Theory, Context & Practice* (Oxford and New York: Oxford University Press).

Wilson, J. (2000), 'Volunteering', *Annual Review of Sociology* 26, 215–40.

— and Janoski, T. (1995), 'The Contribution of Religion to Volunteer Work', *Sociology of Religion* 56, 137–52.

— and Musick, M. (1997), 'Who Cares? Toward an Integrated Theory of Volunteer Work', *American Sociological Review* 62:5, 694–713.

Wuthnow, R. (1990) 'Religion and the Voluntary Spirit in the United States', in Wuthnow and Hodgkinson (eds).

— (1991), *Acts of Compassion* (Princeton: Princeton University Press).

— (1994), *God and Mammon in America* (New York: Free Press).

— and Hodgkinson, V. (eds) (1990), *Faith and Philanthropy in America* (San Francisco, CA: Jossey-Bass).

Index